WRITING QUEER IDENTITIES
IN MOROCCO

WRITING QUEER IDENTITIES IN MOROCCO

Abdellah Taïa and Moroccan Committed Literature

Tina Dransfeldt Christensen

I.B. TAURIS
LONDON • NEW YORK • OXFORD • NEW DELHI • SYDNEY

I.B. TAURIS

Bloomsbury Publishing Plc

50 Bedford Square, London, WC1B 3DP, UK
1385 Broadway, New York, NY 10018, USA
29 Earlsfort Terrace, Dublin 2, Ireland

BLOOMSBURY, I.B. TAURIS and the I.B. Tauris logo are trademarks of Bloomsbury
Publishing Plc

First published in Great Britain 2021
This paperback edition published in 2022

ISBN: HB: 978-1-7883-1585-2
PB: 978-0-7556-3770-6
ePDF: 978-1-7883-1587-6
eBook: 978-1-7883-1586-9

Series: Written Culture and Identity

Typeset by Deanta Global Publishing Services, Chennai, India

CONTENTS

Acknowledgements   vi
Note on transliteration and translation   viii
Introduction   ix

Chapter 1
WRITING THE 'SELF-ABSORBED' AS A SITE OF QUEER COMMITMENT   1

Chapter 2
ABDELLAH TAÏA AS AUTHOR AND ACTIVIST   21

Chapter 3
SUBVERTING 'ETHNOGRAPHIC' READING STRATEGIES:
    DRISS CHRAÏBI'S *LE PASSÉ SIMPLE* AND
    ABDELLAH TAÏA'S *L'ARMÉE DU SALUT*   49

Chapter 4
WRITING TRANSIDENTITY IN THE LANGUAGE OF THE 'OTHER':
    THE *SOUFFLES* MOVEMENT, ABDELKÉBIR KHATIBI'S *AMOUR*
    BILINGUE AND ABDELLAH TAÏA'S *UN PAYS POUR MOURIR*   79

Chapter 5
SHAME, SILENCE AND NATION BUILDING: FATNA EL BOUIH'S
    ḤADĪTH AL-'ATMAH AND ABDELLAH TAÏA'S *INFIDÈLES*   117

CONCLUSION: HYSTERIA AS MASK AND THERAPY   149

Notes   157
Bibliography   179
Index   191

ACKNOWLEDGEMENTS

This book is the outcome of research undertaken from 2012 to 2017 during my time as a PhD fellow at Cultural Encounters, Roskilde University, Denmark. It is the result of hard work, perseverance, a love of literature and the indispensable encouragement, support and guidance of my supervisors, Heidi Bojsen and Joshua A. Sabih. Their critical eyes and engagement in discussing my research both challenged me to substantiate my arguments and confirmed me in the legitimacy and importance of the project. I would like to express my sincere gratitude to Heidi Bojsen for her continuous support and excellent guidance. I would also like to extend a special thank you to Joshua A. Sabih, who has been the most generous and knowledgeable supervisor since I enrolled as a graduate student at Islamic Studies, University of Copenhagen, in 2004. It was from our inspiring dialogues about critical theory, religion, language, philosophy and literature in the Maghreb that this project sprang in the first place.

I have been privileged with an extremely engaged assessment committee, and I sincerely thank Khalid Zekri and Jean Zaganiaris for encouraging me to transform my PhD thesis into book form and for an enriching discussion of my thesis and the most valuable suggestions for revisions. I would also like to thank the series editor, Miriam Cooke, and the peer reviewers at I.B. Tauris. Their questions, comments and suggestions for revisions have been crucial in revising the manuscript into its present form. Thank you also to my editor, Rory Gormley, who has offered much support and guidance during the process.

I am grateful to the editors of *Expressions maghrébines*, *Journal of North African Studies* and *New Geographies: Texts and Contexts in Modern Arabic Literature* for their permission to publish edited versions of some of my previous works. Parts of Chapter 2 were originally published as 'Breaking the Silence: Between Literary Representation and LGBT Activism. Abdellah Taïa as Author and Activist' in *Expressions maghrébines* 16/1 (2017). The analysis of Abdellah Taïa's *L'Armée du salut* in the last part of Chapter 3 appeared in an earlier version as '"Writing the Self" as Narrative of Resistance: *L'Armée du salut* by Abdellah Taïa' in *Journal of North African Studies* 21/5 (2016). An early and significantly different version of the analysis of Fatna El Bouih's *Ḥadīth al-ʿatmah* in Chapter 5 was presented at the Eleventh Euramal Conference at Universidad Autónoma de Madrid, Spain, in 2014 and published as 'Narrating the Unnarratable: The Role of Literary Memory in Moroccan Testimonial Writing' in *New Geographies: Texts and Contexts in*

Modern Arabic Literature (eds. Roger Allen, Gonzalo Fernández Parrilla, Francisco M. Rodríguez Sierra and Tetz Rooke) (UAM Ediciones, 2018).

A special thank you goes to Abdellah Taïa, whom I have met on a number of occasions and informally interviewed in Aarhus in March 2016. I am indebted to the generosity and kindness with which he has shared his personal stories. There are few books that I have read as many times as his, and they continue to surprise me whenever I revisit them.

NOTE ON TRANSLITERATION AND TRANSLATION

I follow IJMES transliteration standards, with the exception of accepted English spellings for Arabic names, both historical figures and living individuals. All translations in this book are mine. I am aware that a number of the French and Arabic texts I quote have been translated into English. However, for the sake of textual precision in relation to my analyses, I have chosen to provide my own translations. Translations of book titles, which are inserted in parenthesis after the first mention of the titles, however, follow the titles of published translations and are written in italics to distinguish them from titles that have not been translated into English.

INTRODUCTION

Café de France, Casablanca, January 2006. Moroccan author and cineaste Abdellah Taïa (b. 1973), who has lived in Paris since 1999, is meeting with a journalist from the Moroccan francophone newsmagazine *TelQuel*, during a promotion tour for his short story collection, *Le Rouge du tarbouche* (The Red of the Tarbouche) (2004). The journalist Chadwane Bensalmia has read *Le Rouge du tarbouche* thoroughly, and she has noticed the theme of homosexuality and the autobiographical underpinnings of some of the short stories. During the interview she therefore asks Taïa if she can interview him about his life as a homosexual in Morocco.

This interview became a turning point in Taïa's life and career, because at that moment he decided to come out publicly. On 28 January 2006, *TelQuel* 210 published the interview under the headline 'J'ai été élevé dans la honte' (I was raised in shame). Two months later Taïa was interviewed for the two arabophone newspapers *al-Ayyam* and *al-Jarida al-Oukhra*, and on 9 June 2007 *TelQuel* 277 ran a front-cover portrait of Taïa under the headline 'Homosexuel. Envers et contre tous. L'histoire poignante du premier Marocain qui a eu le courage d'assumer publiquement sa différence' (Homosexual. Against all odds. The poignant story of the first Moroccan with the courage to assume his difference in public). Taïa soon achieved almost iconic status as the 'first' Moroccan with the courage to defy the anti-homosexuality laws and lay claim to his homosexuality in public. However, whereas this status increased the global interest in his literary production and provided him with space to speak up about LGBT rights, it has simultaneously elevated him to a position of being 'exceptional' despite the fact that he was and is not.

By this I do not intend to pass judgement either on Taïa's choices as author and activist or on those who have seen a potential in him as an 'openly homosexual Arab author'. What I find interesting is instead what insights it may bring to relate his coming-out interview to the public debate about LGBT rights in Morocco and to read his creative writing in dialogue with a longer postcolonial tradition of committed writing in Morocco. In this respect, the ambition of *Writing Queer Identities in Morocco* is to investigate how the position of 'exceptional' has forced Taïa to navigate in a minefield of stereotypes that have haunted Moroccan literature at least since the 1950s – whether stereotypical conceptions of 'authentic Arab sexuality', stereotypical readings of autobiographical literature as ethnographic material, or stereotypical conceptions of French as a language of civilizational and sexual emancipation. Moreover, *Writing Queer Identities in Morocco* investigates how Taïa's literary works are grafted upon the Moroccan postcolonial novel of the 1950s, the Moroccan avant-gardist literature of the 1960s–80s and Moroccan prison testimonies of the 1990s–2000s.

Writing the 'self-absorbed' as a site of queer commitment

Taïa made his literary debut in 2000 with the short story collection *Mon Maroc* (My Morocco), and he has since published a book almost every other year: *Le Rouge du tarbouche* (2004),[1] *L'Armée du salut* (*Salvation Army*) (2006), *Une Mélancolie arabe* (*An Arab Melancholia*) (2008), *Le Jour du roi* (The King's Day) (2010), *Infidèles* (*Infidels*) (2012), *Un Pays pour mourir* (A Country to Die In) (2015), *Celui qui est digne d'être aimé* (He Who Is Worthy to Be Loved) (2017) and *La Vie lente* (The Slow Life) (2019). Moreover, he has published two photo books: *Maroc, 1900–1960: Un certain regard* (Morocco, 1900–1960: A Certain Look) (2007) with Frédéric Mitterrand and *Égypte. Les martyrs de la révolution* (Egypt. The Martyrs of the Revolution) (2014) with Mahmoud Farag and Denis Dailleux. He has edited *Lettres à un jeune marocain* (Letters to a Moroccan Youth) (2009), and he has written several essays and opinion pieces in Moroccan news magazines as well as in international newspapers, cultural magazines and so on. According to his publisher, Le Seuil, his novels and short stories have been translated into more than ten languages,[2] and in 2010 he won the prestigious French literary award for young authors, Prix de Flore, for *Le Jour du roi*. In 2014, he made his directorial debut with a film adaption of his novel *L'Armée du salut*, which won the jury awards of Festival Premiers Plan D'Angers and Festival Tous Ecrans de Geneve, and the Best First Feature Film at Durban International Film Festival.

A recurrent trait in Taïa's creative writing is a preoccupation with what I would call the 'self-absorbed' as a site of queer commitment. Writing openly about his own life as a homosexual in Morocco and later in Paris, he has time and again been accused of exhibitionism and of being more preoccupied with his own fame than with the 'common good' of Morocco. However, Taïa's literary play with the 'self-absorbed' is anything but overtly focused on the self or blind to the other; it is rather an expression of what Abdelkébir Khatibi has termed *pensée-autre*,[3] that is, an 'other' way of thinking about sexuality and marginality. In this respect, writing the 'self-absorbed' is a performative strategy which, instead of claiming space within the norm, insists on the right of the marginalized to be seen and heard without being assimilated into a new normativity. That is, writing 'I' constitutes an effort of writing the self as other in order to expose the existence of queer identities that have been silenced by social, cultural and religious normativity. In this respect, queer commitment – rather than simply commitment – signals that the works studied in *Writing Queer Identities in Morocco* function as stumbling blocks of 'dominant' and 'authoritative' narratives by interlocking narrations of self and other, masculinity and femininity, and heterosexuality and homosexuality.

Writing the self as an act of commitment, while operating on the margins of nations, languages and sexualities, is something Taïa shares with both earlier and contemporary Moroccan writers. The historical and comparative approach of *Writing Queer Identities in Morocco* is therefore meant to underline the importance of prior texts for the creation of new literature – not to identify direct sources of influence, but to investigate how texts are brought to articulate meaning in particular discursive spaces. That is, as an intersection of textual surfaces, a literary text is, as argued by Julia Kristeva, a dialogue among several writings rather than a self-contained system.[4] Thus by tracing the changes in Moroccan literature from the so-called ethnographic novel and the so-called novel of acculturation of the 1950s over the literary avant-gardism of the 1960s–80s to what I would call a 'naive realist literature of dissent' since the 1990s, this book investigates how Taïa's narrations of the 'self-absorbed' as a site of queer commitment rearticulate themes and narrative strategies that have marked Moroccan literature over generations.

Committed literature

Throughout the book I use commitment as the English equivalent of the French *engagement* and the Arabic *iltizām*. However, my conception of commitment is not simply based on Jean-Paul Sartre's *littérature engagé*,[5] but on how the political in literature has been reappropriated and reconfigured in Moroccan literature since the 1950s. That is, in challenging the classical dichotomy between committed art and pure art, I argue that even though the question of representability, that is, the relationship between literary text and reality, has changed significantly since the 1950s, it has not displaced literature as a site of commitment. Of significance instead is how the forms and strategies of 'writing with a cause' have changed along with new experimental representational strategies.[6]

What I, in this respect, find significant about Taïa's literary performance of the 'self-absorbed' is how it is intertwined with questions of literary value, culture, language and identity. The construction of literary value, and the related question of commitment, has been the subject of ongoing discussion within the field of world literature, as it is inextricably related to the question of how to define what makes literature 'world literature'. For this reason, world literature is, as argued by Robert J. C. Young, a heterogeneous field of critical debate rather than a constituted canon.[7] Whereas David Damrosch has defined world literature as 'literary works that circulate beyond their culture of origin, either in translation or in their original language',[8] Rebecca Walkowitz argues in *Born Translated* (2015) that a new transnational genre written for a globalized book industry has – if not replaced – at least supplemented the traditional conception of world literature as books that are born in one language, often in a so-called native language, and then travel out to other languages. Today, many books are written with a global audience in mind, and they are either written in a transnational language and distributed globally or published in several languages at once. What is of interest in relation to Taïa's writing and modern Moroccan literature in general is how their existence as 'born translated' is embedded in the stories they tell, their narrative form and their different expressions of commitment.

Walkowitz has met some critique from postcolonial critics, who have long argued that the most experimental and challenging literature is work that impedes translation and does not travel easily.[9] So-called untranslatable works have been celebrated for their refusal to wear their context lightly in order to enter the pipeline of multinational publishing, whereas works with high mobility have often been vilified for exchanging aesthetic innovation for commercial success.[10] Within this paradigm, literary value is constructed as 'locally committed', as opposed to the detached, but widespread, popular literature of commercial publishing (whether Harry Potter or Scandinavian crime fiction, to mention but two examples). An opposing paradigm is the nineteenth-century French slogan *l'art pour l'art* (art for art's sake), where art is only considered true art if it is divorced from any didactic, moral or utilitarian function. Within this paradigm, locally committed literature is often read reductively as mere ethnographic depictions of a given society, or as approaching political propaganda. However, so-called born-translated works, such as Taïa's, do not necessarily wear their context lightly either as commercial art or as pure art; but their context is not limited to a so-called national culture, and they cannot be reduced to either ethnographic depictions or political propaganda. Instead, born-translated works, as defined by Walkowitz, have multiple affiliations, which complicate their composition.[11]

With respect to Taïa's creative writing, its borderline existence (as Moroccan, Maghrebin, Arab, Mediterranean, francophone, etc.) reveals a hybridity in Homi K. Bhabha's strict sense of the term.[12] That is, Taïa's works do not simply reflect a merging of two or more cultures into a new, but constitute a process of negotiation, contestation and rearticulation in which cultural meaning is both produced and lost. Hybridity is closely intertwined with the context in which a text is inscribed, but, noticeably, a context which cannot mimetically be read off from the content of the text.[13]

Thus by focusing on Moroccan literature – rather than Maghrebin, Arabic, francophone or other transnational categories – I do not seek to reinforce a dualism between national literature and world literature, but acknowledge that transnational critiques of exclusionary notions of national identity are still rooted in the 'nation', however imagined it might be.[14] A specific focus on Moroccan literature will thus reveal the nation as always already transnational, while simultaneously acknowledging the importance of the local context from which committed literature springs. This is of importance over and above Taïa and his engagement in the fight for LGBT rights in Morocco: the Moroccan struggle for independence, post-independence state formation, the Years of Lead during the reign of Hassan II and the political reforms (but with continuing human rights violations) since the ascension of Mohammed VI to the throne have all had a significant impact on literary production in Morocco and by Moroccans outside of Morocco.

A focus on Moroccan literature as rooted in a nation that is always already heterogeneous and transnational, moreover, requires a multilingual approach, acknowledging that Moroccan literary works across languages share political, social, cultural and literary history. I have therefore chosen to include texts in both French and Arabic in my analyses. I am, however, aware that Moroccan literature is also written in Amazigh (Berber), *dārija* (Moroccan colloquial Arabic), Hebrew, Spanish and English; but I have chosen to focus on Arabic and French because these two languages have dominated the literary scene, and because Arabic-French bilingualism is exemplary of both the existence and significance of plurilingualism in Morocco.[15]

Autobiographical writing

Autobiographical literature constitutes a particularly interesting case of committed writing, because its focus on individual life and the psychological state of the narrator has often excluded it from the domain of committed literature. On the one hand, autobiographical writing has been regarded as a 'self-absorbed' genre that emerged in and belongs to the West and to so-called Western norms of literary value (*l'art pour l'art*). This was, for instance, the case with *iltizām* writers such as the Lebanese journalist and literary critic, Husayn Muruwwa (1910–87), who distinguished between 'reactionary' and 'progressive' writers and criticized the former for drawing on Idealist philosophy with its focus on individual reason and consciousness.[16] A similar argument, but with different implications, has been advanced in the study of Maghrebin francophone literature: that not only the genre but the self-conscious 'I' and individualism are borrowed from the West, with no history in the Maghreb prior to colonialism and the French *mission civilisatrice*. Orientalist postures like this are reflected in, for instance, Jean Déjeux's study of francophone Maghrebin literature,[17] and in the work of literary critics within the field of autobiographical theory, such as Georges Gusdorf.[18] On the other hand, autobiographical literature has, because of its alleged referential nature, often been perceived as a sort of documentary literature that provides an inside perspective on an otherwise inaccessible world. This has, however, often reduced autobiographical literature to a window through which to see a given culture and society and, consequently, valued it according to its ability to portray the latter truthfully.

Contrary to these approaches, *Writing Queer Identities in Morocco* explores how Moroccan autobiographical writings operate in-between the two extremes of so-called self-centred art and documentary art, not as a merging of two 'trends', but as hybrid works that are referential and non-referential at the same time: that is, as a literary practice which simultaneously rearticulates both in order to subvert established literary norms and reading practices. Similarly, autobiographical works most often dismantle the dichotomy of 'art for art's sake' and 'art for society's sake' as even what appears to be the most ivory-tower novel of art for art's sake can be an instrument of political action, just as the most expressly politically engaged texts, such as testimonial writing, can be preoccupied with aesthetic experimentation. In this respect, I understand commitment in the broadest sense of the term as an author's engagement in any social, cultural or political concern of his or her time. In Moroccan literature, the question of commitment is thus reflected in how it subverts social, cultural and political structures, certain ways of reading literature, as well as epistemological systems that distinguish between what is imagined and what is real, what is individual and what is collective, what is masculine and what is feminine, as well as between what is French and what is Arabic.

An overview

Writing Queer Identities in Morocco analyses Taïa's literary and extra-literary writing in dialogue with earlier and contemporary Moroccan literature and political activism. The chapters are structured comparatively, historically and thematically in order to trace the multiple discursive regimes within and against which Moroccan authors write.

The difficult task of countering the violence of public obliteration and invisibility without reproducing regulatory regimes through new exclusionary identity categories – whether Arab, Muslim, Moroccan, woman or homosexual – is a concern that authors such as Taïa share with such critics as Khatibi, Bhabha, Réda Bensmaïa, Judith Butler and Sara Ahmed. Thus in order to analyse the different expressions of queer commitment in modern Moroccan literature, Chapter 1 engages with scholarship within the fields of postcolonial studies, literary criticism, and queer and affect theory. What I hope to demonstrate is a kind of *pensée-autre*: one that seeks to displace the false dichotomy between 'Western' and 'Arab' thought by confronting the Eurocentric underpinnings of so-called pure criticism. Of particular interest, in this respect, is how the alignment of Khatibi's double critique with Butler's performativity and Bensmaïa's experimental nations with Yumna al-Eid's critique of Philippe Lejeune's autobiographical pact may offer valuable insights into the experimental representational strategies of modern Moroccan literature.

Chapter 2 explores Taïa's narrations of the 'self-absorbed' as a site of queer commitment in relation to contemporary LGBT activism in Morocco, contemporary Moroccan queer literature, and Taïa's own extra-literary writing and public talks on culture, language, sexuality and identity in Morocco, Europe and the United States. I have found this contextualization important because literary studies rarely take Taïa's position as activist into account or relate his 'coming-out' interview to the public debate about the relation between so-called authentic Moroccan sexuality and so-called universal rights. As Taïa, moreover, is part of a larger literary scene in Morocco, even though he today lives in Paris, I have found it important to outline how a new generation of Moroccan writers, similarly to Taïa, are writing the real through the lens of individual experiences and in a narrative style marked by textual eclecticism and pop culture.

Chapters 3 to 5 explore the dialogic encounter of Taïa's narrations of queer sexualities with earlier works of literature. Within the vast field of modern Moroccan literature, I have chosen to focus on the following works: Driss Chraïbi's *Le Passé simple* (*The Simple Past*) (1954), Khatibi's *Amour bilingue* (*Love in Two Languages*) (1983) and Fatna El Bouih's *Ḥadīth al-ʿatmah* (*Talk of Darkness*) (2001), which I will read comparatively with Taïa's *L'Armée du salut* (2006), *Un Pays pour mourir* (2015) and *Infidèles* (2012). I am aware that my choice of works prioritizes Moroccan francophone literature at the expense of arabophone literature, but as Taïa writes in French, a number of significant questions related to reception and choice of language are indispensable to discussing the different expressions of commitment in his writing. However, as I move back and forth between socio-critique, literary analysis and modern literary history, I will include both arabophone and francophone works in all chapters.

Le Passé simple is a pioneer work in Moroccan literature both in terms of aesthetic innovation and political commitment, and it remains one of the most read and referenced Moroccan novels today.[19] More importantly, *Le Passé simple* is exemplary of how Moroccan literature has interacted with public debates about cultural identity, both under colonial rule and after independence. What I find particularly interesting is how *Le Passé simple* was caught in a heated ideological debate about independence, nation building and cultural identity, and how the father–son conflict in the novel, consequently, often was read reductively as a one-dimensional critique of Moroccan tradition and culture. However, Chraïbi's narration of a 'self-absorbed' protagonist, incapable of really seeing anybody else, encompasses a multilayered critique of both Moroccan and French culture and politics through a parody of the so-called emancipated Arab boy. In this respect, Taïa's narration of the 'self-absorbed' as a site of queer commitment in *L'Armée du salut* is significantly different from *Le Passé simple*. But my comparative reading of the two novels in Chapter 3 reveals how Moroccan literature has been haunted since the 1950s by so-called ethnographic readings and demands for authenticity, and how authors over generations, each in their own way, have sought to dismantle these culturalist stereotypes through their writings.

Amour bilingue has been hailed as inaugurating a new period in Maghrebin francophone literature, because Khatibi in this novel managed to create a literary and linguistic space where Arabic and French 'meet without merging'.[20] The Manichean dualism between colonizer and colonized, between French and Arabic, which dominated early postcolonial novels, is still the subject of *Amour bilingue*, but Khatibi's avant-gardist writing is significantly different from, for instance, Albert Memmi's and Frantz Fanon's approach to the bilingual experience. However, as I argue in Chapter 4, plurilingualism and the accompanying questions of 'cultural alienation' are still central concerns for many contemporary Moroccan authors and critics, despite the fact that *Amour bilingue* has been described as marking a before and an after in the history of Maghrebin writing. Just as Khatibi wrote as a politically engaged intellectual against both institutionalized bilingualism in Morocco and the neocolonial underpinnings of the French promotion of *la francophonie*, Taïa has been outspoken in his critique of both Moroccan 'bourgeoisie' French and *la francophonie*. The continued preoccupation with the bilingual experience is not of course because Khatibi's work lacks significance, but rather an effect of the cultural and political realities within and beyond the borders of Morocco. For this reason, Chapter 4 investigates how rupture and continuity coincide in and around Khatibi's text. Moreover, it analyses how Taïa's subversive mimicry of the idea of France/French as a site of emancipation in *Un Pays pour mourir* is both indebted to and a reaction against the hermetic avant-gardism of Moroccan literature during the 1960s to 1980s.

Within contemporary Moroccan literature, an important archive of committed literature is the recent prison testimonies written by former political prisoners incarcerated during the Years of Lead. Like the contemporary authors who have put pen to paper to challenge sociocultural and religious taboos regarding sexuality, these authors have, in particular since the 1990s, narrated their horrific experiences of arbitrary detention, forcible disappearance and torture to bear witness to a period in Moroccan history that for long has been weighed down by silence. El Bouih's testimony *Ḥadīth al-ʿatmah* is significant because of its resistance to dominant narratives of women as 'silent keepers of memory'. Like the silence to which Taïa had to turn to protect himself as a teenager, the silence of women victims of political violence has the double function of protecting them from social stigmatization and upholding hegemonic narrations of the 'nation'. In this respect, women as 'silent keepers of memory' – and their testimonies as too horrific to be voiced in public – have excluded women from the public sphere by transforming them into untouchable, silent representatives of 'national purity'. Reading El Bouih's work comparatively with Taïa's novel *Infidèles*, I explore, in Chapter 5, how Moroccan authors have (re)articulated the role of shame and silence in the process of national reconciliation and the healing of past wounds.

The Conclusion focuses on how Taïa's two latest novels *Celui qui est digne d'être aimé* (2017) and *La Vie lente* (2019) rearticulate themes that have dominated Taïa's writings since his debut in 2000, particularly the 'self-absorbed' as a site of queer commitment and its symbiotic relation to the mother figure and hysteria. Since the wave of terrorist attacks that swept over Paris and France in 2015 and with a sharpened anti-immigration rhetoric, the space for Arab-Muslim queers has grown even smaller. This claustrophobic space is what Taïa grapples with in his two latest novels, both of which turn his position as 'exceptional' upside down.

Chapter 1

WRITING THE 'SELF-ABSORBED' AS A
SITE OF QUEER COMMITMENT

Within the fields of gender studies, queer studies, postcolonial and diaspora studies, and French and francophone studies, scholars[1] have become increasingly preoccupied with the sexualization of national culture and how a globalized rhetoric of a 'sexual clash of civilizations', to quote Éric Fassin,[2] constructs the Arab-Muslim 'other' as both misogynist and homophobic. Within this homonationalist[3] rhetoric there is little, if any, room for Arab-Muslim queers, because 'being queer' presupposes coming out in public, arriving in the city centre of, for instance, Paris, and leaving one's religion, culture, family and community behind. Both Denis M. Provencher and Mehammed Amadeus Mack have pointed to the 'impossible location' of diasporic Arab-Muslim queers in France and investigated how the politicization of sexuality renders many queer subject positions invisible – whether clandestine and peripheral modes of being queer[4] or queer 'coming and goings' between French and Maghrebin culture.[5] Both Mack and Provencher combine ethnographic fieldwork in France with analyses of cultural productions by contemporary Arab-Muslim authors, artists and film directors in France, and both have included Abdellah Taïa's literary work in their investigation of the lives and stories of Arab-Muslim queers in France.

Writing Queer Identities in Morocco forms part of this growing research field with the ambition of exploring how Taïa's narrations of the 'self-absorbed' as a site of queer commitment is grafted upon earlier literary efforts to contaminate monologic and heteronormative narrations of the nation. That is, the ambition is to contribute with a historical perspective on contemporary autofictional works on queer identity formation and with a specific focus on Morocco in order to emphasize that an author, such as Taïa, is operating in-between Morocco and France; while Taïa today resides in France and is published in French, he is nevertheless deeply indebted to Moroccan literary history, and Moroccan culture and history is an inherent part of his life and writing. Moreover, although writing about homosexuality as an identity category is a relatively recent phenomenon in Moroccan literature, writing about queer desire and narrating queer subject positions is not. Moroccan literature has since the 1950s focused on queer identities that are performed and contested on the thresholds of nations, languages and sexualities.

In order to provide the theoretical foundation for an investigation of how the 'self-absorbed' may function as a site of queer commitment, this chapter engages with postcolonial theory on nation and literary commitment (Homi K. Bhabha, Réda Bensmaïa and Abdelkébir Khatibi); with autobiographical theory on the relationship between social world and literary work (Philippe Lejeune, Yumna al-Eid and Arnaud Schmitt); and with queer and affect theory on identity formation, political activism, nation building and shame (Joseph A. Massad, Judith Butler and Sara Ahmed).

From 'national allegory' to experimental nations

During the 1950s, *iltizām* (commitment) emerged in the Arab Middle East as a response to the need for creating a new postcolonial identity.[6] As Arab nationalism fuelled many struggles for decolonization, the question of nation and national identity became a significant site of contestation in committed literature. As Jarrod Hayes points out, the national Algerian slogan – 'Islam is my religion, Arabic is my language, Algeria is my fatherland' – was an effective battle cry in the Algerian War of Independence, but while this definition of national identity was perhaps necessary to justify the anti-colonial struggle, it was quite exclusionary, as it implied that only Arabic-speaking Muslims could be truly Algerian.[7] The most obvious exclusions were Berbers and Algerian Jews, but the idea of a national identity based on a cult of origin did, as argued by Hayes, not exclude on the basis of ethnicity and religion alone: historically, exclusive notions of nationhood have also been based on political belief, gender and sexual orientation as narrations of the 'nation' have served to legitimize political power by affirming patriarchy and heterosexuality as essential to national identity. Significant in all of these exclusions is, however, that the need to exclude presupposes that the excluded part is already there.[8]

As Homi K. Bhabha has demonstrated with his neologism 'dissemiNation', the fiction of anchoring the nation in an originary past constitutes an act of forgetting, as Ernest Renan pointed out in his famous 1882 Sorbonne lecture 'Qu'est-ce qu'une nation?'[9] – that is, forgetting heterogeneous narratives of the nation that conflict with the linear narration of founding events, from 'birth' to modern nation.[10] Coupling his own experience of migration with Jacques Derrida's 'dissemination', Bhabha challenges traditional historiography by identifying 'the event of the everyday' as an equally important temporality as that of 'the advent of the epochal'.[11] Significantly, he does not substitute everyday time for epochal time, but explores the paradox that links them together: members of a nation live in everyday time, but ground their identity in epochal time. In this sense, people are both the 'objects' of nationalist pedagogy – they are what they learn about 'their' nation in school – and 'subjects' who perform, embody and reproduce the 'nation'. But as historicist narrative disavows everyday time with its discontinuous and heterogeneous narratives, it simultaneously reveals its own incapacity to ground the nation in the people.[12] In this respect, literary depictions of 'sexual transgressions' have, as Hayes has also pointed out, served to contaminate hegemonic narrations of the nation by publicly representing what 'should' be kept private and hidden[13] – in Bhabha's words, forgotten. In Taïa's novel *Infidèles* (2010), for instance, the introducer Saâdia both safeguards and subverts conservative norms of sexual conduct. In *Infidèles* social norms of honour, worth and virginity presuppose the profession of the introducer, who has the power to create a fiction of purity by making sure that blood appears on the sheets of newlywed couples. For this reason, Saâdia is simultaneously needed and feared, because her profession both upholds and radically destabilizes the entire framework of 'norm' and 'deviance'.

Because 'national identity' has been a significant site of contestation in postcolonial literature, a popular analytical strategy within the study of postcolonial Moroccan autobiographical writing has been Fredric Jameson's 'national allegory', which interprets the microcosm of the protagonist as a (multilayered) metaphor of the macrocosm of the people.[14] According to Jameson, 'all third-world texts are necessarily [. . .] allegorical [. . .] *the story of the private individual destiny is always an allegory of the embattled situation of the public third-world culture and society*.'[15] Not surprisingly, Jameson's attempt to place 'all third-world texts' under the same analytical umbrella has met considerable critique. Of particular importance with respect to committed literature is Aijaz Ahmad's critique of the notion 'third world' and its implicit homogenizing tendencies, such that 'the enormous cultural heterogeneity of social formations within the so-called third world is submerged within a singular identity of "experience".'[16] With respect to Maghrebin literature, Réda Bensmaïa has articulated a similar suspicion of Jameson's 'national allegory', arguing that even if an allegorical dimension exists in so-called postcolonial texts, it is almost never the author's primary or sole ambition.[17] Taken together, Ahmad's and Bensmaïa's critiques point towards both the heterogeneous corpus of 'third-world' texts and the multiple determinations within a single 'third-world' text.

However, it is worth noting that this is not all that different from what Jameson argued himself. Jameson directly refuted any simplified 'one-to-one table of equivalences',[18] as he was critical of any presumptuous generalization of the heterogeneous corpus of so-called third-world texts.[19] What is at stake in relation to Jameson's category 'third world' is a question of reading strategy: How to read so-called third-world literature? The problem with Jameson's 'national allegory' might be its unclear position within the dialectic of 'close reading' and 'distant reading'. On the one hand, his 'national allegory' seeks to counter methodological colonialism in literary studies, but on the other, it – perhaps unintentionally – isolates third-world literature in its 'otherness'. Put in other words, Jameson's theory has been attractive in its questioning of the universal applicability of Western literary theory by emphasizing the importance of the colonial and imperial experiences in the formation of 'third-world' literature, but in 'designing' a theory for this literature, it simultaneously runs the risk of reducing so-called third-world literature to a social commentary with little literary merit (the exact opposite of Jameson's declared intention). As argued by Bhabha, 'pure criticism' is in reality highly Eurocentric,[20] but the counterargument that the 'historical and ideological determinants of Western narrative – bourgeois individualism, organicism, liberal humanism, autonomy, progression – cannot adequately reflect'[21] the experiences of the 'colonial subject' subscribes to the same epistemological system, in which the opposition to Western narrative then becomes the unmediated reality that an 'authentic' literary tradition must reveal through mere mimeticism.

The difference between so-called third-world literature and so-called first-world literature intersects with the difference between 'art for art's sake' and 'art for society's sake' and the related discussion of literary value. In this respect, Jameson's national allegory, like Franco Moretti's 'distant reading', acknowledges that the world literature system is 'profoundly unequal'[22] as it mirrors the neo-imperial contours of global capitalism, and as such it sets up a significantly different measure for literary value than Western formalism. While Jameson sought to outline the 'literariness' of so-called third-world literature by defining the relationship of literary texts to political and historical reality, rather than resorting to 'Western' formalism, his 'grand theory' unintentionally supported the reductionist readings of Maghrebin literature that Bensmaïa laments:

> What has long struck me was the nonchalance with which the work of these writers was analyzed. Whenever these novels were studied, they were almost invariably reduced to anthropological or cultural case studies. Their literariness was rarely taken seriously. And once they were finally integrated into the deconstructed canon of world literature, they were made to serve as tools for political or ideological agendas. This kind of reading resulted more often than not in their being reduced to mere signifiers of other signifiers, with a total disregard for what makes them literary works in and of themselves.[23]

The difficult path that an author such as Taïa is treading is precisely between wanting to claim a voice as Moroccan and homosexual and having his literary works reduced to anthropological and cultural case studies. What Bensmaïa in this respect seeks to bring to light is the originality of the aesthetic strategies developed by Maghrebin authors as a means to reappropriate and reconfigure their history, territory, language and community,[24] and it is in this respect that he coins the term 'experimental nations':

> Under today's postmodern conditions, it is not geographical or even political boundaries that determine identities, but rather a plane of consistency that goes beyond the traditional idea of nation and determines its new transcendental configuration. And it is in this sense that I use the term experimental nations. My nations are experimental in that they are above all nations that writers have had to imagine or explore as if they were territories to rediscover and stake out, step by step, countries to invent and to draw while creating one's language.[25]

What is significant about Bensmaïa's conception of experimental nations is that it, while acknowledging the centrality of 'national identity' as a site of contestation, simultaneously displaces Jameson's national allegory in order to provide room for an analysis of the experimental representational strategies in Maghrebin literature. In so doing, Bensmaïa's experimental nations – like Abdelkébir Khatibi's 'transnation', as I will elaborate in Chapter 4 – deconstruct any neatly defined national boundaries by focusing on the multiple affiliations of Maghrebin authors and on how their linguistic, cultural and social experiences transcend the idea of the 'nation'.

Like Bhabha's 'double movement' between everyday time and epochal time as a potential site for resisting totalizing and exclusive ideas of the nation, a double critique in Khatibi's sense of the term can serve to dismantle the false dualism between 'art for art's sake' and 'art for society's sake' that either deems so-called non-Western literature an imitation of Western literature or reduces it to depicting an unmediated reality and, consequently, labels it 'poor literature'. Khatibi developed his double critique in *Maghreb pluriel* (1983) as a methodological tool with which to subvert the relation and discernibility between centre and periphery:

> le savoir arabe actuel opère à la *marge* de l'épistémè occidentale; ni donc à son intérieur, puisqu'il lui est plutôt subordonné, déterminé par elle, ni non plus à son extérieur, puisqu'il ne pense pas le *dehors* qui le fonde. Marge, limite aveugle, en fait. La double critique consiste à opposer à l'épistémè occidentale son dehors impensé tout en radicalisant la marge, non seulement dans une *pensée en arabe*, mais dans une pensée-autre qui parle *en langues*, se mettant à l'écoute de toute parole – d'où qu'elle vienne.[26]

> (current Arab knowledge operates on the *margin* of the Western episteme; neither from the inside, as it is rather subordinated, determined by it, nor from the outside, as it does not think the *outside* which founds it. Margin, blind limit, in fact. Double critique consists in opposing the Western episteme to its unthought outside while radicalizing the margin, not only as a *thinking in Arabic*, but as an other-thought which speaks *in languages*, listening to every speech – wherever it is from.)

By defining double critique as a method consisting in 'opposing the Western episteme to its unthought outside while radicalizing the margin', Khatibi relates the process of decolonization to the Derridean deconstruction and the Foucauldian genealogy. Instead of feeding the opposition between inside and outside, colonizer and colonized, double critique seeks to radicalize the margin, so as to constitute a thinking in languages (*pensée en langues*). On a textual level, double critique seeks to reveal the arbitrariness of binary oppositions such as that between national literature and world literature, pure art and committed art, and Arabic and French. On a historical level, double critique is preoccupied with the arbitrariness of the historical emergence of specific hegemonic practices and hierarchical relations such as that between so-called Western and Arab thought. Consequently, Khatibi argues that we need a *thinking in Arabic* that can pursue an 'archeology of silence'[27] because Arab societies – as long as they are not heard in their difference – constitute silent societies. That is, to deconstruct the relation between inside and outside, the outside must first be given a voice and be heard. However, as an instance of deconstruction, double critique moves beyond a reversal of established hierarchies to a *thinking in languages* – that is, an other-thought that is neither inside nor outside, neither centre nor periphery. In this respect double critique is significant because it draws attention to how Moroccan authors operate on the margin, not only of the nation but also of multiple hegemonic literary-linguistic systems – be they Arabic literary traditions, French literary traditions or postcolonial literary traditions.

The dual function of self-narration

With respect to autobiographical theory, the question of representation is particularly interesting because Moroccan autobiographical writing often has been read both allegorically (the 'I' as an allegory of a 'we') and mimetically (depicting an 'unmediated' reality), while simultaneously being accused of reproducing a literary form that is deemed 'Western'.[28] However, we are, as argued by Debra Kelly, confronted with several prevailing discourses about how to consider the forms and strategies employed by Maghrebin authors in autobiographical texts.[29]

Since Philippe Lejeune introduced his 'autobiographical pact' in 1971,[30] most literary critics have, as Arnaud Schmitt has pointed out, been preoccupied with the relation between fiction and fact in autobiographical writing.[31] Many have opted for either a fictional approach or a referential approach. Textually, Lejeune's point of departure is that of the reader, and he defines autobiography as a 'récit rétrospectif en prose qu'une personne réelle fait de sa propre existence, lorsqu'elle met l'accent sur sa vie individuelle, en particulier sur l'histoire de sa personnalité' (retrospective narrative in prose made by a real person about his own existence, while emphasizing his individual life, in particular the history of his personality).[32] Lejeune's 'autobiographical pact' is a referential pact. The essence of the pact is the silent agreement made by the reader with the author of the text, that author, narrator and protagonist are the same.[33] This pact can be derived either indirectly through the paratext (i.e. title, subtitle or preface) or directly in the main text if the name of the author, the narrator and the protagonist is the same.[34] An autobiography is in this sense written 'under oath', and, according to Lejeune, any discrepancy between text and reality must therefore be considered not fiction but a lie. According to Lejeune, autobiography is an unambiguous, referential discourse based on empirical data, just like biographical, scientific and historical texts.[35] If the text appears ambiguous to the reader, it is, accordingly, solely because the latter lacks the necessary information to determine whether it is fiction or fact.

On the one hand, Lejeune's autobiographical pact has been a useful tool with which to understand the generic properties of autobiography and its distinction from related genres, such as biography, memoirs, diary and novel. But as his genre theory, on the other hand, is based on a structural difference between autobiography and fiction, it fails to account not only for those experimental works which challenge traditional genre categorizations but also for those works that operate in-between 'conformity with authority and lack of it',[36] whether the authority is a repressive regime or a hegemonic epistemological system, as I will elaborate in the following.

When Serge Doubrovsky coined the term 'autofiction' in 1977, it was intended precisely to criticize Lejeune's definition of autobiography as an unambiguous genre. Doubrovsky loosely defined autofiction as 'fiction, d'événements et de faits strictements réels' (fiction, about events and facts that are strictly real),[37] in order to underline that fiction is a constitutive element of any writing about the self, which makes it both impossible and undesirable to maintain that fiction and fact belong to two different ontological spheres. Similarly, Taïa has, in interviews, argued that fiction and fact are interlocked when writing the self:

> There isn't a distinction. I mean, what is the difference? Every morning I wake up. That is reality. But as I lay in bed I need time to construct a narrative: who am I, where am I, and so on. The answers to these questions aren't necessarily objective. So, we all live in something that is autobiographical and fictitious at the same time.[38]

According to Doubrovsky, narrating your life story is a speech act that creates identity as much as it describes it. His neologism is therefore based rather on a 'contradictory pact' than an autobiographical or a referential pact.[39] The reader must accept that it cannot be determined whether a text is fiction or fact, as it is in fact both. What is significant about Doubrovsky's 'autofiction' is its inherent hybridity: it is neither a merging of two genres into a new, nor is it two genres taking turn (i.e. this part fiction, this part fact), but a 'hybrid monster'[40] that is referential and non-referential at the same time.

However, since Doubrovsky coined the term 'autofiction', the referentiality of autobiographical literature has been questioned on equal terms with the referentiality of fiction, which died definitively with Roland Barthes's proclamation of the death of the author in 1967.[41] The author is born along with the text: life is no longer just the cause of the literary work, but also the product of the author's self-narration. Both Derrida[42] and Paul de Man[43] have questioned the very possibility of defining autobiography as a genre, because all actual examples appear to be an exception to the rules of the genre. According to de Man, it is impossible to distinguish between fiction and autobiography. Autobiography thus becomes a particular reading strategy, rather than a regular genre.[44] The reference to reality is a construction created by the reader on the basis of the ability of a text to reproduce the rules and norms of the genre. Moving further away from Doubrovsky's conception of autofiction as hybrid, Gérard Genette[45] and Vincent Colonna[46] have defined autofiction as all those works in which an imaginary character is given the author's name. Nothing but the name need be referential. Autofiction is thus definitively removed from autobiography. The recurrent pronouns *I, you, he* and *she* then become self-referential, linguistic instances referring only to the imaginary universe of persons, time and space created by the narrative. It thus becomes impossible to explain the I of the narrative by referring to an extra-textual author.

In response to what he saw as a growing misconception of Doubrovsky's neologism, Arnaud Schmitt coined the term 'self-narration'.[47] According to him, a postmodern confusion has displaced the ambiguous nature of autofiction in favour of an all-fictional approach to any writing about the self. To counter this trend, he has therefore reintroduced Doubrovsky's textual practice, while arguing for a new terminology on the grounds that the substantive 'fiction' component of autofiction emphasizes the non-referential part of the personal discourse at the expense of the referential part.[48] Consequently, he defines self-narration as a loosely referential literary genre vacillating between the autobiographical and the fictional:

> Referential because there is no protective distance between the narrator and the author, consequently there is also a degree of assumed responsibility for the text's content. Literary because it resorts to every formal weapon offered by novels and does not make it one of its duties to be true to life.[49]

What is particularly interesting about Arnaud Schmitt's conception of self-narration is his emphasis on a double reading strategy that takes both the referential and the non-referential aspects of the text seriously: 'the text's interaction with my paratextual knowledge of the author resulted in a position enhancing the intensity and the complexity of the personal account that the game of generic doubting would have spoiled.'[50]

Two things are at stake with respect to this double reading strategy: the relationship between author and text, and the relationship between text and reader. On the one hand, referentiality implies an ethical and a legal responsibility for the content of a literary text when the author writes in his or her own name. On the other hand, referentiality implies a particular reading strategy whereby the reader's paratextual knowledge is acknowledged as an analytical asset along with formalist analysis. If we return to Taïa, this is particularly interesting with respect to his coming-out interview in 2006. When Chadwane Bensalmia, the journalist from *TelQuel*, asked if she could interview him as a homosexual, he assumed responsibility for his literary works by identifying with the narrator. He has subsequently argued that he felt he could no longer 'hide' behind fiction, but that he had to be truthful to his writing: that he had no right to write something in a book, publish it and then afterwards act as if it were not in the book.[51] Consequently, he decided to come out publicly in that interview, and that act in turn constructed new paratextual information that has affected the reception of his works and reinforced their function as committed literature.

It is noteworthy, however, that this assumption of responsibility simultaneously in itself reflects a changing public sphere in Morocco. As I will show in Chapter 4, Moroccan authors during the 1960s–80s were not less courageous than Taïa, but writing under the repressive regime of King Hassan II forced authors to operate in between conformity with authority and lack of it, which Yumna al-Eid has argued is a condition many authors in the Arab world have to live with:

> Speaking about sex, religion and politics in the Arab countries is still relatively prohibited and many of the books which deal with these subjects are still banned,

even when they claim to be fictional works. Verdicts of expulsion, killing and arrest are still delivered to many writers and authors. [. . .] Accordingly, it would seem that the fictional imagination is a more authentic mask for presenting autobiography since, by keeping its pact secret, it can be more daring in its revelation of the self.[52]

Importantly, however, political reality can only in part explain the changes that took place on the literary scene during the 1960s–80s, as Gonzalo Fernández Parrilla has also argued.[53] While I acknowledge that the political changes of the 1990s, and in particular since the coronation of Mohammed VI in 1999, have had an effect on both literary production and LGBT activism, there is, as I will argue in Chapters 2 and 4, more at stake in the difference between the opacity of literary avant-gardism during the 1960s–80s and the 'naive' realism of authors such as Taïa and Rachid O.

Nevertheless, al-Eid's study of Arabic novelistic art (*fann al-riwāyah al-'arabiyyah*) and the relation between aesthetics (*fanniyyah*) and lived experience (*tajribah ḥayātiyyah*) reveals a number of shortcomings in so-called Western literary theory that are not dissimilar to Bhabha's critique of the Eurocentric nature of so-called pure criticism. First of all, al-Eid's 'secret pact' is a direct critique of Lejeune's autobiographical pact and its inability to account for instances where either author or reader violates the pact.[54] According to al-Eid, literary interpretation cannot presuppose the presence of a shared agreement between author and reader, making it impossible to neatly distinguish between novel, autobiographical novel and autobiography. All three 'genres' must instead be approached via a double reading strategy that is attentive to both aesthetic strategy and reference to a lived reality.

Thus far, Arnaud Schmitt's conception of self-narration and al-Eid's conception of a dialectic relationship between aesthetics and referentiality have much in common. However, despite his preoccupation with referentiality and a double reading strategy, Arnaud Schmitt hardly takes the public sphere and its effect on self-representation in literary production into account. Consequently, referentiality – as an analytical asset – is still limited to a question of the reader's paratextual knowledge about the author. However, the public sphere, whether under a repressive regime or within a democracy, is controlled by rules and norms that influence literary production. These rules and norms determine not just what can be said unpunished but also what is in vogue at a given time. Analysing modern Moroccan autobiographical writing as sites of queer commitment, therefore, requires attention to how the Moroccan public sphere – and its transformation over time – has affected aesthetic strategies, that is, choice of genre, thematic focus, orchestration of voices and so on.

Since her first publications in the mid-1970s, al-Eid – like Jameson, Bhabha, Bensmaïa and Khatibi – has been preoccupied with the relationship between social world and literary work. According to her, a literary work is always a product of a given reality.[55] That is, specific historical circumstances produce specific literature, and literary critique consequently is required to combine structural analysis with socio-critique.[56] Inspired by Marxist thought, al-Eid already in her early writings defined the role of the author with reference to the painter Paul Klee (1849–1940): 'rendre visible ce qui est invisible' (making that which is invisible visible),[57] and this conception of the role of the author has run through her work since:

يحيل المقروء لدى القراءة على مرجعي هو, في حال الرواية العربية المعيش الذي شكّل الحافز الأساسي لكتابة الرواية, أو الذي استدعتْ حكايتُه [. .] فنأ يرويه ولا ينقله, أو فنأ يسمح متخيِّله بقولِ غير المرئي, المختلف, أو بقول ما لا يُسمَح بقوله.[58]

(In the act of reading, the read refers to a referential which, in the case of the Arabic novel, is lived life; lived life, which constitutes the primary motivation for novelistic writing, or the story of which requires [. . .] an art that narrates it and does not reproduce it; that is, an art that allows imagination to enunciate the invisible, the different, or to enunciate that which is not allowed to be said.)

But what makes the invisible visible? According to al-Eid, it is through language and literary expression that an author can reveal reality. Like Bhabha, al-Eid argues that literature produces signification through a creative and aesthetic production of meaning in response to historical and ideological discourses. Form, content and lived reality thus become indissociable, and literary analysis therefore needs to pay attention to how aesthetic strategies and referentiality interplay in literary texts. As I will show throughout this book, changing relations of power have affected how the self is both constructed and deconstructed, how silence is broken and how the invisible is made visible in Moroccan autobiographical writing. This is so regardless of whether power is expressed in hegemonic and exclusionary conceptions of culture, language and sexuality, or in direct political violence and torture.

Along with several other literary critics,[59] al-Eid has long argued that novel, autobiography and autobiographical novel are modern genres in the Arab world. One of the challenges faced by Arab authors, consequently, has been the question: 'How should I enunciate?' (*kaifa 'aqūl*) without succumbing to either imitation (*taqlīd*) of their predecessors' narrative form (the *maqāmah*) or mimesis (*muḥākāh*) of the Western novel.[60] This of course does not imply that Arabic novelistic or autobiographical writing cannot benefit from either Arabic literary traditions or Western literary traditions; simply that Arab authors have been forced to consider how to develop aesthetic strategies through which to tell *their* stories; that is, a narrative form that can enunciate their memory, history and experience.[61]

As argued by Sabry Hafez, one may understand the relation of modern Arabic narrative to Western narrative discourse and classical Arabic archetypal fiction as one of dynamic intertextuality rather than imitation or mimesis.[62] As an analytical tool, intertextuality has precisely the double focus to which al-Eid points. On the one hand, intertextuality, as coined by Julia Kristeva, 'calls our attention to the importance of prior texts, insisting that the autonomy of texts is a misleading notion and that a work has the meaning it does only because certain things have previously been written'.[63] On the other hand, rather than seeking to identify prior texts as direct sources of influence, it investigates a text's participation in a discursive space.[64] According to Kristeva, the literary text is an intersection of textual surfaces: that is, a dialogue among several writings rather than a self-contained system.[65] In the context of modern Moroccan autobiographical writing, an intertextual analysis would imply focusing on the discursive spaces in which these texts participate, including how Moroccan authors write in dialogue with earlier and contemporary literary, linguistic, cultural, social and political practices. In Taïa's novel *L'Armée du salut* (2006), for example, the mother figure simultaneously parodies earlier literary depictions of the submissive wife and contemporary stereotypical representations of the oppressed Arab woman while drawing on hysteria as site for queer resistance and as a means to question what it means to be in power.

Queering the nation

As noted at the beginning of this chapter, national identity and the fiction of anchoring the nation in an originary past has excluded not only on the basis of ethnicity and religion but also on the basis of political belief, gender and sexuality. However, as Hayes argues, the need to actively exclude the queer from the narration of the 'nation' presupposes that the queer is always already there.[66] In this respect, I agree with Hayes that sexual 'transgressions' in Maghrebin novels contaminate monologic and heteronormative narrations of the nation. Common to all of Taïa's works, for instance, is a preoccupation with non-normative sexual practices that official discourses consider shameful and whose existence they seek to deny. By centring his works around sexual 'transgressions' and the local spaces where these 'transgressions' take place, Taïa exposes the existence of queer characters who have been silenced by 'the Hetero-Nation', that is, a national identity that foregrounds patriarchy and compulsory heterosexuality.[67] Moreover, as born-translated Taïa's works are preoccupied with the impossible location of Arab-Muslim queers on both sides of the Mediterranean, and with the hegemonic conceptions of national identities implicit in the globalized rhetoric of a sexual clash of civilizations as outlined by Fassin.[68]

While I am aware that 'queer' is a loaded term and one that originated in the West, and that it is important to be attentive to potential sexual differences between cultures, I agree with Hayes that warning against any exportation of the term 'might lead to an Anglo-American monopoly on queerness that repeats exclusionary gestures many constructionists have used to define Western homosexuality'.[69] Arno Schmitt and Jehoeda Sofer's *Sexuality and Eroticism Among Males in Moslem Societies* (1992) is such an example of a work which warns against exporting so-called Western terms, such as homosexuality, to the Muslim world. In his introductory essay, Arno Schmitt argues that in Muslim societies 'there are no homosexuals, there is no word meaning homosexual, there is no such concept in people's minds'.[70] Basing his study of modern sexuality on medieval texts he argues, in an ahistorical and culturalist way, that the absence of Arabic words to describe homosexuality implies that there is no such thing as homosexuality in Muslim societies despite the existence of male-male sexuality:

> To most Muslims anal lust is not really unnatural. One has to avoid getting buggered precisely in order not to acquire a taste for it and thus become addicted. It is like an infectious disease: once infected it is difficult to get rid of it. Men stop getting fucked at the age of 15 or 16 and 'forget' that they allowed/ suffered/enjoyed it earlier.
>
> In spite of all this activity I say there are no 'homosexuals' and there is no (indigenous) word for 'homosexuality'.[71]

As this quote indicates, Arno Schmitt's study of 'Muslim sexuality' is highly Orientalist and based on a static conception of an 'Oriental difference' whereby male-male desire is described by combining an active/passive or sodomitical model with a transgenerational model of pederasty, as Hayes also emphasizes.[72] Arno Schmitt bases his study on sociocultural normativity – that is, on exclusionary narrations of the nation as well as of Islam – while simultaneously reproducing stereotypical depictions of Muslims as a homogenous group of people who always have and always will live according to conservative interpretations of the Qur'an. Within this narrative, men are strong and in control, whereas women are weak and emotional, and those who do not fit into these gender identities are deviant exceptions to the norm:

> [In Muslim societies] there is a strong separation between the domestic sphere of women and children and the public sphere of men.
>
> This separation is not a matter of 'separate but equal' as Muslim apologists want us to believe. Men consider themselves to be stronger, physically, intellectually, and morally, and to be able to control instinct and emotion – unlike women, children, slaves, serfs, eunuchs, barbarians, hermaphrodites, and transvestites.
>
> All of these groups and non-Muslims are discriminated against – in the economy, in ritual, in law, in the political sphere, as well as in matters of sex. It is the right of men to penetrate and their duty to lie on top.[73]

With this construction of masculinity in place, Arno Schmitt argues that male-male sexuality is tolerated as long as the relation is between a 'man' and a 'less-man', as there is, according to him, 'no social role of male-wants-to-fuck-male-and-wants-to-get-fucked-by-another-male'.[74]

The shortcomings of Arno Schmitt's exoticizing gaze on 'Muslim sexuality' have been addressed by many,[75] and in *Desiring Arabs* (2007) Joseph A. Massad provides a welcome critique of Orientalist discourses on so-called Arab sexuality. According to Massad, Western representations of Arab sexual desires are – in both their culturalist and their universalist outlooks – highly Orientalist and Eurocentric. Focusing on how discourses about sex are produced and how they relate to concepts such as culture and civilization, Massad argues that not only culturalist stereotypes about licentious Arab sexuality (as opposed to Victorian puritanism) and repressed Arab sexuality (as opposed to a sexually open West) but also supposedly universalist human rights discourses are a product of Western hegemony. According to Massad, the Gay International[76] has, in an Orientalist and social Darwinist manner, imposed on the Arab world a Western epistemology in which LGBT rights are – at this moment in history – the 'highest step' on the evolutionary ladder. Through the Arab elite, which, according to Massad, has adopted this epistemology, the Gay International has enforced the very hetero/homo binary on the Arab world:[77] '[I]t is the very discourse of the Gay International, which both produces homosexuals, as well as gays and lesbians, where they do not exist, and represses same-sex desires and practices that refuse to be assimilated into its sexual epistemology.'[78]

Whereas I recognize the importance of being attentive to what the hetero/homo binary renders invisible (i.e. sexual desires that do not fit into these identity categories),[79] as I will elaborate throughout this book, Massad's argument is replete with generalizations about the highly diverse human rights movements in both the West and the Arab world, and it makes Taïa's homosexual identity both 'inauthentic' – as homosexuality within this logic equals 'Westernization' – and impossible – because he grew up in a poor family, and both 'Arab homosexuality' and advocating LGBT rights are said to be an invention of *the elite* in the Arab world. Moreover, while I agree with Massad that homosexuality is a modern concept that originated in the West, I find it important to underline that we cannot opt out of the hetero/homo binary. By acknowledging that we are all conditioned by and through it, we can instead shift our attention to how this binary can be – and already is – resisted and renegotiated from the inside, for instance in literary texts.

In this respect, I agree with Jean Zaganiaris that a focus on those identities that are performed and contested on the thresholds of nations and sexualities cannot be reduced to 'Western interventions':

Si les apports de *Desiring Arabs* au niveau de la déconstruction de la rhétorique universaliste sont importants, l'absence d'une prise en compte effective des pluralités, des hybridités, des métissages, des ambivalences identitaires du monde arabe est problématique, surtout lorsqu'il s'agit de penser les pratiques homosexuelles. A partir du moment où il y a exercice des pratiques de pouvoir, il y a également des formes de résistances qui se mettent en place, notamment au niveau de l'expression artistique ou bien du militantisme féministe et LGBT. Considérer ces modes d'action comme des ingérences 'occidentales' au sein des pays anciennement colonisés est une posture réductrice, incapable de prendre en compte les coalitions hybrides susceptibles de se former entre des personnes appartenant à différentes aires géographiques.[80]

(If the contributions of *Desiring Arabs* to the deconstruction of universalist rhetoric are important, the absence of an effective consideration of the pluralities, hybridities, métissages, and identity ambivalences in the Arab world is problematic, especially when thinking about homosexual practices. As soon as power practices are exercised, forms of resistance also take place, particularly in terms of artistic expression or feminist and LGBT militancy. Considering these modes of action as 'Western' interferences in formerly colonized countries is a reductive posture, incapable of taking account of the hybrid coalitions likely to be formed between people belonging to different geographical areas.)

Self-narration as gender insubordination

In the essay 'Imitation and Gender Insubordination',[81] Judith Butler explores how identities such as 'homosexual' and 'heterosexual' are constructed as a relation of copy to original, and how such categories function as sites of regulation, because identity formation always is a result of exclusion and concealment. Tellingly, Butler simultaneously acknowledges that identity categories are indispensable to political action. According to Butler, 'identity categories tend to be instruments of regulatory regimes, whether as the normalizing categories of oppressive structures or as the rallying points for a liberatory contestation of that very oppression'.[82] Thus, like Michel Foucault in *Histoire de la sexualité* (1976),[83] she argues that the affirmation of 'homosexuality' might in itself be an extension of homophobic discourse. But discourse is also the starting point of resistance, because it is simultaneously an instrument and a stumbling block of power. In this respect, the hetero/homo binary is a product of the heterosexual matrix that constructs sex, gender and desire as interdependent: that is, if you are biologically female, you are expected to display female traits and desire men. Homosexuality, in turn, is constructed as that which is not heterosexual; placed outside the normative, it should either be obliterated or be made invisible.

To counter the violence of public obliteration and invisibility, the discourse of 'coming out' has functioned as affirmative resistance. While Butler acknowledges the purpose and importance of this discourse, she is nevertheless primarily preoccupied with what 'outness', when claimed, risks oppressing itself. As I will elaborate in Chapter 2, Taïa's 'coming-out' interview in 2006, on the one hand, constituted a significant political action that pushed the public debate about homophobia and LGBT rights; but on the other, his 'coming out' has simultaneously been trapped within a hetero/homo binary (i.e. the heterosexual matrix, or heteronormativity) replete with culturalist stereotypes as well as with Western hegemonic conceptions of 'universal' rights and with exclusionary conceptions of homosexuality (i.e. homonormativity).

If we relate this to al-Eid's definition of the role of the author as one who makes the invisible visible, Butler adds that rendering visible simultaneously institutes new exclusions or invisibilities. With respect to 'coming out', a risk is that homosexuals themselves end up trapped in an exclusionary identity category which is defined by and through the heterosexual matrix:

There is no question that gays and lesbians are threatened by the violence of public erasure, but the decision to counter that violence must be careful not to reinstall another in its place. Which version of lesbian or gay ought to be rendered visible, and which internal exclusions will that rendering visible institute? Can the visibility of identity *suffice* as a political strategy, or can it only be the starting point for a strategic intervention which calls for a transformation of policy?[84]

Noticeably, Butler does not call for a return to silence or invisibility, but urges that we make use of a provisional identity category that can constantly be called into question. It is 'in avowing the sign's strategic provisionality (rather than its strategic essentialism), that identity can become a site of contest and revision, indeed, take on a future set of significations that those of us who use it now may not be able to foresee'.[85] This is of significance not only with respect to future openings but also with respect to cultural differences, and as such Butler's conception of performativity and imitation is not only of interest in terms of how homosexuality *as copy* deconstructs heterosexuality *as origin* but also in terms of how homonormativity is deconstructed through imitation.

According to Butler, gender is a performative construct. That is, 'there is no gender identity behind the expression of gender; [. . .] identity is performatively constituted by the very "expressions" that are said to be its results'.[86] This, moreover, implies that there is no pre-discursive 'natural sex' behind the cultural inscription of gender. Bodies are gendered from the beginning of their social existence, and it is therefore impossible to retrieve a 'natural body' pre-existing gender inscriptions. In line with Foucault, Butler maintains that discourses produce the subjects they subsequently claim to represent: 'The performative invocation of a nonhistorical "before" becomes the foundational premise that guarantees a presocial ontology of persons who freely consent to be governed and, thereby, constitute the legitimacy of the social contract'.[87] As there is no position outside the field of power, this is a condition of political resistance as well.

Like the concepts of patriarchy and heterosexuality, identity categories such as woman, gay and lesbian are produced as subjects of identity politics through exclusionary practices. Whereas feminist theory initially sought to establish the term 'woman' as a category that could encompass all women as the most effective means of political action, it has been criticized ever since by both third-world feminism and queer theory for assuming that the term 'woman' denotes a common identity and that the oppression of women has a singular form. Instead of insisting on a stable subject of feminism, Butler therefore argues that we must pursue a feminist genealogy of the category 'woman' if the relations of domination and exclusion that control representational politics are to be avoided.[88] In other words, as the stable notion of gender is an effect of a heteronormative discourse, invoking the subject 'woman' will both reinforce what feminism seeks to resist and risk doing violence to the women it claims to represent.

If we return to Khatibi, this is precisely what is at stake with his double critique. In opposing the Western episteme to its unthought outside while radicalizing the margin, double critique points to the arbitrariness of binary oppositions. While the silenced or invisible part (Khatibi = Arabs, the colonized, etc.; Butler = women, homosexuals, etc.) first of all needs a voice and an identity to be seen and heard, double critique moves beyond a reversal of hierarchies to a thinking in languages (*pensée en langues*) – an other-thought (*pensée-autre*) that is neither inside nor outside, but a radicalization of the margin. Relating the question of gender performativity to double critique, I argue, opens the possibility for an analysis of queer identities in Moroccan autobiographical writing as not simply resisting the 'Hetero-Nation' but also unsettling categories such as homosexual, gay, lesbian and transgender. This is precisely what is at stake in Khatibi's novel *Amour bilingue* (1983) and its literary play with homosexuality and androgyny. In *Amour bilingue* Khatibi narrates the bilingual experience through a love story that continually disturbs the difference between 'he' and 'she', between 'mother tongue' and 'foreign language', between 'eroticism' and 'bestiality'.

The fact that we are all discursively constructed thus does not imply that resistance is impossible, but rather that 'representation' will make sense only if the subjects 'woman', 'gay', 'lesbian' and so on are nowhere presumed.[89] 'Representing' the unrepresentable is, according to Butler, pursued through imitation and parody: 'The professionalization of gayness requires a certain performance and production of a "self" which is the *constituted effect* of a discourse that nevertheless claims to "represent" that self as a prior truth.'[90] In this respect, 'being' lesbian is a repeated play through which the lesbian 'I' is established, instituted, circulated and confirmed.[91] Paradoxically, however, this repeated play is also what reveals the instability of the category: 'For if the "I" is a site of repetition, that is, if the "I" only achieves the semblance of identity through a certain repetition of itself, then the I is always displaced by the very repetition that sustains it.'[92] That is, the coherence of the 'I' or its self-identity is both constituted and contested by the repetition and the failure to repeat an identity. With respect to the relation between heterosexuality and homosexuality, the heterosexual matrix has established heterosexuality as 'real', 'natural' and 'authentic', whereas homosexuality is constituted as 'a copy, an imitation, a derivative example, a shadow of the real'.[93] But this regulatory regime can be subverted through repetition, imitation and parody. This is particularly clear in the parodic performance of the drag, who by imitating gender reveals the imitative structure of gender itself.[94] In other words, imitation produces the imitated, implying that heterosexuality as 'natural' and 'original' is an effect of imitative strategies:

> [I]f it were not for the notion of the homosexual *as* copy, there would be no construct of heterosexuality *as* origin. Heterosexuality here presupposes homosexuality. And if the homosexual *as* copy *precedes* the heterosexual as *origin*, then it seems only fair to concede that the copy comes before the origin, and that homosexuality is thus the origin, and heterosexuality the copy.
>
> But simple inversions are not really possible. For it is only *as* copy that homosexuality can be argued to *precede* heterosexuality as the origin. In other words, the entire framework of copy and origin proves radically unstable as each position inverts into the other and confounds the possibility of any stable way to locate the temporal or logical priority of either term.[95]

If imitation does not copy that which is prior, but produces and inverts the very terms of priority and derivativeness, it simultaneously makes room for a subversion of the relation between 'Arab' homosexuality *as* copy and 'Western' homosexuality *as* original while unsettling the very category 'homosexual' through an expansion of the boundaries of homosexual desires. In Taïa's novel, *Un Pays pour mourir* (2015), the story of Aziz/Zannouba (both before and after his/her gender reassignment surgery) is the story of a man who wants to return to childhood obliviousness in order to resist homonormativity and its heterosexual mimicking. Moreover, by parodying the role he is expected to play as effeminate, passive and exoticized 'other', Aziz's drag performance displays an effeminate man that is as virile as anyone.

Shame and (hetero)normativity

As noted by Massad[96] and, before him, Edward Said,[97] the excessive focus on the oppressive role of so-called shame–honour culture in Arab societies when discussing sexual rights is highly Orientalist and tends to reduce Arabs to an emotionally driven group of people devoid of reason (as opposed to 'rationally acting Western individuals'). But all cultures have a moral system that defines what is shameful and what is honourable. Shame is, in all societies, central to moral development and the reproduction of social norms, in particular norms of sexual conduct. The question is therefore: How do we analyse narrations of non-normative sexual practices, which official discourses in Morocco consider shameful and whose existence they seek to deny, without succumbing to culturalist stereotypes about Morocco as a shame–honour culture?

One of the strengths of affect theory is its displacement of the hierarchy between reason and emotion, and Sara Ahmed's study, in *The Cultural Politics of Emotion* (2004), of how emotions produce social relationships (which in turn determine the rhetoric of the nation) provides insightful perspectives on how shame functions both as an essential part of subject formation and as a possible strategy for queer resistance. According to Ahmed emotions are cultural practices, not psychological states. Inspired by Butler's conception of performativity, she is, therefore, concerned with what emotions 'do' rather than what they 'are'. Shame can thus neither be reduced to a psychological or social phenomenon, nor simply be described as both psychological *and* social:

> In suggesting that emotions create the very effect of an inside and an outside, I am not then simply claiming that emotions are psychological *and* social, individual *and* collective. My model refuses the abbreviation of the 'and'. Rather, I suggest that emotions are crucial to the very constitution of the psychic and the social as objects, a process which suggests that the 'objectivity' of the psychic and social is an effect rather than a cause. In other words, emotions are not 'in' either the individual or the social, but produce the very surfaces and boundaries that allow the individual and the social to be delineated as if they are objects.[98]

Just as Butler questions the distinction between sex and gender, Ahmed problematizes the distinction between affect and emotion, between the non-discursive and the discursive. What then does shame do? According to Ahmed, it is 'an intense and painful sensation that is bound up with how the self feels about itself, a self-feeling that is felt by and on the body'.[99] When a person feels shame, it is because he or she has done something he or she feels is bad. Shame is usually experienced before another, and therefore the double play of concealment and exposure is crucial to the work of shame:

> Shame certainly involves an impulse to 'take cover' and 'to cover oneself'. But the desire to take cover and to be covered presupposes the failure of cover; in shame, one desires cover precisely because one has already been exposed to others. Hence the word 'shame' is associated as much with cover and concealment, as it is with exposure, vulnerability and wounding. On the one hand, shame covers that which is exposed (we turn away, we lower our face, we avert our gaze), while on the other, shame exposes that which has been covered (it un-covers). Shame in exposing that which has been covered demands us to re-cover, such a re-covering would be a recovery from shame.[100]

Shame thus both conceals and reveals, and as such it requires a witness, or at least an imagined witness. However, anybody cannot be a witness, or cause somebody to feel shame. According to Ahmed, the subject only feels shame if there is a prior love or desire for the 'other', who catches the subject doing something bad. 'Shame is not a purely negative relation to another: shame is ambivalent.'[101] When I feel shame, it is the imagined view of the other – an other whose view matters to me – that I take on in relation to myself. In this sense, shame reveals a complex relation between self and other:

> In shame, I am the object as well as the subject of the feeling. Such an argument crucially suggests that shame requires an identification with the other who, as witness, returns the subject to itself. The view of this other is the view that I have taken on in relation to myself; I see myself *as if I were* this other. My failure before this other hence is profoundly a failure of myself to myself. In shame, I expose to myself that I am a failure through the gaze of an ideal other.[102]

On the one hand, shame reveals a failure to live up to an ideal; on the other, it confirms a commitment to this ideal in the first place. Because 'the fear of shame prevents the subject from betraying "ideals", while the lived experience of shame reminds the subject of the reasons for those ideals in the first place',[103] shame has been considered crucial to moral development. When we refrain from doing something out of fear of shame, we simultaneously reproduce social norms. Thus feeling shame reveals how subject formation takes place under the constant threat of exclusion. Both the fear of shame and the feeling of shame produce subjects and social relations through constant processes of inclusion and exclusion.

If shame is crucial to subject formation and the reproduction of social norms, how can it simultaneously function as a strategy for queer resistance? It is precisely in the relation between shame and exclusion that Eve Sedgwick has identified a queer political potential, as both shame and queer represent a position outside of the normative. Following Butler's conception of performativity, shame, according to Sedgwick, both generates the queer subject and repeats past associations with what is considered queer. As such, shame constitutes a sort of speech act that calls certain subjects into existence. As shame is crucial to queer subject formation, it is, according to Sedgwick, impossible to separate queer from shame, and a resistance strategy with that purpose would therefore be futile: 'If queer is a politically potent term, which it is, that's because, far from being capable of being detached from the childhood scene of shame, it cleaves to that scene as a near-inexhaustible source of transformational energy.'[104] Sedgwick argues that we instead search for forms of political protest which maintain an anti-normative position by formulating alternatives to 'freedom from shame'.[105] Rather than operating within a 'shame/pride' paradigm, where the object of political activism is to replace shame with pride, Sedgwick argues that the strategy of resistance lies in the performative potential of shame, which – rather than reclaiming space within the norm – seeks to undermine the norm. While shame as an anti-normative political strategy can raise awareness of practices of social exclusion, postcolonial critics, such as Ahmed, have, however, criticized Sedgwick for circular reasoning and for idealizing shame:

> I am not sure how it is possible to embrace the negative without turning it into a positive. To say 'yes' to the 'no' is still a 'yes'. To embrace or affirm the experience of shame, for instance, sounds very much like taking a pride in one's shame – a conversion of bad feeling into good feeling.[106]

Moreover, saying 'yes' to shame presupposes that you have a choice between saying 'yes' and 'no'. But not everyone is this privileged. To some, shame is an inescapable condition of life which is not easily turned into political resistance, whereas others are not even recognized as subjects who can feel shame. In Taïa's novel *Un Pays pour mourir*, the question of feeling shame or feeling pride is intertwined with the characters' desperate efforts to reinvent themselves. But as they are not privileged with a voice in the public sphere of political resistance, this reinvention is trapped between desiring and deferring death. The novel is in this way simultaneously an effort to embrace experiences of shame and marginalization (in order to voice them as positions of political resistance) and a narrative that reveals the impossibility of such a political resistance (as no one within the narrative sees or recognizes any of the characters). Thus along with Maja Mons Bissenbakker-Frederiksen, I argue that reading shame as a strategy for queer resistance needs to pay attention to the relations of inequality that shame both conditions and is conditioned by.[107]

To return to the beginning of this chapter, shame is also crucial to the formation of the nation as ideal. As Ahmed argues, shame plays a significant role in the process of reconciliation and the healing of past wounds. This is quite significant with respect to Morocco's process of reconciliation after the Years of Lead and the ruling elite's insistence on the need to 'turn the page' (*ṭayy al-safḥah*).[108] But what do expressions of national shame do? And who is entitled to feel shame? According to Ahmed, national shame over past injustices works as a form of nation building. By 'coming to terms' with its own past, the nation can reconcile with itself; that is, by feeling bad the nation is allowed to feel better.[109] However, by projecting injustice and wrongdoings onto the past, the collective shame of the nation is, as Ahmed argues, represented as a shame that does not affect individuals in the present despite its being expressed right there in the present, which is haunted by the wrongdoings of the past. Thus '[d]espite its recognition of past wrongdoings, shame can still conceal how such wrongdoings shape lives in the present. The work of shame troubles and is troubling, exposing some wounds, at the same time as it conceals others.'[110] In this respect, shame represents an expressed desire to move on. That is, the exposure of the nation's failure to live up to its ideals in the past becomes the ground for a narrative of recovery, which enables the nation to 'live up to' its ideals in the present.[111] However, the expression of national shame risks repeating the same hegemonic structures that caused past wrongdoings, because it consolidates the distinction between inside and outside the nation. Only those who are entitled to feel shame are 'in' the nation and a part of national recovery. As I argue in Chapter 5, Moroccan authors, intellectuals and human rights activists have struggled against such exclusionary practices of national shame, because they both conceal injustices committed in the present and exclude those who do not fit into the narrative of the nation as ideal from being a part of the reconciliation process.

Chapter 2

ABDELLAH TAÏA AS AUTHOR AND ACTIVIST

Despite an increasing academic interest in Abdellah Taïa's work, literary studies rarely take his position as activist into account or relate his creative writing to LGBT activism in Morocco. However, Taïa's narrations of the 'self-absorbed' as a site of queer commitment form part of a larger struggle to counter the violence of public obliteration and invisibility. For this reason, this chapter explores his position as author and activist in relation to contemporary LGBT activism in Morocco, contemporary Moroccan queer literature and his own extra-literary writing and public talks on culture, language, sexuality and identity in Morocco, Europe and the United States.

Even though Taïa is not part of an organized activist group, his coming-out interview in 2006 nevertheless constituted a significant political action, and he has since actively pushed the public debate about homophobia and LGBT rights through interviews in newspapers and on television, in essays and opinion pieces, both inside and outside Morocco. Living in-between Morocco and France, Taïa's coming-out interview has formed part of a larger public debate about the relation between so-called authentic Moroccan sexuality and so-called universal rights. Taïa has not simply faced homophobia and accusations of having assumed a sexual identity that is foreign to Morocco, but also Islamophobia and a French homonormative rhetoric that leave Arab-Muslim queers invisible and marginalized because they can only be seen as queers if they renounce their religion and culture.[1] For this reason, Taïa is not only preoccupied with queering the 'Hetero-Nation' through a subversion of the relation between heterosexuality *as origin* and homosexuality *as copy*, through his literary works and public performances he also dismantles the relation between 'Western' homosexuality *as origin* and 'Arab' homosexuality *as copy*, while unsettling the very category 'homosexual' through extending the boundaries of homosexual desires.

Moreover, Taïa's extra-literary public performances can inform our conception of his creative writing as committed literature because commitment is a question of not only writing but also how writing is activated in the public debate. Somewhat paradoxically, literary representation in French has been regarded as politically less dangerous than public debate in Arabic, even though Taïa's literary accomplishments are precisely what have paved the way for his position in the public debate. Moreover, in contemporary Moroccan literature, writing the 'real' through the lens of individual experiences has become a site of commitment to the struggle to secure the right to individual liberty. In this respect, Moroccan authors such as Taïa, Rachid O., Bahaa Trabelsi, Karim Nasseri and Nedjma are neither overtly focused on the self nor blind to the other. Instead, their various literary plays with the 'self-absorbed' as a site of queer commitment constitute ethical acts of writing the self as other. That is, through an intentionally 'naive' narrative style marked by textual eclecticism and pop culture, they are infiltrating hegemonic narrations of the Moroccan 'nation' through everyday stories that reveal a heterogeneous world that fits into neither 'authentic' Moroccan culture nor 'universalist' discourse about individual rights.

Significant in this respect is how the question of silence – which surrounds homosexuality in Morocco – relates to a larger debate about so-called authentic Moroccan culture. As I have argued in Chapter 1, the impulse to take cover and keep silent is closely related to the workings of shame and its role in moral development. Both LGBT activism and literary representations of queer identities are closely intertwined with the work of shame as a double play of concealment and exposure. As Ahmed has demonstrated, shame is ambivalent, and reveals a complex relation between self and other. On the one hand, it reveals a failure to live up to an ideal, but on the other, it confirms a commitment to that ideal in the first place. In this respect, refraining from concealing what social norms have deemed shameful – which authors such as Taïa and LGBT activists make a virtue of – often comes across as self-absorbed and exhibitionist to those who seek to uphold the norm, because the act of displacing the workings of shame equals displacing the established moral system and the relation between self and other. Thus what is at stake in both the discourse of 'coming out' and the question of writing the 'self-absorbed' as a site of queer commitment is a reconfiguration of the relation between self and other, between individual and community.

Breaking the silence[2]

Despite the fact that Taïa is repeatedly introduced as the first Moroccan to profess his homosexuality publicly – and he should of course be credited with his courage – many others are equally courageous in their struggle for LGBT rights in Morocco. At the time Taïa came out, the public debate about homosexuality had already begun. The ascension of Mohammed VI to the throne in 1999 had sparked hope for liberalization in the country, especially among young Moroccans, and this hope resonated in the Moroccan media, which saw an opening of a space for democratic debate.[3] Under the headline 'Être homosexuel au Maroc. Quoi qu'on pense d'eux, ils existent. Et ils se cachent. Et si on les écoutait?' (Being homosexual in Morocco. Whatever one thinks of them, they exist. And they hide. And what if we listened to them?), *TelQuel* 120 on 4 April 2004 addressed the conditions of homosexuals in Morocco with unprecedented outspokenness. As noted by Florence Bergeaud-Blackler and Victor Eck, *TelQuel*'s coverage moved beyond the scandalous and anecdotal by embarking on a social analysis, in addition to publishing personal testimonials by Moroccan homosexuals.[4] Moreover, the front-page illustration challenged two of the principal stereotypes about homosexuals in the Arab world – the transgenerational relation (between an object-boy and a mature male) and the active–passive relation (between a masculine man and a feminine man) – by depicting the back of two men of approximately same age and equally 'masculine', the one with his hand on the neck of the other.

The two common goals of the four main LGBT movements in Morocco – KifKif, MALI, 'Aṣwāt and Akaliyat – are to improve the living conditions of LGBT persons and to urge the Moroccan government to repeal Article 489 of the Moroccan penal code, according to which an indecent act or an act against nature with an individual of the same sex is a criminal offence and punishable with six months to three years of imprisonment and a fine of 200 to 1,000 dirhams. However, KifKif, MALI, 'Aṣwāt and Akaliyat have approached these goals in significantly different ways.

In 2004 the LGBT movement KifKif (Equal to Equal, or same-same) was founded as a Facebook group in reaction to an incident in Tétouan where forty-three people were arrested on 1 June 2004 and accused of 'indecent behaviour' (thirty-three men dressed in women's clothes and ten women dressed in men's clothes were singing and dancing at a birthday party). After their arrest a group of young Moroccan homosexuals launched an international protest campaign in order to effect their release, and KifKif was created to coordinate this campaign.[5] In 2006 the movement unsuccessfully applied for official legal status, and today KifKif is based in Madrid, where it has been recognized as a NGO since 2008. According to Samir Bargachi, the founder and coordinator of KifKif, the principal strategy of the movement is perseverance and dialogue. That is, in order to change the living conditions of LGBT persons in Morocco, silence must be broken and a dialogue be opened.

In 2010 Bargachi and KifKif were behind another key event: the publication of the first Arabic-language gay print magazine not only in Morocco but, according to the Moroccan francophone news magazine *Actuel* 44, in the Arab, African and Muslim world in general.[6] In April 2010 200 copies of the first issue of *Mithly* (Like me) were printed and distributed clandestinely so as to avoid the attention of the authorities. Most Moroccan journals showed little interest in covering the print publication or the ensuing online publication (last updated in July 2011), confining their coverage to the negative reactions of the Islamist right, such as the PJD (Parti de la justice et du développement).[7] However, *Mithly* was well received by *Actuel* and *TelQuel*, both of which are known for editorial lines that are critical of the Moroccan government and intent on breaking the silence surrounding social, cultural and religious taboos.

The ambition of *Mithly* was to establish a new and non-pejorative vocabulary in Arabic for talking about homosexuality. The neologism *mithly*, with its connotations of exemplarity and sameness, had already been in use among Arab homosexuals since around 2000, to begin with in Lebanon.[8] The intention of the magazine was thus to start a debate about linguistic practices and to advance *mithly* in the public debate as the proper Arabic term to describe homosexuals. The articles in the magazine consequently used the terms *mithliya* (homosexuality), *mithliyine* (male homosexuals) and *mithliyat* (female homosexuals) instead of the more commonly known term *shādhdh al-jinsī* (sexual deviant), Arabic pejoratives such as *zamel* (faggot) and the English 'gay' or 'lesbian'. Despite the fact that *shudhudh al-jinsī* (sexual deviance) is still the most commonly used term in the media and *mithliya* (homosexuality) primarily is known to the LGBT community, the latter has gained ground as a term contesting homophobia.[9]

However, KifKif and the francophone Moroccan news magazines are not the only ones to address the conditions of homosexuals in Morocco. On 24 August 2009 'Mouvement alternative pour les libertés individuelles' (MALI; Alternative movement for individual liberties) was founded on Facebook by two young Moroccans, journalist Zineb El Rhazoui and psychologist Ibtissame Lachgar. Their activism began with debates on Facebook about individual freedom in Morocco (freedom of cult and consciousness, freedom of expression, sexual freedom and freedom to choose your private life).[10] They have generally been more confrontational in their activism, and their first effort to mobilize the public was the organization of a symbolic picnic during Ramadan on 13 September 2009 in the Mohammédia forest, north of Casablanca. With this event they wanted to spark a debate about the right to break the fast in public during Ramadan and push for the abrogation of Article 222 of the Moroccan penal code, which stipulates that a Muslim person who breaks the fast in public during Ramadan is liable to six months of imprisonment and a fine between 12 and 120 dirhams.[11] Even though the local authorities in Mohammédia managed to disrupt the picnic before it took place, MALI became famous for its efforts and – in a somewhat reductive way – also known under the name 'Dé-jeûners de ramadan, *Ouakallin ramdan* (en marocain)'.[12] However, as Zineb El Rhazoui underlines in an interview with *Afrik*, MALI is not 'un mouvement qui appelle à la rupture publique du jeûne, mais qui défend le droit de ceux qui ne jeûnent pas, pour des raisons qui leurs sont propres, à exister en toute légalité' (a movement that calls for breaking the fast in public, but a movement that defends the right of those who do not fast, for reasons of their own, to exist legally).[13] MALI has also been campaigning against Article 489 under the headline 'Homophobia is a crime, not homosexuality', for instance in relation to the homophobic assault on two men in their private home in Beni Mellal (March 2016) and in relation to the two girls who were arrested for kissing in Marrakesh (October 2016), to mention but two examples.

In 2012 yet another Arabic-language gay magazine, ˀAṣwāt (Voices), saw the day. The online magazine and its activist arm, ˀAṣwāt LGBTI Association, were created by a group of volunteers who felt a need for more information about the everyday struggles and triumphs of homosexuals in Morocco. In 2014, the founder and president of ˀAṣwāt, Marwan Bensaid, began to produce a series of short films under the title *Kaynīn* (They exist), with the hope 'to create a dialogue and break through the barrier of silence around sexual orientation and gender identity in Morocco'.[14] Filmed with his own camera and without any financial support, these YouTube videos provide a number of personal testimonies by Moroccan homosexuals about their lives and the violence and discrimination they encounter because of their sexuality.[15] Moreover, as part of their campaign 'al-ḥubb laysa jarīmaʾ (love is not a crime) on the occasion of the international day against homophobia, ʾAṣwāt produced yet another video in 2014, this time with journalists, academics and activists, among other academics, author and literary critic Abdellah Baida and professor of sociology Abdessamad Dialmy.[16]

A significant part of ʾAṣwāt's activism consists in providing legal assistance to LGBT persons in prison and to raise awareness about the basic legal rights that every Moroccan citizen, regardless of his or her sexual orientation or gender identity, has when he or she is under police investigation.[17] For this reason, there is also a significant difference between ʾAṣwāt's and MALI's perception of the effect of public happenings and the interference of international organizations in Morocco. This is perhaps best reflected in how they reacted to the Femen happening 'In gay we trust'.

On 2 June 2015 two topless Femen activists from France kissed in front of the Hassan Tower in Rabat to protest against the conviction of three homosexuals to three years of imprisonment by the court in Taourirt. The two activists were quickly expelled from Morocco, but the next day two Moroccan men imitated the happening by kissing in the same spot. They were immediately arrested. The two happenings sparked a number of protests lead by a new group called 'Touche pas à mes moeurs' (Hands of my mores), and as the Moroccan national TV channel broadcasted photos of the two men, around twenty protesters gathered outside the home of one of the men and threatened his family.[18]

'By broadcasting a photo of these two men, national television deliberately put them in harm's way. Rabat is a small city, making it all too easy for their critics to identify them. This protest in front of one of their homes was a genuine incitement to hatred.'[19] Lachgar from MALI did not only find the actions of the national TV channel deeply problematic but also criticized the authorities for not monitoring the protests and protecting the families of the two arrested men. However, despite the subsequent protests, Lachgar welcomes happenings such as 'In gay we trust': 'Je pense que cela fait sauter des boulons, brise des tabous, ouvre des débats. Le fait que ce soit devant une mosquée interpelle la symbolique des religions ou des pratiquants religieux qui sont homophobes [. . .] Il faut secouer le cocotier pour obtenir des droits et faire évoluer les mentalités.' (I think that it makes bolts jump, breaks taboos, opens debates. The fact that it is in front of a mosque challenges the symbolism of religions or religious practitioners who are homophobic [. . .] We must shake the coconut tree to obtain rights and change the mentalities.)[20] As to whether happenings such as 'In gay we trust' could be counterproductive, Lachgar's answer is: 'Nous n'avons pas le temps de penser à cela. La désobéissance civile est nécessaire pour dénoncer la loi et la société homophobes.' (We don't have time to think about that. Civil disobedience is necessary to renounce the law and the homophobic society.)[21]

Contrary to this, ʾAṣwāt has been more critical towards these kinds of confrontational happenings. In a press release they wrote that they 'ne peuvent guère adhérer à une activité similaire à celle de Femen au Maroc. [Cette action] va à l'encontre de notre vision d'un engagement et d'une lutte pacifiste' (can hardly adhere to an activity similar to that of Femen in Morocco. [This action] goes against our vision of a pacifist commitment and struggle).[22] An anonymous representative of 'Aṣwāt further explained to *TelQuel*: 'Le choc et la provocation dans notre contexte précis peuvent nuire à la cause, ce qui constitue un pas en arrière. Cette action à certes créée une polémique au niveau du Maroc et sur le plan international, mais à-t-elle pu libérer les deux Marocains arrêtés le lendemain?' (The shock and provocation in our specific context can harm the cause and constitute a step backwards. This action has certainly created a controversy both in Morocco and internationally, but has it been able to free the two Moroccans that were arrested the following day?)[23]

The youngest LGBT organization in Morocco is Akaliyat (Minorities), which is dedicated to defending the rights of religious and sexual minorities. On 14 November 2016 Akaliyat announced that it had created a commission to prepare for a general assembly in late December 2016 in order to apply for official legal status. However, in January 2017 the wali of the Rabat-Salé region rejected their application on the grounds that the authorities had not been properly informed about their general assembly.[24] Today Akaliyat operates as an unofficial organization similarly to MALI and 'Aṣwāt.

However, despite the growing number of people advocating equal rights for all, the anti-homosexuality law still forces LGBT activists to work below the radar of the government to avoid censorship and prosecution. Aside from a few bars in cities such as Casablanca, the internet is still the primary place for homosexuals to meet and organize as participants of online communities in which they can retain anonymity and thus avoid the risk of exposure. Whereas Article 489 is rarely enforced, as it requires proof of same-sex sexual intercourse, the accusations can often be as harmful as a conviction because the exposure of the accused's identity can lead to loss of one's job or being ostracized from one's family. The law is thus as much a method of social control as it is a means of punishment, and the problems that LGBT persons face are as much a question of public opinion as it is a lack of legal rights.[25] Moreover, homophobia seems to have surged in the public sphere, perhaps in response to the increasing visibility of LGBT rights activists, and perhaps also along with the increasing popularity of Islamist political parties such as the PJD, which currently holds the position of head of government and which regards homosexuality as a sin and a deviance testifying to the country's moral decay.

Another event, which reveals not only how emotional a subject homosexuality still is but, more importantly, how social acceptability of homosexuality, in some cases, seems to be inversely proportional to its visibility, is an incident in Ksar El Kébir, a city located between Rabat and Tangier.[26] On 19 November 2007 an inhabitant held a private soirée during which a man dressed as a woman danced. The event was filmed and uploaded on YouTube as a 'gay wedding' by an anonymous user. Two days later the Moroccan press reported that 'uncontrollably' angry citizens in the thousands were demonstrating in the streets while chanting homophobic slogans.[27] The Friday sermon stirred the crowds, and while shops were attacked during demonstrations, rumours spread and passing individuals were assaulted by protesters.[28] The affair ended as quickly as it had begun. Six people were arrested, and the interior minister, Chakib Benmoussa, assured the public that no 'gay marriage' had taken place and that the party had been nothing but 'charlatanism'. This official version was adopted without question by all the political parties in Morocco and demonstrated that not even the left wing was ready to enter into a debate about Article 489 and a decriminalization of homosexuality, even though a part of the press had paved the way.[29]

Moreover, as Bergeaud-Blackler and Eck's 2009 interviews of Moroccan homosexuals in Sidi Ali, Fez and Casablanca show, there is far from being a consensus among Moroccan homosexuals with respect to the need for 'breaking the silence'. As one of their interviewees, Hichem from Fez, said:

Ils [les médias] veulent que la société soit entre parenthèses 'ouverte'. Moi je suis d'accord qu'elle soit fermée, mais fermée avec respect car on est islamique, l'Islam est contre ça (l'homosexualité); et moi je pense qu'il viendra un jour ou j'arrêterai tout ça, je vais pas rester gay. On (nous, les homos marocains) est fermé avec respect, ça veut dire qu'on veut pas attire l'attention, on est normal, on s'habille normalement, et dans ce cas on doit être respecté. [. . .] Si c'est ouvert on va avoir des problèmes sociaux. Pour le moment il y a des homo qui font la rue, c'est à peu près 5%, mais si c'est ouvert, il y en aura partout et on n'aura plus une société marocaine, on n'est pas des Européens ni des Américains, on vit en Afrique au Maroc. On garde toujours nos origines. C'est contre la religion et contre la société, il y a une ligne rouge.[30]

(They [the media] want society to be, in brackets, 'open'. I think that it should be closed, but closed with respect because we are Islamic, and Islam is against it (homosexuality); and I think that one day I will stop all that; I will not stay gay. We (us, the Moroccan homos) are closed off by respect, meaning that we do not want to attract attention, we are normal, we are dressed normally, and in this case we should be respected. [. . .] If it is out in the open, we will have social problems. At the moment, some homos are out in the street, they make up around 5 percent, but if it is out in the open, it will be everywhere, and we will no longer have a Moroccan society, we are neither Europeans nor Americans, we live in Africa in Morocco. We always guard our origins. It is against our religion and against our society; there is a red line.)

As the quote by Hichem shows, not everybody wants to come out of the shadows. Even a repeal of Article 489, which will allow homosexuals to live without fear of imprisonment, does not necessarily imply more 'openness' about sexual orientations, as 'coming out' would still be at the risk of being ostracized.

Two things are at stake with respect to the difference between positions such as Hichem's and those of LGBT activists and authors such as Taïa: the conception of Moroccan 'authenticity', and the risk of violent sexual harassment. According to Hichem, silence protects the 'honour' and privacy of men like him, while simultaneously guarding Moroccan cultural and religious specificity. That is, silence both protects those who have homosexual relations from being judged by society and protects society from being infiltrated by 'inauthentic' sexuality. However, while some find freedom in being 'invisible', as they can have same-sex sexual relations without necessarily identifying as homosexual, others experience a loss of dignity, as they are prevented from identifying as homosexual and being respected for who they are. To Taïa and others, the demand for 'authenticity' is not only a direct impediment to individual liberty but also an exoticization of Morocco.

However, at the core of this conflict lies a more difficult question about violence: that is, the relation between silence and violence, as well as between visibility and violence. On the one hand, silence protects some from violence insofar as social acceptability is inversely proportional with visibility. For many, homophobic assaults and harassment are legitimate concerns and suffice to argue against 'openness' and activism, as they feel the stakes are too high. On the other hand, however, homosexuals such as Taïa have been subject to both harassment and rape, with nowhere to seek protection – people might know what is going on, but because of the taboos surrounding homosexuality, nobody talks about it, and nobody interferes.

'Coming out' in Morocco

It is within this context that Taïa as author and activist must be understood. In interviews and essays, Taïa has pointed to two childhood experiences of violence and shame that forced him into silence and became formative of his life, writing and activism. In an essay in the *New York Times* in 2012, Taïa describes how, as a child, he was an effeminate boy whom everybody in his neighbourhood called 'the little girl' – even the teenagers who once took part in the same sexual games as him.[31] Already at the age of ten he knew what happened to boys like him: they became the easy sexual objects of frustrated men, because homosexuality was a taboo, claimed as non-existent in the 1980s in Morocco, and therefore no one would interfere.[32] The only protection family and friends could offer him was to urge him into silence. At the age of twelve when his body started to change from 'effeminate' boy into 'effeminate' man, attempts at rape and abuse multiplied. It culminated in 1985, when he realized that no one would save him:

> It all came to a head one summer night in 1985. It was too hot. Everyone was trying in vain to fall asleep. I, too, lay awake, on the floor beside my sisters, my mother close by. Suddenly, the familiar voices of drunken men reached us. We all heard them. The whole family. The whole neighborhood. The whole world. These men, whom we all knew quite well, cried out: 'Abdellah, little girl, come down. Come down. Wake up and come down. We all want you. Come down, Abdellah. Don't be afraid. We won't hurt you. We just want to have sex with you.'
>
> They kept yelling for a long time. My nickname. Their desire. Their crime. They said everything that went unsaid in the too-silent, too-respectful world where I lived. But I was far, then, from any such analysis, from understanding

that the problem wasn't me. I was simply afraid. Very afraid. And I hoped my big brother, my hero, would rise and answer them. That he would protect me, at least with words. I didn't want him to fight them – no. All I wanted him to say were these few little words: 'Go away! Leave my little brother alone.'

But my brother, the absolute monarch of our family, did nothing. Everyone turned their back on me. Everyone killed me that night. I don't know where I found the strength, but I didn't cry. I just squeezed my eyes shut a bit more tightly. And shut, with the same motion, everything else in me. Everything. I was never the same Abdellah Taïa after that night. To save my skin, I killed myself. And that was how I did it.

I began by keeping my head low all the time. I cut all ties with the children in the neighborhood. I altered my behavior. I kept myself in check: no more feminine gestures, no more honeyed voice, no more hanging around women. No more anything. I had to invent a whole new Abdellah. I bent myself to the task with great determination, and with the realization that this world was no longer my world. Sooner or later, I would leave it behind. I would grow up and find freedom somewhere else. But in the meantime I would become hard. Very hard.[33]

I have quoted Taïa's own description at length because it pinpoints how the internalization of heteronormativity is linked to silence, invisibility and obliteration. To save himself, Taïa had to obliterate himself.

The second and related key event that happened that same summer is recounted by Taïa in an interview with Aaron Hicklin from *Out*.[34] On a hot afternoon when he was supposed to be taking his afternoon nap, Taïa went out looking for friends to play with, but ran into a group of older boys who wanted to have sex. Rather than complying, he ran off and only stopped to catch his breath when he was almost home. At that moment he touched a high-voltage generator and passed out.[35] When he woke up an hour later, his family and the whole neighbourhood were grieving by his bedside, believing that he was dead. The story of how he died and rose again became a local legend, and Taïa became known as 'the miracle boy'. However, for Taïa the story had different implications. He defied death and would keep on doing it, as a teenager by withdrawing from everything and keeping silent, and as an adult by speaking up and reclaiming his right to exist.

After these two incidents, Taïa stopped seeing his friends in the neighbourhood and lived a teenage life in solitude and silence. 'All was completely silent and filled only with studying and movies because as a homosexual I knew that Moroccan society would only destroy me.'[36] From the age of thirteen to twenty-two he experienced the violence of public erasure, but during these years of isolation he became a silent spectator of life, developing his own creative way of viewing society. Thus, and through his fascination with especially Egyptian films by film directors such as Salah Abou Seif (1915–96), Youssef Chahine (1926–2008) and Yousry Nasrallah (1952–), his dream of becoming a filmmaker was born:

Since the age of thirteen my dream was to become a filmmaker and transform my Moroccan reality into images, with no words. Only images. I discovered that in Paris there's a great school, La Fémis, where you could learn how to make movies.

I was living with my family, who are really very poor, but I decided that one day I would go. At the same time, I made another decision: to start learning French seriously, to master it. Not love it. To make it my own by putting into it all that I am, and the world that I come from.[37]

When Taïa was enrolled at Rabat University in 1992, where he studied French literature, he began writing a diary to practice his French, and it was through this diary that he discovered his ability to write and put images into words: 'a crazy diary where I wrote all that I wanted in French. I put into that diary and into French my identity, my dreams, my silliness, my panic attacks, my tears, my cleverness, and my sexuality, without shame.'[38]

There are several questions at stake in how Taïa, in interview and essays, constructs his position and function as author and activist. By linking a teenage life in silence with the discovery of his ability to write and put images into words he, on the one hand, constructs solitude as a space both of violent erasure and of productive creativity. On the other hand, he positions himself as someone who, unlike Hichem in Bergeaud-Blackler and Eck's study, found protection in silence only insofar as self-annihilation can be defined as protection. In this respect, his literary works and his coming-out interview function as acts of affirmative resistance as defined by Butler; they are counternarratives to those who claim to protect 'authentic' Moroccan culture by forcing him into silence and erasing him from the public sphere.

Significantly, Taïa has never depicted his teenage life in his novels,[39] but his literary works are, I would say, eulogies for the innocent, naive and spontaneous 'effeminate' boy who was forever lost when he became a teenager, and for all other queer lives that have been forcibly silenced by cultural and religious norms, whether in Morocco or in France. Tellingly, silence, invisibility and obliteration are, in Taïa's works, not simply countered by giving voice to the silenced and invisible; they have formed his style of writing, which is dominated by seemingly self-absorbed internal monologues by protagonists who are more or less isolated in their solitude. In this respect, silence and invisibility are not simply fought off but constitute an inescapable condition of life, one that is maintained as a multilayered position of resistance. Moreover, in allowing his characters to appear both self-absorbed and naive, Taïa's self-narrations unsettle prevailing identity categories, such as homosexual/heterosexual and male/female. His characters never have and never will fit into these categories, and their identity performances are deliberately oblivious of them, even though they are formed by and through them.

It is against this background of childhood and teenage experiences – and within the above context of the public debate – that Taïa's coming-out interview must be understood. A mere couple of months before the events in Ksar El Kébir, *TelQuel* 277 ran a front-cover portrait of Taïa with a renewed focus on his coming-out interview. Not surprisingly, the 2006 interview had incited heated debate, and the focus of the 2007 feature article was precisely on the reactions to Taïa's public persona. In the lead paragraph, the journalist Karim Boukhari quotes the following reactions to catch the attention of the reader: 'Il a accepté de donner son c . . . pour se faire connaître,' 'Il est publié et on parle de lui parce qu'il est homo,' 'Il se prostitue pour plaire à l'Occident,' 'C'est son postérieur qui parle, pas lui,' 'Il nuit à l'image du Maroc et de l'islam,' 'Si nous étions réellement en terre d'islam, on le lapiderait' ('He has accepted to give his a . . . to make himself known,' 'He is published and we talk about him because he is homo,' 'He prostitutes himself to please the West,' 'It is his posterior that talks, not him,' 'He harms the image of Morocco and Islam,' 'If we were really in the land of Islam, we would stone him').[40] In the article, Boukhari accuses Rachid Niny (editor, publisher and star columnist of *al-Massae*, Morocco's largest newspaper) of practically calling for Taïa's lynching, while both Niny and *Attajdid*, PJD's official newspaper, openly criticized *2M*, the largest national francophone TV channel in Morocco, for spending Moroccan taxpayers' money on airtime for Taïa. However, whereas PJD and *Attajdid* have been outspoken in their critique of Taïa, they have simultaneously sought to downplay his influence by insisting that he 'ne représente pas grand-chose, il ne vend pas – encore – assez de livres' (does not represent much, he – even – does not sell that many books).[41]

Nevertheless, when Taïa was invited to speak at al-Jadida University in May 2012, Islamist university professors and students from *al-tajdīd al-ṭullābī* (Student Renewal), PJD's university student organization, organized a protest against the talk, which was eventually cancelled.[42] However, within the last couple of years, probably reflecting its current position as ruling party, the PJD has changed its strategy towards Taïa. When his film, *L'Armée du salut*, was screened at the Moroccan national film festival in Tangier in February 2014, the Islamic party MUR (Movement of Unity and Reform) declared in the newspaper *ʾAkhbār al-Yaum*: 'Nous avons pris la décision il y a deux ans de ne plus commenter ce genre de films. [. . .] Nous avons découvert à travers une étude que nous avons menée sur le terrain, que les auteurs de films médiocres, tentent de palier à ce manque de qualité, en essayant de faire de leurs productions une affaire politique.' (Two years ago, we decided no longer to comment on films like this. [. . .] We have discovered through a study we conducted in the field that authors of mediocre films attempt to overcome this lack of quality by trying to make their productions a political case.)[43] Thus rather than addressing the question of homosexuality, MUR strategically seeks to turn the focus towards Taïa's alleged exhibitionism and lack of interest in Morocco's 'common good'.

Unlike *al-Massae* and *Attajdid*, *2M* had found in Taïa a poignant story – the Moroccan 'fils de pauvre' (son of the poor) becoming an acclaimed author in Paris – while more or less ignoring his 'sexual orientation' and the explicit focus on homosexuality in his novels.[44] *TelQuel* had yet another interest in Taïa. As a 'fils de pauvre' and a homosexual, they found in him a voice that contradicted the conception of homosexuality as a Western phenomenon adopted by the elite in the Arab world: born into a poor family, Taïa had identified as homosexual long before 'the West' meant anything to him.

Last, but not least, Taïa's coming-out interview significantly moved the focus on homosexuality from being 'something fictional' to becoming 'real': 'J'ai eu un nœud à l'estomac au moment de l'entretien. L'heure de mon coming out avait sonné. Vous pouvez dire ce que vous voulez dans les livres, mais à partir du moment où vous le dites dans les journaux, cela devient l'affaire de tous, vous avez franchi le point de non-retour.' (I had a knot in my stomach at the time of the interview. The time of my coming out had come. You can say what you want in books, but at the moment you say it in the newspapers, it becomes everyone's business, you've crossed the point of no return.)[45] This shift from 'fiction' to 'reality' was further enhanced when, a couple of months after his *TelQuel* interview, Taïa was interviewed for the arabophone newspapers *al-Ayyam* and *al-Jarida al-Oukhra*: 'Cela a tout changé, puisqu'on est passé de la langue des riches (le français) à la langue de tout le monde (l'arabe). Un peu comme si on était dans la pure théorie, et que là, d'un coup, on atterrissait dans le réel.' (That has changed everything, because we have passed from the language of the rich (French) to the language of everyone (Arabic). A bit as if we were in pure theory, and there, suddenly, we landed in reality.)[46]

La génération du 'je'

While literature is often considered a closed space where anything can be said because it is 'fiction', it can – precisely because of this status – engender debate on topics that are otherwise considered 'taboo'. That is, while literature might not change society in and of itself, it can inspire people to do so. In this respect, Taïa is part of a larger literary scene in Morocco where the focus is on writing the real through the lens of individual experiences, and in a narrative style marked by textual eclecticism and pop culture.

In Morocco, a veritable explosion of 'l'écriture de soi' (writing the self) has taken place since the 1990s. As the Moroccan journalist and expert in Moroccan literature, Adil Hajji, notes, in Morocco 'le "je" a été considéré pendant longtemps comme quelque chose d'indécent. Seule une personne très importante, un philosophe ou un scientifique pouvait utiliser la première personne du singulier. Aujourd'hui, ce n'est plus le cas' (the 'I' has for a long time been considered something indecent. Only a very important person, a philosopher or a scientist, could use the first-person singular. Today this is no longer the case).[47]

The first-person narrative – both the fictional and the autobiographical – is of course not a new phenomenon in Moroccan literature in either Arabic or French.[48] But characteristic of contemporary Moroccan authors is how they orient their reader towards the individual as an autonomous subject capable of living a non-normative life in the midst of Moroccan society. Authors such as Taïa, Rachid O., Bahaa Trabelsi, Siham Benchekroun and the author behind the pseudonym Nedjma simultaneously narrate the complicated life of women and anyone who wants to live a life outside of heteronormativity and depict a society where everyday life is anything but a mirror of cultural and religious normativity. The postmodern collapse of 'grand narratives' is of course not foreign to them, and as Khalid Zekri argues, they seem to renounce the position of spokesperson or representative of a specific ideological position.[49] However, this renunciation is, I would argue, in itself an expression of positioning. Centring creative writing around non-normative forms of life is not simply a question of subverting collective norms, but an explicit point of commitment to authors such as Taïa: that is, a commitment to the struggle to secure the right to individual liberty.

Consequently, the new voices on the contemporary literary scene have been named 'la génération du "je"', and it is just as much because of their adamant individuality and condemnation of collective values as it is because of the sexual content that the works of authors such as Rachid O. and Taïa are bothersome to some Moroccans. Their style of writing is both what makes them fun to read and what makes them come across as self-absorbed and exhibitionist. However, neither Taïa's nor Rachid O.'s writings are overtly focused on the self or blind to the other. Instead, their literary play with the 'self-absorbed' constitutes an ethical act of writing the self as other. They are not simply writing the self as an individual's confrontation with collective norms; rather, they are infiltrating hegemonic narrations of the Moroccan 'nation' by means of everyday stories that reveal a heterogeneous world that fits neither hegemonic traditions nor Orientalist stereotypes. In an article in *TelQuel* 249 (2007) with the title 'La génération du "je"', Moroccan journalist Ilham Mellouki has characterized these authors through the leitmotif 'osons être nous-mêmes . . . sans pour autant renier l'autre' (daring to be ourselves . . . without denying the other). As Moroccan author Trabelsi has underlined, writing 'I' is 'un acte de libération. Elle a signifié que nous pouvions aussi exister autrement' (an act of liberation. It signified that we could also exist in another way).[50]

In this respect, writing the self is not simply a question of writing autobiographically, and it is more than a question of hiding an autobiographical pact behind fiction. Through 'l'écriture de soi' many contemporary Moroccan authors are challenging the very distinction between autobiography and fiction. Their writings can be characterized as textual eclecticism;[51] they are mixing genres such as essay, short story, novel and autobiography in order to position themselves in the literary field and underline their subjective point of view. In contrast to the omniscient narrator of earlier post-independence novels, such as Abdelkrim Ghallab's *Dafannā al-māḍī* (*We Have Buried the Past*) (1966) and the linear narration of Abdelmajid Benjelloun's *Fī al-ṭufūlah* (In Childhood) (1957), contemporary authors experiment with genres and narrative techniques.

However, as I argue in Chapter 4, this textual eclecticism is reminiscent of the 'poetics of violence' (Mohammed Khaïr-Eddine) and the 'linguistic and textual violence' (Abdellatif Laâbi) of the *Souffles* movement. From the late 1960s, both francophone and arabophone authors embarked on a linguistic and poetic guerrilla in an effort to split off from 'nationalist realism' and the traditional narrative mode of authors such as Ghallab.[52] The hermetic nature of this literary avant-gardism is, however, also what distinguishes it from the young generation of contemporary authors. The textual eclecticism of authors such as Taïa and Rachid O. is almost anti-intellectual, insofar as their eclecticism is reflected in a mixture of literature with, for instance, storytelling and film culture rather than an academic deconstruction of literary models often inaccessible to 'ordinary people'.

Contemporary Moroccan authors are still preoccupied with the real, but sociopolitical themes are now treated from the subjective point of view of the narrator or the protagonist of the story, and often in an ironic or satiric tone. Here, in contrast to novels such as *Dafannā al-māḍī* (which is a thinly fictionalized historical novel), historical and sociocultural events are not treated as objects in themselves, but are rather staged through a fiction of miming the real and the social languages.[53] That is, instead of serving ideological or didactic purposes, the insertion of historical events, names and places primarily functions by alluding to official narratives, which are then contaminated by the narration of non-normative life. In this respect, a distinguishing feature of post-1990 novels is an intentional naivety that functions parodically. These novels neither accurately depict reality nor feed Western stereotypes through self-orientalizing gestures, as they are sometimes reductively accused of doing. Instead, their naive style of writing and the naivety of their characters function as a double critique, which simultaneously subverts Western stereotypes through imitation and queers the nation through a style of writing in which the non-normative comes to haunt the idea of the 'Hetero-Nation'.

However, while this differs considerably from Ghallab's *Dafannā al-māḍī*, there are points of comparison with, for instance, Driss Chraïbi's *Le Passé simple* (1954), Mohammed Khaïr-Eddine's *Agadir* (1967), Mohamed Choukri's *Al-khubz al-ḥāfī* (*For Bread Alone*) (1973/1981), Abdellatif Laâbi's *Le Chemin des ordalies* (*Rue du Retour*) (1982), Leila Abouzeid's *'Ām al-fīl* (*Year of the Elephant*) (1983) or Mohamed Berrada's *Lu'bat al-nisyān* (*The Game of Forgetting*) (1987), to mention but a few. In these pre-1990 novels, which differ considerably from one another in theme, genre and narrative technique, the narration of historical events serves neither an ideological nor a didactic purpose, but nevertheless anchors fiction in reality and functions as the backdrop against which everyday events are narrated. Whereas pre-1970 Moroccan novels in both Arabic and French have had young, secular and modern male intellectuals as protagonists and tended to exaggerate the split between 'tradition' and 'modernity', Moroccan novels from the beginning of the 1970s and in particular the 1980s have moved the male intellectual from the centre to the margin of the narrative, to rewrite and challenge the dominant narrations of the nation from a class- and gender-sensitive perspective. Moreover, as Gonzalo Fernández Parrilla argues in his analysis of the Arabic-language Moroccan novel, this movement was accompanied by formal experimentation and everyday realism, as well as an explicit intertextual dialogue that functioned as an open reply to earlier literary models.[54]

Whereas the 'nationalist realism' of *Dafannā al-māḍī* reflects a period of natural euphoria, depicting the 'glorious' past of the independence struggle in a highly ideological fashion, the new generation of authors who entered the literary scene during the 1960s and 1970s shifted attention to social reality, because they were profoundly disappointed with the nationalist-salafi ideology that had come to dominate political life.[55] This is what is at stake in Abouzeid's novella *'Ām al-fīl*, which rewrites national history from a class- and gender-sensitive perspective; but this is also what distinguishes it from the hermetic avant-gardism of, for instance, Abdelkébir Khatibi's *Amour bilingue*, published the same year. Since the 1990s the opacity of literary avant-gardism has, in general, been replaced by an intentionally 'naive' realism which appears more direct in its critique of social norms and political reality. This, however, implies neither that contemporary authors have returned to a novelization of history, nor that their literary works are thinly fictionalized political messages. On the contrary. Like Abouzeid, Rachid O., for instance, opens *L'Enfant ébloui* (The dazzled child) (1995) with a preamble staging the novel as an oral narrative in Arabic that has been put into writing by a French friend. Moreover, the preamble opens with the narrator recalling that his childhood dream was to become the hero of a novel. Just as Abouzeid has sought to give voice to the voiceless of literature, Taïa and Rachid O. centre their stories around characters who are rarely the protagonists in novels. In this respect, the representational strategies of the young generation of contemporary authors form part of a longer literary tradition of reappropriating and reconfiguring their (trans)national history, territory, language and community. As experimental nations, Taïa's and Rachid O.'s novels both contaminate monologic and heteronormative narrations of the 'nation' and subvert supposedly universal identity categories.

Transgression of heteronormativity

Rachid O.'s *L'Enfant ébloui* is often identified as the first Moroccan novel to question 'the norms of society from a sexuality standpoint'.[56] The political changes that have taken place since the 1990s have unquestionably affected the literary landscape and have made room for voices once absent from public discourse, and in these post-Lead Years, Rachid O. is one of the first to write about homosexuality as an identity category. However, I am less preoccupied with Rachid O. as one who 'founded the gay voice of Morocco'[57] than with how he and other contemporary authors write in dialogue with an earlier corpus, both Arabic and French, in an effort to rearticulate themes that have haunted Moroccan literature at least since the 1950s.

Both in *Fiction du réel* (2006) and in a later article entitled 'Le Sujet et son corps dans le roman marocain' (2011), Zekri has identified two bodily markers of heteronormativity – circumcision and expulsion from the female hammam[58] – which are repeatedly represented as exerting a symbolic violence on homosexual life. This is so for, for instance, the narrator-protagonists in Karim Nasseri's *Noces et funérailles* (Wedding and funeral) (2001) and in Rachid O.'s *L'Enfant ébloui*, to mention but a few. As rites of passage, the purpose of circumcision and expulsion from the female hammam is to fix boys in a particular sexual order in which they are expected to orient their desire towards the opposite sex.[59] According to Zekri, 'le corps est ainsi "normé" et "sociabilisé" à travers des rituels dont le choix échappe au sujet qui les subit. Le corps est ainsi assujetti à la loi de la communauté qui tente de le priver de son autonomie.' (The body is thus 'normed' and 'socialized' through rituals to which the subject is subjected without choosing. The body is thus subject to the law of the community which attempts to deprive it of its autonomy.)[60]

However, as Zekri demonstrates in his analysis, the narrativization of these ritualized practices effectively subverts the naturalization of the heteronormative order. That is, these heteronormative markers reveal, in themselves, those who are unable to conform to them, and as such they subvert the same social order they are meant to reinforce. By writing the self as 'other', authors such as Taïa, Rachid O., Nasseri, Trabelsi and Nedjma are not only reclaiming autonomy by giving voice and room to non-normative sexual relations; they are disturbing the very relation between 'origin' and 'copy' – between what is 'natural' and what is 'unnatural' – through a parodic performance that reveals how rites of passage such as circumcision and expulsion from the female hammam serve to uphold a regulatory regime through forced repetition.

Like Zekri, Jean Zaganiaris is, in his study *Queer Maroc* (2013), preoccupied with the multifaceted literary representations of sexuality, gender and identity in contemporary Moroccan literature. A central figure in literary efforts to queer the 'nation' is the mother and her symbiotic relationship with the father figure. In Taïa's works, the mother figure functions as a revolutionary figure, and the representation of the mother as 'whore' constitutes a subversive category, as argued by Zaganiaris:

> Chez Taïa, les termes 'prostituée' ou 'pute' n'incarnent pas forcément les travailleuses du sexe, dont il sera question dans son dernier roman *Infidèles* (2012). Dans *Le jour du roi*, il s'agit plutôt de désigner par ce vocable ces femmes que les hommes traitent de 'pute' car elles refusent d'être prisonnières des contraintes sociales ou des règles de bienséance que leur impose leur genre.[61]

> (In Taïa's works, the words 'prostitute' and 'whore' do not necessarily embody sex workers, which is the case in his latest novel *Infidèles* (2012). In *Le Jour du roi*, it is rather a question of designating, with this term, those women whom men treat as 'whores' because they refuse to be imprisoned by social constraints or rules of decorum imposed by their gender.)

As I will elaborate in my analysis of the mother figure in *L'Armée du salut*, becoming a 'whore' in Taïa's works represents an act of emancipation: despite the social stigmatization, becoming a 'whore' implies finally being able to enjoy sexual freedom.[62] With *Infidèles*, however, the mother figure as 'whore' is simultaneously made more explicit and rendered complicated. Both Saâdia and Slima are sex workers; being a 'whore' is thus no longer simply a question of enjoying sexual freedom by refusing to succumb to cultural and religious norms, but a professional business, which reveals the hypocrisy of a society simultaneously relying on and ostracizing women like Saâdia and Slima.[63]

Contesting and rearticulating normative gender roles through mother and father figures are literary traits that Taïa shares both with earlier and contemporary Moroccan authors. But while Taïa's focus is on the mother as a revolutionary figure, with a father who is either absent or defeated, authors such as Rachid O. and Nasseri have rearticulated a long tradition of repressive father figures. In this respect, *L'Enfant ébloui* is noteworthy because it 'normalizes' homosexuality, depicting the transgenerational relationship between an older man and a younger boy as something of common occurrence in Morocco and as a more or less unproblematic relationship that both friends and family can accept. By drawing a father figure who understands and protects both his homosexual son and his daughter who became pregnant outside of marriage, Rachid O. dispels the macho homophobia often associated with father figures. Unlike Chraïbi's authoritarian 'Seigneur' in *Le Passé simple* and Choukri's violent and tyrannical father in *Al-khubz al-ḥāfi*, Rachid O. depicts the father as someone who can assume the nurturing role normally associated with the mother figure and can accept an alternative lifestyle. According to Rachid O., sexuality 'est un sujet tabou et tellement tabou que justement, aussi bizarre que ça puisse paraître, c'est ce qui permet plein de choses' (is a taboo subject and is so taboo that, as bizarre as it may seem, it is what permits many things).[64] In this respect, what is uncommon here is neither non-normative sexuality nor the father's acceptance of alternative lifestyles, but the public representation of them in a literary work.

By contrast, Nasseri's 'Dictateur' in *Noces et funérailles* mirrors Chraïbi's 'Seigneur' in authoritarianism and Choukri's father figure in violence. While Taïa and Rachid O. each in their way displace the gendered space of traditional patriarchy by narrating mothers and fathers who do not fit into normative gender roles, Nasseri contests the validity of patriarchal authoritarianism by displaying its violent underpinnings, just as Chraïbi and Choukri did in their early works. Another significant aspect of *Noces et funérailles* is the protagonist's fascination with the forbidden book of his childhood, *Al-khubz al-ḥāfi*, which was banned until 2000. This mirrors a general fascination with Choukri among the young generation of contemporary Moroccan authors. Idriss, the protagonist, is shocked by the social realism of *Al-khubz al-ḥāfi*, a style of writing beyond his imagination. He instantly feels a kinship with the protagonist of *Al-khubz al-ḥāfi* and is fascinated by its novelistic style, which defies ethnographic and exotic depictions of Morocco:

> Choukri aurait pu étaler tout un Maroc imaginaire. Un Maroc exotique où la misère, la violence, la prostitution féminine et surtout masculine, l'inégalité et l'injustice n'auraient pas existé. Un Maroc où tout était possible. Un Maroc qui aurait été le meilleur des mondes. Mais l'honnêteté de Choukri a triomphé.
> Par sa sincérité et sa spontanéité, il a su ébranler le monde littéraire.[65]

> (Choukri could have displayed a whole imaginary Morocco. An exotic Morocco where misery, violence, feminine and especially male prostitution, inequality and injustice would not exist. A Morocco where everything was possible. A Morocco which would have been the best of all worlds. But Choukri's honesty triumphed.
> Through his sincerity and spontaneity, he has shaken the literary world.)

Both intertextual references and direct mentions of Choukri and *Al-khubz al-ḥāfi*, as in *Noces et funérailles* and in Taïa's *L'Armée du salut*,[66] reveal a commitment to writing the real through the lens of individual experiences of non-normative sexuality. When Choukri wrote *Al-khubz al-ḥāfī*, he himself argued that it was 'a semi-documentary about a social group'.[67] This characterization of *Al-khubz al-ḥāfī* is significant, because it contains a double critique. That is, a critique of Arabic literature trapped in 'politics, religion, and morality',[68] and of Western 'artistic' autobiographies with the psychological state of the protagonist at the centre of the narrative.

However, while to the protagonist of *Al-khubz al-ḥāfī*, sex and prostitution are a form of escapism from hunger and political ignorance, reflecting a relation of colonial domination, in contemporary writings queer sexualities are inserted as identity categories, which are then constantly unsettled. In *Al-khubz al-ḥāfī*, sexual freedom is neither immoral (as cultural and religious norms would have it) nor subversive (as in a modernist view), but a symptom of oppressive socio-economic conditions, as Nirvana Tanoukhi has also argued.[69] Sex functions as a site of resistance insofar as its violent underpinnings reveal a loss of human values. The protagonist finds freedom from his violent and tyrannical father in the rough and violent life of the street, where the norms of society have been turned upside down.

In contradistinction to this, a novel such as Trabelsi's *Une Vie à trois* (A Life of Three) (2000) depicts how cultural and religious norms imprison people in a heteronormative order that ultimately makes them reproduce the same oppressive gender roles that they initially sought to displace. In this respect, queer sexualities are not a symptom of oppression, but the subject of oppression in the first place. In *Une Vie à trois*, the threesome – Adam, Jamal and Rim – is the outcome of Adam trying to hide his homosexuality from fear of shame and ostracism. Whereas Jamal has been disowned by his family because of his homosexuality, and poverty has forced him into prostitution, Rim is young, naive and dreaming of marrying 'Mr Perfect'. Both end up being nothing but pieces in Adam's charade puzzle. However, in his effort to mask his sexual identity, Adam ends up reproducing the same regulatory regime that has forced him to live a life in secret, but 'allows' him to dominate both Rim and Jamal because he is male and upper class. Ultimately, all three of them are left marginalized, with no prospect of that changing.

Homosexuality 'à la marocaine'

Because writing about queer sexualities in Moroccan literature has been inextricably linked to questions about cultural identity and cultural differences between the 'West' and the 'Arab world', authors such as Taïa and Rachid O. have not been preoccupied solely with subverting the relation between heterosexuality *as origin* and homosexuality *as copy*, but also the relation between 'Western' homosexuality *as origin* and 'Arab' homosexuality *as copy*, while unsettling the very category 'homosexual' through expanding the boundaries of homosexual desires. In this respect, their creative writings effectively dismantle the false dualism between 'Moroccan authenticity' and 'Western emancipation', neither of which leaves any room for homosexuals with Arab, Muslim, Moroccan or poor backgrounds. However, while Taïa's literary play with the 'native informant' trope thwarts ethnographic readings of his works, as I will elaborate in Chapter 3, his extra-literary performances are more direct in their critique of culturalist conceptions of 'Arab sexuality' – whether internalized homophobia, exoticizing gazes on 'Arab sexual desire' or the politicization of sexuality in France where Arabs and Muslims are represented as inherently misogynist and homophobic.

'L'Homosexualité expliquée à ma mère' (Homosexuality Explained to My Mother), written by Taïa and published in *TelQuel* 367 in April 2009, is one of his most well-known essays. The title of the essay is significant for at least two reasons. First, it contains a hypotextual reference to Éditions du Seuil's collection 'Expliqué à' which, according to Le Seuil, 'aborde des grands thèmes de société sous forme de questions-réponses entre un spécialiste et un enfant. Les sujets, traités de façon claire, simple et concise, invitent aussi bien les enfants que les enseignants et les parents à la réflexion' (addresses major themes in society in the form of questions and answers between a specialist and a child. The topics, treated in a clear, simple and concise manner, invite children as well as teachers and parents to reflect).[70] In Morocco, one of the better-known 'expliqué à' publications is Taha Ben Jelloun's *Le Racisme expliqué à ma fille* (*Racism Explained to My Daughter*) (1998). Despite the fact that Taïa's essay does not follow the question–answer structure, it is still constructed as a text in which he – as an expert *qua* his lived experience – explains his homosexuality to someone with limited knowledge on the topic:

> Expliquer ma démarche, ce que je suis, ce que j'écris et pourquoi je le fais. Expliquer?! Oui, expliquer davantage parce que j'en ressens la nécessité intérieure et parce que vous, ma famille, n'avez pas pris la peine de lire, de bien lire, ce que j'ai publié – livres, articles, interviews. . . . Expliquer parce que depuis longtemps c'est ce qui nous manque au Maroc: qu'on nous considère enfin comme des êtres dignes de recevoir des explications, qu'on nous implique vraiment dans ce qui concerne ce pays et qu'on cesse de nous humilier jour après jour.[71]

> (To explain my approach, what I am, what I write, and why I do it. To explain?! Yes, to explain first of all because I feel an inner necessity, and because you, my family, did not bother to read, really read, what I've published – books, articles, interviews. . . . To explain because for a long time this is what we have been missing in Morocco: that we are finally considered beings worthy enough to receive explanations, that we are really involved in what concerns this country, and that we will no longer be humiliated day after day.)

As this paragraph indicates, Taïa's agenda is not simply to explain homosexuality, but to talk about it in the first place. As homosexuality is a taboo subject, silence must first of all be broken in order to turn homosexuality into a 'major theme in society' that merits explanations.

Second, the essay is written in the form of a letter to his family – in particular to his mother, who does not understand French and who cannot read. Though he is addressing his family in this 'letter', its publicity clearly indicates that it concerns the Moroccan people and the authorities in general. However, besides the obvious fact that the 'letter' is published in a news magazine, Taïa's mother, sisters and brothers are also presented as having internalized the societal norms and taboos, and as such they become representatives of those Moroccans who have not 'really read' what Taïa has published because they have turned a blind eye to the centrality of homosexuality in his books. Thus the letter/essay is a supplement in the Derridean sense.[72] Taïa is retelling his life story over and over again using different literary genres in order to force people to acknowledge that – rather than a self-absorbed and exhibitionist author obsessed with the scandalous because he craves attention – he is an engaged author who is being sincere about his own life as a homosexual because breaking the silence, for him, is the necessary first step to secure LGBT rights:

> Je sais que je suis scandaleux. Pour vous. Et pour les autres autour de vous: les voisins, les collègues au travail, les amis, les belles-mères. . . . Je sais à quel point je vous cause involontairement du 'mal', des soucis. Je m'expose en signant de mon vrai prénom et de mon vrai nom. Je vous expose avec moi. Je vous entraîne dans cette aventure, qui ne fait que commencer pour moi et pour les gens comme moi: exister enfin! Sortir de l'ombre! Relever la tête! Dire la vérité, ma vérité! Être: Abdellah. Être: Taïa. Être les deux. Seul. Et pas seul à la fois.[73]

> (I know that I'm scandalous. To you. And to others around you: neighbors, colleagues at work, friends, mothers-in-law. . . . I know how I involuntarily cause you 'harm', worries. I expose myself by signing with my real first name and my real family name. I expose you with me. I drag you along on this adventure that has just begun for me and people like me: to finally exist! Come out of the shadow! Raise the head! Tell the truth, my truth! Be: Abdellah. Be: Taïa. Be both. Alone. And not alone at the same time.)

There is something ambiguous to the sentence 'I know how I involuntarily cause you "harm"'. Taïa is perfectly aware that he is exposing his family without their consent, but he maintains that it is a necessary evil, because his self-exposure and the exposure of his family are part of a greater cause: to fight for his right 'to finally exist' both as an individual and as a part of a family and a community. In addition, exposing himself serves the purpose of giving homosexuality a human face, while simultaneously resisting stereotypical representations of Moroccans and 'Moroccan sexuality':

> Au-delà de mon homosexualité, que je revendique et assume, je sais que ce qui vous surprend, vous fait peur, c'est que je vous échappe: je suis le même, toujours maigre, toujours cet éternel visage d'enfant; je ne suis plus le même. Vous ne me reconnaissez plus [. . .] je me révèle autre, quelque chose que vous n'avez pas prévu, vu venir. Un monstre. En plus, à côté de vous, j'ai toujours été tellement gentil, tellement studieux et bien élevé.[74]

> (Beyond my homosexuality, which I claim and assume, I know that what surprises you and scares you is that I elude you: I am the same, still thin, still this

eternal baby face; I am no longer the same. You no longer recognize me [. . .] I reveal myself as other, something you had not anticipated, did not see coming. A monster. Moreover, by your side, I have always been so gentle, so bookish, so well-behaved.)

By drawing attention to the uncomfortable position of his family, who behind his 'monstrous' sexual identity still recognizes their gentle, bookish, well-behaved son and brother, he reveals how absurdly silence works as a way to 'normalize' the 'deviant'. He is of course still the same; what has changed is the knowledge of those around him, who now know that he is homosexual.

A year later, in the essay 'Le Retour du maréchal Lyautey' (The Return of Marshal Lyautey), Taïa addresses how exoticizing gazes on 'Arab sexual desire' trap Moroccans in an Oriental invention. This essay is a response to a response, and a few words about the context are therefore required. In April 2010, the cover of the francophone Moroccan newsmagazine *Actuel* 44 showed two men embracing each other with the accompanying text: 'Homosexuels. Pourquoi tant de haine?' (Homosexuals. Why so much hate?). Inside the magazine the editorial and pages 42–4[75] were dedicated to debating a number of seemingly unrelated events, which nevertheless had something in common: an increasing tension between homophobic voices and violent acts, and the growing presence of LGBT rights activists in the public debate. Among other events, the editorial mentions the upcoming Elton John concert (in May 2010 he played in front of 40,000 fans at the Mawazine festival in Rabat, despite protests from the PJD, but with high security) and the publication of *Mithly* as the first of its kind in the Arab world. Moreover, the editorial critically questions the hypocrisy behind Morocco's ratification of the International Covenant on Civil and Political Rights, which is supposed to protect the right to respect for the individual's private life, while Article 489 of the Moroccan penal code still criminalizes homosexual relations between consenting adults.

In *Actuel* 47, published in May 2010, Jean-Pierre Péroncel-Hugoz, a former reporter at the French daily *Le Monde*, was invited to write a piece about *Actuel*'s coverage of homophobia and LGBT rights, which had engendered heated debates. Taïa (who had been interviewed in 44) was invited to respond to Péroncel-Hugoz's piece. The opening of Péroncel-Hugoz's article, 'Pédérastie et pudeur: le prêt-à-penser a encore frappé . . .' (Pederasty and modesty: Ready-to-think has struck again . . .), asserts that *Actuel*, which prides itself on being anti-conformist, has succumbed to what he calls a 'politically correct homophilic compassion',[76] thus turning the pro-LGBT rights position into a conformist one, as opposed to the then supposedly anti-conformist Moroccan authorities. However, according to Péroncel-Hugoz, it is unnecessary for Morocco to 'glisser sur cette pente ridicule [. . . qui] commence par la liberté d'afficher ses goûts intimes et [. . .] finit par l'adoption d'enfants par des couples des mêmes sexe, en passant par l'égalité juridique avec le couple hétéros' (slide down this ridiculous slope [. . . which] begins with the freedom to display one's intimate tastes, and [. . .] ends with the adoption of children by same-sex couples, passing through legal equality with heterosexual couples),[77] because Islam has taken care of homosexuality once and for all in a modest and discreet manner:

'Ni vu ni connu. Ni étalage ni tapage. Et nul ne s'est jamais plaint d'avoir été déniaisé par son grand cousin ou un collégien aîné.' (Neither seen nor known. Neither display nor fuss. And no one has ever complained that he has been initiated by his cousin or an older schoolmate.)[78] And he continues, 'Cette invisible filière entre garçons a notamment permis, depuis un millénaire et demi, que la plupart des filles musulmanes arrivent vierges au mariage.' (This invisible bond between boys has, for a millennium and a half, notably enabled that the majority of Muslim girls are virgins at the time of marriage.)[79]

The second half of his article is dedicated to a less than subtle critique of Taïa and authors, such as Rachid O. and Nasseri, who have also settled in Paris and dedicated their writing to depicting queer sexuality:

> Aujourd'hui, au nord de la Méditerranée, une toute petite poignée de plumitifs maghrébins sans autre sujets d'inspiration que le gigolisme ou des parties de touche-pipi dans des toilettes publiques, ont calculé qu'en posant en victimes de leur pays d'origine dans le Marais (ce quartier parisien où en plein jour, on peut voir des personnes du même sexe se patiner à pleine bouche, s'enlacer, se tripoter . . .) ou sur les Ramblas de Barcelone, il y avait là un moyen idéal pour flatter leur ego et faire fructifier leur gloriole et les ventes de leur répétitives plaquettes autobiographiques . . . [. . .]
>
> Et tel écrivaillon des bords du Bouregreg aux airs de Mater dolorosa publie des tribunes larmoyantes dans la grande presse parisienne. . . . Espérons que les autorités marocaines ne se laisseront pas intimider – car c'est ce qui est recherché – par des chantages du type: 'Si on est en démocratie, on doit pouvoir crier ses préférences sexuelles sur les toits et même se promener en ville avec des plumes sur le postérieur.' Puisse le Maroc rester fidèle à ses traditions spécifiques, en l'occurrence la retenue et la pudeur, ce qui n'interdit pas la volupté, bien au contraire car, comme le répétait Coco Chanel: 'Quand on déballe tout, on n'a plus envie de rien.'[80]

(Today, north of the Mediterranean, a small handful of Maghrebin scribblers with no other subject of inspiration than gigolism or 'playing doctor' in public toilets, have calculated that posing as victims in their country of origin in le Marais (this Parisian district where you, in broad daylight, can watch people of the same sex give blowjobs, hugging, fiddling . . .) or on Las Ramblas in Barcelona was an ideal way to flatter their egos and make their vainglory and the sales of their repetitive autobiographical leaflets grow . . . [. . .]

And this scribbler from the banks of Bouregreg publishes, like some *mater dolorosa*, tearful tribunes in the great Parisian press. . . . Hopefully, the Moroccan authorities will not be intimidated – because that is what is sought – by extortions such as: 'If we have democracy, we must be able to shout our sexual preferences from rooftops and even walk around town with feathers on the back.' May Morocco remain faithful to its specific traditions, namely restraint and modesty, which does not prohibit pleasure, on the contrary, because as Coco Chanel repeated: 'When you unpack everything, you no longer crave for anything.')

Péroncel-Hugoz's overall view of 'Muslim sexuality' is profoundly Orientalist, and his romanticization of Morocco and Islam is not only misogynist and homophobic but also neocolonial. In his response to Péroncel-Hugoz, Taïa focuses primarily on the ahistorical and neocolonial implications of his Orientalist position while he hardly takes offence at the accusation of exhibitionism. This is noteworthy, because going into that debate would imply accepting the premises of Péroncel-Hugoz's argument, which – in a manner strikingly similar to the PJD – seeks to displace the actual subject of the debate, namely homophobia and LGBT rights, by shifting focus to an alleged exhibitionism as the underlying motivation of authors and activists such as Taïa. This, I argue, is in turn what necessitates an insistence on the right to assume the position as 'self-absorbed', because it is only through the 'self-centred' position of refraining from concealing what collective norms have deemed shameful that queer identities can come into existence, as Eve Sedgwick has also argued.

Thus instead of addressing the question of exhibitionism, Taïa addresses the troubling fact that Péroncel-Hugoz, by asking Moroccans to remain 'modest and restrained', is failing those young Moroccans who have finally found the courage to break the silence: 'Ce Monsieur lui demande de ne pas relever la tête, de se soumettre encore et encore. De se taire. De se fondre dans des traditions qui n'ont plus aucun sens. De ne surtout pas parler.' (This *monsieur* asks them not to raise their head, to submit again and again. To keep silent. To blend with traditions that no longer make any sense. Especially not to speak.)[81] Rather than supporting the young generation of Moroccans, Péroncel-Hugoz is effectively imprisoning them in an Orientalist invention, according to Taïa:

> On ne peut pas s'y tromper, il s'agit du fameux Maroc éternel inventé par les orientalistes au XIXe siècle, figé par le maréchal Lyautey au début du XXe. Un Maroc qui n'a jamais vraiment existé et qui, pourtant, continue de faire fantasmer un grand nombre de français (et pas seulement les Français).[82]

> (There is no doubt about it, it is the famous, eternal Morocco invented by Orientalists during the nineteenth century, fixed by Marshal Lyautey at the beginning of the twentieth. A Morocco which never really existed and about which a great number of French people (and not only the French) continue to fantasize.)

Drawing a line to 'L'Homosexualité expliquée à ma mère', this so-called Orientalist invention, Taïa argues, is precisely the ahistorical, folkloric conception of Moroccan culture that seeks to 'normalize' the 'deviant' through silence. Within this 'authentic' culture men (and only men) can practice homosexuality freely – of course in silence and hidden – as long as they return to the social and cultural order at the end of the day. That is, as long as they do not identify as homosexuals, but simply practice homosexuality to protect the honour of women. However, the problem is not only that this folkloric conception of Moroccan culture traps Moroccans outside of history and thus prevents them from changing (as any change – be it women's rights, LGBT rights and so on – would be a betrayal of one's cultural specificity), but also that it reinforces a neocolonial relation between Moroccans and 'Westerners':

> Un Maroc où des privilégiés occidentaux peuvent aujourd'hui goûter tranquillement, les yeux bien fermés, à la 'dolce vita', avoir Fatima comme cuisinière, Mohamed comme jardinier, Saïd comme chauffeur, Rachid ou Meryem comme objet sexuel. Le tout pour quelques dirhams seulement. Ces gens, déçus de l'Occident, on peut les comprendre. . . . Allez, allez, faisons un effort . . . ils sont tellement gentils, ils aiment tellement le Maroc, ils restaurent nos riads, nous soignent parfois, donnent à nos enfants du travail. . . . Ils ne nous veulent que du bien. N'est-ce pas. . . . Pour les remercier, il n'y a presque rien à faire: être 'authentiques', être à leur disposition, être exactement comme dans un tableau d'Eugène Delacroix. Être vide, loin de soi, loin de toute possibilité d'exister par soi-même. Ne pas réfléchir. Ne jamais devenir un adulte. Esclave à vie.[83]

> (A Morocco where privileged Westerners today can taste the 'dolce vita' quietly with their eyes firmly shut, can have Fatima as a cook, Mohamed as a gardener, Saïd as a chauffeur, and Rachid or Meryem as a sexual object. All for a few dirhams. These people, disappointed with the West, we can understand them. . . . Come on. . . . We should make an effort, they are so nice, they love Morocco so much, they restore our riads, sometimes they take care of us, give our children work. . . . They only want the best for us. Right. . . . To thank them we hardly need to do anything: be 'authentic', be at their disposal, be precisely like a painting by Eugène Delacroix. Be empty, far from ourselves, far from any possibility of existing by ourselves. Not think. Never become adult. Slave for life.)

However, despite the efforts to 'trap' Moroccans in their 'cultural specificity', which play right into the agenda of, for instance, the PJD, young Moroccans have begun to speak up, and within this context, self-exposure functions as a means to tell 'my truth' as one among many truths in Morocco. By claiming his right to exist as an individual, as he does in 'L'Homosexualité expliquée à ma mère', Taïa is simultaneously fighting for his right to be homosexual and countering the conviction that there is such a thing as one true, authentic Moroccan culture.

There is a noticeable discrepancy between 'Le Retour du maréchal Lyautey', which is concluded with 'Demain, je relirai De l'Orientalisme d'Edward Saïd' (Tomorrow I will reread *Orientalism* by Edward Said),[84] and Taïa's insistence, in his conversation with Dale Peck at PEN World Voices Festival in 2011, that his generation has nothing to do with colonialism – that earlier generations dealt with that, whereas the problem preoccupying him and his generation is how the Moroccan government and the rich Moroccans have abandoned the Moroccan people to illiteracy and poverty.[85] Of course, I acknowledge both the legitimacy and the importance of shifting focus from blaming the French protectorate for everything that is wrong in Morocco, to confronting the authorities and demanding that they take responsibility for, for instance, human rights violations in Morocco. This shift in focus is, however, not all that different from what Moroccan intellectuals during the 1960s and 1970s did within a postcolonial frame of reference.[86] But nevertheless, since 2010/11 Taïa has moved towards a postcolonial repositioning that sheds new light on Khatibi's conception of double critique from the standpoint of an Arab, Muslim, Moroccan, poor, immigrant, homosexual subject.

First, Taïa has been forced to deal with accusations that homosexuality does not belong in the Arab world, supposedly because it is a Western phenomenon adopted by a 'Westernized' Arab elite. This argument is put forth not only by conservatives such as Péroncel-Hugoz or Islamists such as the PJD but somewhat paradoxically also by postcolonial critics such as Joseph A. Massad, as I have demonstrated in Chapter 1. In '"Sortir de la peur": construire une identité homosexuelle arabe dans un monde postcolonial' (Quitting Fear: Constructing an Arab Homosexual Identity in a Postcolonial World) – an interview with the French literary magazine *Fixxion*, published in June 2016 – Taïa criticizes both the so-called Gay International and positions such as Massad's. On the one hand, he maintains that 'Je ne peux pas dire à un jeune homosexuel marocain qui habite à la campagne et qui aspire à l'émancipation: "Arrête, tu n'as pas le droit de rêver à cela."' (I cannot tell a young Moroccan homosexual who lives in the countryside and who aspires to emancipation: 'Stop, you don't have the right to dream about this.')[87] On the contrary, Taïa insists that everyone has the right to fight for their individual liberty, regardless of their cultural, religious or ethnic origin. But, on the other hand, he does not support the 'universality' behind the Gay International:

> De la même manière, alors que j'ai pu inventer ma propre liberté dans cet espace occidental, je n'ai pas le droit de véhiculer une vision idyllique de Paris. L'enjeu principal se trouve là: des occidentaux veulent le bien des homosexuels du monde entier, tout en ignorant presque tout de leur pays. On a parfois l'impression qu'ils n'acceptent les homosexuels que quand ces homosexuels correspondent à la definitions de l'homosexualité établie par l'Occident.[88]
>
> (In the same way, whereas I have been able to invent my proper freedom in this Western space, I have no right to convey an idyllic vision of Paris. The main challenge is here: Westerners want the best for homosexuals all over the world, while ignoring almost all of their countries. It sometimes feels like they only accept homosexuals when these homosexuals correspond to the definitions of homosexuality established by the West.)

By rejecting both the Gay International and the alleged existence of an 'authentic' Moroccan culture, Taïa seeks to create a space for an 'Arab' homosexuality which is neither assimilated into 'Western culture' nor isolated in its own 'cultural specificity'. Noticeably, however, Taïa is, like Khatibi and Butler, careful not to install new exclusions and invisibilities by claiming that 'Arab' homosexuality denotes a common identity or a singular form of oppression. Just as Khatibi's double critique moves beyond affirmative resistance through a *pensée-autre* that unsettles the very binaries of inside/outside, national/transnational, homosexual/heterosexual, Taïa is preoccupied with the plurality of queer sexualities.

Second, and along the line of the Gay International, Taïa has time and again been confronted with the argument (which resonates especially within francophone studies[89] and among French journalists) that he and others like him have somehow been saved by the French language, in which they are free to express themselves as homosexuals, and by France, where they can openly live as homosexuals. However, as Denis M. Provencher rightly states,

> Taïa and other queer Maghrebi French speakers do not depend on the assumed teleology of a North African subject who simply leaves the Maghreb once and for all to chart a postcolonial and queer diasporic path to Paris where he 'comes out' as a gay author, and 'French' writer, never to return to or write again of his homeland. In fact the author's work is not exactly full of 'coming outs', but it is more precisely replete with 'coming and goings' or 'performative encounters' between and 'disidentifications' with the Maghreb and France.[90]

It is precisely the simplified deduction that writing in French and living in Paris has effected his emancipation that Taïa confronts in the interview in *Fixxion*.[91] When the journalist from *Fixxion* begins the interview by asking, 'Vous vous présentez souvent comme un écrivain gay, marocain, arabe, musulman. Parfois vous précisez: vivant à Paris. Cette identité que vous affirmez aujourd'hui, vous l'avez toujours pensée comme telle?' (You often present yourself as a gay, Moroccan, Arab, Muslim writer. Sometimes you specify: living in Paris. This identity, which you affirm today, have you always thought about it as such?),[92] Taïa turns the question upside down:

> Non. Je pense que plus je vieillis – j'ai maintenant 42 ans – plus j'entreprends une déconstruction de toutes identités dans lesquelles j'ai avancé ou que j'ai volontairement affirmées, pour arriver à tel ou tel résultat, dans ma vie ou bien dans ce qu'on pourrait appeler ma carrière littéraire en France. Depuis 2010 à peu près, j'essaye de détruire tous les murs, de détruire toutes définitions qui m'ont aidé pour arriver jusqu'à Paris et pour me dire 'je suis un être digne de faire telle ou telle chose, de publier un livre, de contacter une maison d'édition' ou 'être homosexuel et arabe, le fait de le dire, ça va intéresser les gens, ça va les toucher'. À un moment donné, j'ai dû faire tout cela, d'une manière totalement décomplexée, sans me rendre compte que je m'enfermais moi-même dans des définitions qui, forcément, ne rejoignaient pas toute la vérité autobiographique, toute la complexité de ma vérité. Mais tout ça je l'ai fait, et je le fais comme une suite de quelque chose qui est en train de se passer dans ma vie, je veux dire suite aux événements de ma vie et non pas suite à une évolution intellectuelle.[93]

(No. I think the older I get – I am now 42 years old – the more I have undertaken a deconstruction of all identities in which I advanced or that I deliberately affirmed in order to arrive at such and such a result in my life or in what might be called my literary career in France. Since 2010 or so, I have tried to destroy all the walls, to destroy all definitions that have helped me come to Paris and say 'I am a being worthy to do such and such, to publish a book, contact a publishing house' or 'a homosexual and Arab being, the fact of saying it, that it will interest people, that it will touch them'. At a certain point, I had to do all this, in a completely uninhibited manner, without taking into account that I enclosed myself in definitions which, necessarily, did not encompass the whole autobiographical truth, the whole complexity of my truth. But all that I did, and I do it as a sequel of something that is happening in my life, I mean a sequel of events in my life and not a sequel of an intellectual evolution.)

Rather than answering when he started to identify as gay, Arab, Moroccan and Muslim, Taïa addresses when he began to question these easily defined identity categories. That is, Taïa is well aware that identity categories such as 'Arab homosexual' are produced through exclusionary practices, and that it is necessary to move beyond affirmative resistance to avoid the relations of domination and exclusion, which control representational politics.

By turning the interviewer's question upside down, Taïa is able to critically reassess his position as 'token Arab homosexual' – he has neither represented his own autobiography fully, nor is he a representative of other Arab homosexuals. Before he became a recognized author and activist, Paris represented cultural power, book industry, human rights, and thus the possibility of 'making it' as an author and cineaste.[94] In this respect, Taïa took advantage of the possibilities Paris offered him as a platform for artistic expression and political resistance. Importantly, however, he maintains that France has not liberated him as his initial affirmative resistance remained caught within culturalist stereotypes of 'Arab sexuality' and Western hegemonic conceptions of universal rights. Moreover, by insisting that the course of his life – not his intellectual evolution – has determined the transformation of his self-representation, Taïa indirectly argues that before the notion 'Arab homosexuality' or 'Muslim homosexuality' can be deconstructed, the category itself must be created, and that this creation can only take place through lived performance. That is, first of all it is necessary to live out and speak up without fear of misrepresentation; then, when silence is broken through affirmative resistance, it is possible to start deconstructing the category 'Arab homosexuality'.

Whereas this argument could easily be dismissed as a retrospective legitimization of the choices he has made as author and activist in the past, it nevertheless reflects a necessary movement from affirmative resistance to parodic performance as defined by Butler. That is, through affirmative resistance, Taïa has succeeded in starting a debate about LGBT rights, and today his position as a recognized and award-winning author and cineaste makes it possible for him to question any readily established identity categories, and thus contribute to the continuing creation of a space to debate LGBT rights in Morocco and France.

Chapter 3

SUBVERTING 'ETHNOGRAPHIC' READING STRATEGIES

DRISS CHRAÏBI'S *LE PASSÉ SIMPLE* AND
ABDELLAH TAÏA'S *L'ARMÉE DU SALUT*

Authors, such as Abdellah Taïa and Rachid O., have often been accused of self-orientalization and of perpetuating the 'native informant' trope, because their literary 'disclosures' correspond to a consumption demand on the French literary market. In responding to a market demand of testimonial literature about clandestine Arab sexuality, these writers have, moreover, been caught in a long and arduous debate about authenticity and the 'right' representation of Moroccan culture and sexuality. But are they exoticizing themselves for a French audience with no resonance in Morocco, as a journalist such as Jean-Pierre Péroncel-Hugoz has argued?[1] Or do their works function as parodic performances of cultural stereotypes and obfuscate national, linguistic and sexual borders? Reality is that they are – and probably will continue to be – read in both ways.

As Mehammed Amadeus Mack has also argued, these writers are 'treading a difficult path between wanting to claim a voice as members of a minority group and having their work defined by this ethnic'[2] or sexual identity. In this respect, their works form part of a longer literary tradition. Historically, the works of Maghrebin authors have often been reduced to anthropological and cultural case studies with little, if any, focus on what makes them literary works in and of themselves, as Réda Bensmaïa has pointed out.[3]

However, similarly to how Rachid O. in *L'Enfant ébloui* (1995) parodies the expectations of his readers by letting the narrator engage in sexual storytelling that his audience – a group of French homosexual tourists – revel in while the narrator himself is excluded from their fascination because he is not young enough,[4] Driss Chraïbi in *Le Passé simple* (1954) thwarts his own position as 'native informant' through a parodic performance of an Arab storyteller who will change his story the minute he risks losing his audience. Both Rachid O. and Chraïbi have nevertheless been accused of self-orientalization and of reproducing French stereotypes about Moroccan society in order to find readers. Moreover, whereas *Le Passé simple* has often been read as a one-sided critique of Moroccan patriarchal tradition and culture, Taïa has been criticized for contributing to 'a reductive civilizational divide in which Arab sexual intolerance stands in opposition to Western sexual liberation'.[5] Reception history testifies to the difficult path that Moroccan authors are treading and to their struggles to escape the persistent dichotomy of colonizer versus colonized or of Western enlightenment and sexual liberation versus Arab backwardness and sexual intolerance.

In order to investigate the difficult path that Moroccan authors are treading as inevitable 'native informants', this chapter outlines the changing definitions of the 'ethnographic novel' and the 'novel of acculturation' since Abdelkébir Khatibi first introduced the terms in *Le Roman maghrébin* in 1968. Against this background the chapter further analyses Chraïbi's *Le Passé simple* and Taïa's *L'Armée du salut* (2006) in order to discuss how writing the 'self-absorbed' – both as someone who is completely blind to the 'other' and as someone who, as marginalized 'other', comes into existence through an excessive focus on the self – plays into questions about testimony, ethnographic depiction, authenticity and self-orientalization.

'Generation 54': Beyond ethnography and acculturation

In Morocco, the novel is a modern genre generally said to date back to Chraïbi's *Le Passé simple*, Ahmed Sefrioui's *La Boîte à merveilles* (The Box of Wonders) (1954) and Abdelmajid Benjelloun's *Fī al-ṭufūlah* (1957).[6] During the 1950s in the Maghreb (and in particular in Algeria), it was primarily, but not only, francophone authors who adopted the novelistic genre, which provided them with a new narrative form through which to express themselves and make themselves heard outside of their country. The first Maghrebin francophone authors were, among other things, motivated by a wish to provide a counter image to the exotic portraits of Maghrebins in French literature.[7] Moreover, as argued by Khatibi, these authors filled a void for the leftists in France who were supportive of the liberation movements.[8] With a wish to 'exprimer le drame d'une société en crise' (express the drama of a society in crisis) through themes of alienation and depersonalization,[9] willingly or not, these authors spoke directly into the French political debate. Consequently, the works of these authors were celebrated by the leftists to the point where every French publishing house had what some saw as their 'Arabe de service' (token Arab). At the same time the right wing was offended by what they considered an expression of 'ingratitude' and an insult to the French in their own language.[10] In this respect, these authors were successful, but their works were often read reductively as mimetic representations of the Maghreb, because everybody at the time – whether left or right, French or Maghrebin – seemed to agree that the role of the works of these authors should be that of testimonies, 'reflecting' the situation in the Maghrebin countries more or less truthfully.[11]

In the sense that every literary work is a testimony of its time, this definition is tautological, as Khatibi notes.[12] What is of importance is rather how the label testimony relates to representation and reception. These authors did not simply hold the 'power of representation'. They were forced to navigate between the expectations of the French publishing houses, Orientalist stereotypes about the Maghreb among the readers and nationalist sentiments in their home countries during the struggle for independence. As I will demonstrate later, the reception of *Le Passé simple* is an insightful example of how these authors were often caught in a heated ideological debate about the 'right' representation of Morocco (or the Maghreb). Maghrebin francophone authors were, as argued by Khatibi, simultaneously caught in the French language and in their national culture,[13] and what I find of interest is how these authors sought to deconstruct these regulatory regimes through experimental representational strategies.

Despite the fact that the so-called first Moroccan novels were written in French, arabophone authors soon adopted the novelistic genre. In contrast to authors of French expression, they discovered the novel through the short story (*qiṣṣah qaṣīrah*) and the literary traditions of the Middle East.[14] Some of the first Moroccan novels in Arabic were actually originally published in serialized form, for instance Benjelloun's autobiographical novel *Fī al-ṭufūlah*, which was serialized in the journal *Risālat al-Maghrib* (Morocco's Message) between 1949 and 1951,[15] and Abdelkrim Ghallab's *Dafannā al-māḍī* (1966), which was serialized in *al-ʿAlam* (The Banner), the Independence Party's (*ḥizb al-Istiqlāl*) official newspaper, between 1963 and 1965. Moreover, at the time of independence and during the following decade, novels written in Arabic were closely related to the nationalist cause. Whereas the publication of *Le Passé simple* provoked 'a long and arduous debate on who is entitled to represent Morocco's national culture, under what conditions and what kind of ideological positions they should have towards the country's national language, history and identity',[16] *Dafannā al-māḍī* was considered a model of 'nationalist realism' and 'praised as a literary memory of one of the most decisive periods in modern Morocco'.[17]

Nevertheless, despite the difference between novelistic writing in French and Arabic at the time, Moroccan authors across both languages had more than simply the genre in common. Whether in Arabic or French, Moroccan novelistic writing during this period showed a strong autobiographical tendency; and in a time marked by anti-colonial struggle, Moroccan authors were naturally preoccupied with the relation between colonizer and colonized, and with the construction of postcolonial 'national' identities. Thus writing the 'I' (or thinly fictionalized third-person novels, such as those found in Ghallab's writing) during this period was combined with a thematic focus on the nature of Moroccan identity and culture, and all authors struggled with what they saw as stereotypes and misconceptions about Morocco.

The 'ethnographic' novel

As argued by Khatibi, the so-called folkloric or ethnographic type of literature that dominated the literary scene in the Maghreb during the years preceding independence corresponded with a consumption demand in the Metropolitan as well as a nationalist demand for a literature that was faithful to 'authentic' culture in the respective countries.[18] What is particularly interesting in this respect is how the reception history subsequently reduced the label 'ethnographic' to a value judgement, rather than a category by which to describe the cultural and political conditions of literature at the time. This shift in focus had a considerable impact on the conception of literary representation in works labelled 'ethnographic' and reflects the particular ideological reality in which authors and critics were navigating at the time.

In *Le Roman maghrébin*, Khatibi identified three defining traits of the so-called ethnographic novel: (1) these authors' proclaimed aim was to provide their own vision of their self, territory and culture; (2) this was provided through a realist technique, that is, linear narration with focus on both biography and social chronicle; and (3) on a thematic level their meticulous description of daily life revealed an obsession with detail.[19]

In Morocco, the two autobiographical novels frequently referred to as ethnographic are *La Boîte à merveilles* and *Fī al-ṭufūlah*. However, whereas Khatibi was preoccupied with the cultural and political conditions of the Maghrebin novel, his definition of the ethnographic novel was soon reduced to a thematic obsession with detail,[20] and the label ethnographic has more often than not been used to discredit these novels as naive auto-exoticism of little literary merit.[21] In *La Violence du texte* (1981), Marc Gontard, however, contests the alleged unengaged nature of *La Boîte à merveilles* by arguing that the absence of the colonizer in the text should be interpreted as 'une volonté de négation de l'Autre, une sorte de meurtre scriptural du colonisateur' (a will to negate the Other, a sort of scriptural murder of the colonizer).[22] However, whereas he points to the arbitrary application of the label ethnographic, he does not question the so-called ethnographic nature of the novel:

> Sefrioui a été classé par une sorte de consensus propre à l'idéologie dominante (ici, celle des milieu intellectuels de gauche) dans la catégorie 'écrivains ethnographiques', le même consensus donnant un sens péjoratif à cette détermination. Or, dès que le regard s'attache à la vie quotidienne, il devient nécessairement ethnographique et l'on peut se demander pourquoi une telle appellation n'a jamais été appliquée au romancier algérien iconoclaste, Rachid Boudjedra, par exemple, dont *La Répudiation* offre pourtant un bel exemple du genre[23]

> (Sefrioui was classified by a sort of consensus that suited the dominant ideology (here, the milieu of left-wing intellectuals) in the category 'ethnographic writers'; the same consensus that gave a pejorative meaning to this determination. But as soon as the eye focuses on everyday life it necessarily becomes ethnographic, and one may wonder why such a designation has never been applied to the Algerian iconoclastic novelist, Rachid Boudjedra, for example, whose *La Répudiation*, nevertheless, provides a fine example of the genre.)

Gontard's conception of 'ethnographic' is pragmatic: any literary description of everyday life should be labelled ethnographic, regardless of the 'truth value' of the text. Along this line, Kaye and Zoubir included both Chraïbi and Tahar Ben Jelloun among 'ethnographic' authors, but in contrast to Gontard their application of the word 'ethnographic' is pejorative and reflects, according to them, a self-orientalizing gesture by which the author naively reproduces French stereotypes about Moroccan society in order to find readers.[24]

Within the last few decades scholars have, however, started to question these reductive ethnographic readings, and in *Aspects du roman marocain* (*1950-2003*) (2006), Abdallah Mdarhri Alaoui indirectly returns to Khatibi's description of the so-called ethnographic novel. That is to say, Mdarhri Alaoui's interpretation of *La Boîte à merveilles* resembles Khatibi's analysis considerably, but he defines the ethnographic novel along different lines than Khatibi. According to Mdarhri Alaoui, the defining trait of 'la récit ethnographique' is the testimonial function of the text, dedicated to a 'truthful' depiction of the observed society from a 'neutral' position of enunciation that places a maximum limit on the author's individual experience and subjectivity.[25] This definition is considerably different from Khatibi's, but adequately describes how the subsequent use of the label ethnographic has been closer to anthropological definitions than to Khatibi's. With this definition in mind, Mdarhri Alaoui argues that *La Boîte à merveilles* is not ethnographic. First, the novel reflects an individualized and partial view of a Moroccan social milieu during colonization – the popular milieu.[26] Second, the point of view is not neutral.[27] Third, the value of the text, according to Mdarhri Alaoui, lies not in its capacity of 'documenting' but in its 'construction of a certain truth'. Thus Mdarhri Alaoui's characterization of *La Boîte à merveilles* is the same as Khatibi's, but he displaces the label 'ethnographic' because the characterization of a novel as ethnographic has come to reflect a particular conception of culture where 'authenticity' is a desired goal of literary production. That is, the 'ethnographic writer' is either mocked as naive for seeking to convey 'authenticity' or accused of misrepresenting 'authentic' Moroccan culture.

The novel of 'acculturation'

Chraïbi's *Le Passé simple* is often singled out as the archetypal representative of the so-called novel of acculturation in Morocco.[28] Broadly speaking, acculturation refers to the process of adopting the values and customs of another culture after a prolonged contact with that culture. In this respect, acculturation is based upon a rather static conception of cultures as monologic entities which can then be merged if they come into contact with one another. In Khatibi's typology, the novel of acculturation is closely related to Albert Memmi's[29] and Frantz Fanon's[30] conception of the colonized as caught in colonial Manichean structures that situate the colonizer's 'enlightened' culture in opposition to the colonized's 'backward' culture. That is, the so-called novel of acculturation emerged along with an intensification of the nationalist struggle and a growing exasperation with the colonial system, constituting a reaction to assimilation and experiences of depersonalization. These authors were more rebellious than earlier ones, and they were set on dismantling 'les mécanismes de l'oppression coloniale, de la crise des structures sociales traditionelles et des déperditions de la personnalité nationale' (the mechanisms of colonial oppression, the crisis of the traditional social structures and the loss of national character).[31] In the so-called novels of acculturation, the protagonist is, according to Khatibi, portrayed as struggling with the problem of uprootedness and loss of identity, as he finds himself split between cultures.

Moreover, this literature remained caught within and governed by harsh acculturation because it was closely tied to the 'Metropole' and thus primarily an object of foreign consumption, as argued by Abdellatif Laâbi: 'Le colonisé ne découvre pas encore sa culture pour lui-même. Il la montre pour convaincre le camp de l'oppresseur. La culture est un objet d'exhibition.' (The colonized has yet to discover his culture for his own sake. He displays it to convince the oppressor's camp. Culture is an object for exhibition.)[32] Because of low literacy rates and poor publishing possibilities in Morocco,[33] these early postcolonial novels were both preoccupied with the problem of acculturation and caught in a cultural reality of acculturation.

If we turn to Chraïbi, he has often been accused of auto-exoticism and self-orientalization, despite the explicit focus of *Le Passé simple* on alienation and its implicit double critique that effectively dismantles the dichotomy between the French civilizing mission and traditional social, cultural and religious norms and practices. When Chraïbi published *Le Passé simple* in 1954, the novel was considered treasonous and was banned (until 1977), and Chraïbi was accused of betraying his country during the struggle for independence.[34] These angry responses resulted, quite surprisingly, in Chraïbi renouncing the novel in a repentant letter to the editor of *Démocratie*, the periodical of the nationalist Parti Démocratique d'Indépendence (PDI) in 1957.[35] A few weeks later, Ahmed Sefrioui wrote in the same paper:

> *Le Passé simple* a été une tentative pour traduire les sentiments qui agitent les Marocains de sa génération. Mais Driss Chraibi n'a pas pu observer la vie marocaine qui est assurément toute poésie. Et quoi que l'on ait pu dire, *Le Passé simple* n'est ni le Maroc ni les Marocains, c'est Driss Chraibi.[36]

> (*Le Passé simple* was an attempt to translate the feelings that stir the Moroccans of his generation. But Driss Chraibi has not been able to observe Moroccan life, which is surely all poetry. And whatever one may say, *Le Passé simple* is neither Morocco nor the Moroccans, it is Driss Chraibi.)

What was at stake at the time was not so much whose literary representation of Morocco was closer to the 'truth', but rather a struggle about who had the defining power. Chraïbi later argued in *Souffles* 5 (1967) that he renounced the novel because of the right wing in France who, just like the Moroccan nationalists, completely disregarded how the novel criticized the French protectorate, and took it as an argument to uphold France's presence in Morocco:

> Voici ce qui s'est passé pour les attaques. Un éditeur mange, gagne de l'argent. Il a fait paraître mon roman en pleine crise marocaine. Du coup, c'est la presse de droite qui s'en est emparée. La presse de droite française – et la presse de droite au Maroc, dirigée par des Marocains. [...] Oui, j'ai eu un moment de faiblesse, je

l'avoue, quand j'ai renié 'Le Passé simple'. Je ne pouvais pas supporter l'idée qu'on put prétendre que je faisais le jeu des colonialistes. J'aurais dû tenir bon, avoir plus de courage. Mais je vous le demande: en 1967, est-ce que les problèmes posés par ce livre n'existent pas encore?[37]

(So, this is what happened regarding the attacks. A publisher consumes, makes money. He published my first novel in the midst of the Moroccan crisis. As a result, the right-wing media seized it. The French right-wing press – and the right-wing press in Morocco, led by Moroccans. [. . .] Yes, I did go through a moment of weakness, I confess, when I renounced *Le Passé simple*. I couldn't bear the thought that people could claim that I was playing the game of the colonizers. I should have held out, have had more courage. But I ask you this: in 1967, don't the problems raised by this book still exist?)

In Morocco, the thrill of independence left no room for a novel like *Le Passé simple*, in particular because it aligned the national elite and the monarchy with the colonial power, as Jarrod Hayes has also argued.[38] But by 1967 things had changed dramatically, and a growing discontent with the political situation, which had become increasingly corrupt and repressive, made intellectuals join forces to establish a voice of resistance, and shortly after the literary journal *Souffles* was launched[39] Chraïbi was rehabilitated by Laâbi:

En ce sens, il est vraisemblablement le seul écrivain maghrébin et arabe qui ait eu le courage de mettre tout un peuple devant ses lâchetés, qui lui ait étalé son immobilisme, les ressorts de son hypocrisie, de cette auto-colonisation et oppression exercée les uns sur les autres, le féodal sur l'ouvrier agricole, le père sur ses enfants. Le mari sur son épouse-objet, le patron libidineux sur son apprenti.[40]

(In this respect, he was probably the only Maghrebin and Arab writer who has had the courage to confront a whole people with their cowardice, who laid out before them their immobilism, the mechanisms of their hypocrisy, of this auto-colonization and oppression that they exert on each other, the feudal on the agricultural worker, the father on his children. The husband on his object-wife, the libidinous master on his apprentice.)

Moreover, during the repressive reign of King Hassan II, the father–son conflict in *Le Passé simple* gained new relevance. One year after Laâbi's rehabilitation of Chraïbi, Khatibi's *Le Roman maghrébin* was published, in which Khatibi accorded a special place to Chraïbi and *Le Passé simple*. However, whereas Khatibi, on the one hand, seemed to buy into the same logic as Sefrioui by arguing that the political unrealism of Chraïbi's writing was flagrant, on the other hand he insisted that Chraïbi's writing could not be judged on this ground alone.[41] According to Khatibi, Chraïbi never intended to provide an objective analysis of a historical and political situation because his uprootedness prevented him from reconciling with his country, and his works should therefore be read psychologically.[42]

Nevertheless, despite this rehabilitation – or maybe somehow because of the nature of this rehabilitation, which focused on acculturation and the father–son conflict as a rather one-dimensional critique of traditional values and family life, and as such differed from the immediate reception of the book only in its focus on psychoanalysis and in its appraisal of the book – some critics have continued to read *Le Passé simple* through an ethnographic lens and to judge it according to its (in)ability to reflect Moroccan society. Whereas some critics have concluded that *La Boîte à merveilles* is a flight of fancy, trying to preserve a world in danger of disappearing, at the same time as they have accused it of auto-exoticism because the implied reader is 'French', Chraïbi has, through similar academic readings, been accused of being so enmeshed in 'French modernist discourses' that he apparently fails to see that the classical tale of a son's revolt against his father is alien to Morocco:

> This apparent attack on patriarchy, transcribed in the idiom of French modernist discourses, touts the availability of the text's incorporation into paradigms of generational conflict and oedipal motivation which are totally alien to Morocco.[43]

But *Le Passé simple* was not simply a product of Chraïbi's imagination, as argued by Ahmed Sefrioui; nor can it be reduced to a self-orientalized Oedipus complex, as by Kaye and Zoubir. On the one hand, it was a harsh critique of certain political currents prevalent at the time, and it was precisely this fact that made the novel controversial. As argued by Ellen McLarney, 'the hero's patricidal fantasies assume connotations of regicide, a kind of blasphemy in Moroccan politics at the time the novel was published.'[44] Whereas Chraïbi wrote *Le Passé simple* during the period leading up to the exile of Sultan Mohammed V, by the time the novel was published in 1954 the political scene had changed dramatically. By then, the exile of the sultan had generated a unifying cause and sparked a more violent resistance against the French protectorate.[45]

On the other hand, however, *Le Passé simple* subverts the idea that the novel is an example of acculturation just because it allegedly has adopted the classical rules of the nineteenth-century French novel. Even though *Le Passé simple* is somewhat social realist, follows classical linear narration and offers a traditional plot through the father–son conflict, reducing it to an Oedipus complex and an expression of self-orientalization glosses over how the novel is aimed polemically at the recognized literary language, as alluded to indirectly by the narrator through a parody of the difference between Western education (or novelistic art) and the Arab storyteller:[46]

> En dépit de mon instruction occidentale, je continuais de vivre, d'agir et de juger par parabole, à la manière de ces conteurs publics qui s'installent dans un coin de rue, munis en tout et pour tout d'un estomac creux et de leur fatalisme, mais en qui la moindre rire, le moindre geste déclenche une histoire, une giclée d'histoires – qu'au hazard d'une controverse ou d'un silence sceptique ils enjoliveront, interromprent ou adapteront à la mesure de tout chacun.[47]

(In spite of my Western education, I continued to live, act and judge through parables, just like the public storytellers who install themselves on a street corner, provided in all and for all with an empty stomach and their fatalism, but in whom the slightest laughter, the slightest gesture triggers a story, a spurt of stories – that at the risk of controversy or a skeptical silence they embellish, interrupt or adapt to the measure of everyone.)

In this passage the narrator, on the one hand, recalls his literary affiliation with Arabic storytelling and narration through parables rather than with French novelistic writing. On the other hand, however, Chraïbi mocks the traditional storyteller by questioning his reliability by constructing him as someone who will change his story the minute he fears controversy and risks losing his audience. In this respect, *Le Passé simple* functions as a double critique of French and Arabic literary traditions while simultaneously thwarting the narrator's position as 'native informant'.

Nobody sees anybody: Driss Chraïbi's Le Passé simple

The principal voice in *Le Passé simple* is the narrator-protagonist, Driss Ferdi. As other critics have argued, the novel is essentially a story about the ambiguous position of French-educated intellectuals at the time of independence in Morocco.[48] Roughly speaking, these intellectuals were trapped between contesting cultural discourses: the French, on the one hand, seemed to ignore their political aspirations and treat them as cultural informants about 'native life', whereas their compatriots, on the other hand, often accused them of collaborating with the colonial power and adopting so-called French values.[49]

In *Le Passé simple* Driss is depicted as a self-absorbed, disillusioned and angry young man, at once rebelling against and 'pushed around' by two seemingly incompatible societies and value systems. On the one hand, Driss takes everything as a pretext to hit out violently against whoever crosses his way. On the other hand, on multiple occasions he cynically presents himself as nothing but an effect of his surroundings; that is, his agency seems almost predetermined by the oppression of his authoritarian father, *le Seigneur*, and the hypocrisy of the French colonial power. This causal determinism is further emphasized by the titles of the novel's five chapters, each of which corresponds with a stage in a scientific experiment governed by a set of predetermined laws.

The reason for Driss's anger is above all his mother's misery, but his violent behaviour is exacerbated by the fact that he is caught between two seemingly incompatible cultures:

Imaginez-vous un Nègre du jour au lendemain *blanchi* mais dont, par omission ou méchanceté du sort, le nez est resté noir. J'étais vêtu d'une veste et d'un pantalon. Aux pieds une paire de chaussures. Une chemise. Une ceinture à la taille. Un mouchoir dans ma poche. J'étais fier. Comme un petit Européen! Sitôt parmi mes camarades, je me trouvais grotesque. Et je l'étais.[50]

(Imagine a Negro who from one day to the next *turns white* but whose nose, either by omission or a vicious fate, remains black. I was wearing a vest and a pair of trousers. On my feet, a pair of shoes. A shirt. A belt around my waist. A handkerchief in my pocket. I was proud. Like a little European! As soon as I was with my comrades I felt grotesque. And I was.)

At school his classmates mock him because his trousers are short-legged and his shirt unironed, whereas his father, who wears *babouches*, refuses to understand why he needs socks: 'Tu n'en as pas besoin non plus, fils. Tes souliers te couvrent entièrement les pieds. Nous, nous avons le talon dehors.' (You don't need any either, son. Your shoes cover your feet entirely. We have our heels free.)[51] This is the classical example of 'acculturation'. Driss has adopted the dress code of the French, but instead of assimilating into French culture, his appearance becomes a parody of both Moroccan and French dress codes and reveals the arbitrariness with which it is established when it is proper to wear socks.

Whereas Driss's revolt against his father is an integrated part of the narrative line, his revolt against the French is primarily verbal and articulated through a disruption of the narrative line, for instance through his essay for his baccalaureate exam. At the lycée where his father has sent him to get acquainted with the 'arms of the enemy',[52] Driss soon realizes that he will never be accepted as an equal. For his baccalaureate, he is to write an essay about the French slogan 'Liberté, Egalité, Fraternité' (Freedom, Equality, Fraternity),[53] and it is from the 'Arab' or 'colonized' point of view that he deconstructs the premises of the exam theme:

Je n'ignore point, messieurs les examinateurs, qu'une copie d'élève doit être anonyme, exempte de signature, nom, prénom ou marque propre à en faire reconnaître l'auteur. Je n'ignore point non plus cependant qu'une toile révèle aisément le peintre. C'est dire qu'il y a quelque temps déjà que vous avez percé ma personnalité: je suis arabe. Permettez en conséquence que je traite ledit sujet en tant qu'arabe. Sans plan, sans technique, gauche, touffu. Mais je vous promets d'être franc.[54]

(I don't ignore, gentlemen examiners, that a student's copy should be anonymous, without a signature, name, first name or any mark revealing the author. Nor do I ignore that a canvas easily reveals the painter. That is to say, that already some time ago you pierced my personality: I'm an Arab. So, allow me to treat the said subject as an Arab. Without a plan, without a technique, awkwardly, dense. But I promise you to be frank.)

Acknowledging that his voice will never be neutral or anonymous, the protagonist insists on treating the subject as an Arab. Not 'like an Arab', as in what the French would expect from an 'Arab', but as a Butlerian parodic performance. Thus the question remains: What is an 'Arab'? When Driss promises to proceed 'without a plan, without a technique, awkwardly, dense', he parodies French stereotypes about Arabs as if his mind – and the Arab mind in general – mirrors the Orientalist conception of the Arab city as an irrational labyrinthine web of narrow streets and alleys.[55] But according to the protagonist, this 'authentic' Arab no longer exists – if he ever did. What is left is an Arab 'dressed as a Frenchman'.[56] Neither the 'authentic' Arab nor the 'assimilated' Arab exists in the no man's land of the protectorate.[57] Driss remains a parody of both. As the protagonist sarcastically notes in his essay, it was never the intention of the colonial power to fully 'civilize' the Moroccans:

> Un vieux bonze de mes amis, nommé Raymond Roche, m'a dit hier soir: 'Nous, Français, sommes en train de vous civiliser, vous, Arabes. Mal, de mauvaise foi et sans plaisir aucun. Car, si par hazard vous parvenez à être nos égaux, je te le demande: par rapport à qui ou à quoi serons-nous civilises, *nous*?'[58]

> (An old bonze of my friends, named Raymond Roche, said to me last night: 'We, French, are in the process of civilizing you, Arabs. Badly, in bad faith and without any pleasure. Because if by chance you succeed in becoming our equals, I ask you: compared to whom and to what shall we be civilized, *us*?')

Paradoxically, however, it is precisely this reluctance to fully 'civilize' that turns Driss into a grotesque parody of the French, and ultimately unsettles the narrator-protagonist's position as 'native informant' as the so-called 'authentic' Arab is simultaneously irrational and inexistent and thus impossible to retrieve reliable information from.

At this point in his essay the protagonist argues that he is not qualified to talk about 'Freedom, Equality, Fraternity', and that he will therefore replace the subject with another more familiar to him: 'Muslim Theocracy'. Up to this point he has demonstrated that he as a colonized subject is neither free, equal nor a 'brother' to the French, and that the slogan – despite the French civilizing mission – does not apply to him. Instead, it reveals a discrepancy between French humanism and French colonial oppression. Now, however, Driss embarks on a critique of the five pillars of Islam and the hypocrisy with which Moroccans approach these five commandments. Thus he replaces one slogan with another, and concludes with the statement 'devise aussi rouillé que la nôtre' (motto as rusty as ours).[59]

The reaction of the headmaster to his essay almost anticipates the French reception of the novel when it was first published. Whereas the headmaster opens his conversation with Driss by praising him as a Moroccan Luther, who makes him laugh, is skilled and in possession of an erudite tone and a 'serious' violence,[60] he soon reveals that he has understood nothing of the essay written by the protagonist. Driss's subtle critique of 'Freedom, Equality, Fraternity' is lost on the headmaster, who reads the essay only as a critique of Moroccan cultural and religious traditions, as if there were no relation between the different sections of his essay. The irony that Driss passes 'with distinction',[61] despite the fact that the headmaster cannot see any relation between Driss's critique of 'Muslim Theocracy' and 'Freedom, Equality, Fraternity', underlines the protagonist's impossible position. He is simultaneously trapped in a stereotypical conception of the 'irrational Arab' and in the 'exceptional' position of being the only 'evolved Arab' who, according to the headmaster, can see what the French can see: that the Arabs are in need of the colonial powers and their 'civilizing mission'.

The father–son conflict

While Driss's aggressive behaviour reflects a young man who is desperately trying to claim his right to self-definition and agency, he comes to realize towards the end of the novel that he is nothing but a billiard ball[62] being propelled around by everybody else, all of whom to his knowledge are puppeteered by *le Seigneur*. Even though the narrator-protagonist arrives at this recognition only towards the end of the novel, it runs through the narrative line from the beginning.

Le Seigneur has chosen Driss 'parmi une demi-douzaine d'enfants de sexe masculine pour "le monde nouveau"' (among half a dozen male children for 'the new world'),[63] underlining from the beginning that Driss, as a French-educated intellectual, is his father's creation. During their long conversation in chapter five, *le Seigneur* furthermore states that he did not choose Driss because he was special; he chose him by chance only: 'Un jour j'ai fermé les yeux, pointé l'index' (One day I closed my eyes, pointed my index finger),[64] and combined with the utterance 'tu n'es pas le seul. Je ne connais pas un jeune de ta génération qui ne te ressemble' (you are not the only one. I don't know a youth of your generation that doesn't resemble you),[65] this statement serves to underline that there is nothing special about the narrator-protagonist. He is one among many in Morocco.

This alignment with the young generation in Morocco further serves to position the narrator-protagonist vis-à-vis *le Seigneur*. On the one hand, the narrator-protagonist is, as a French-educated intellectual, part of a small elite having almost no contact with the 'oppressed masses'. The distance between Driss and the Moroccan people is repeatedly emphasized by reference to his 'Christian' (i.e. European) outlook which, according to his father, makes him blend in in the European part of the city;[66] which makes his uncle mistake him for a foreigner;[67] and which gives rise to gossip at the funeral of his brother Hamid.[68] On the other hand, the narrator-protagonist identifies with the masses, aligning himself with the ostracized of society, the beggars[69] and the Jews,[70] to underline his low position vis-à-vis the autocracy of *le Seigneur*. As argued by McLarney, Driss's identification with the oppressed masses appears tactical and ideological: 'It emphasizes his low place in the social hierarchy as an adolescent who has not yet come into his own authority', and it serves to align the intelligentsia with the oppressed masses.[71] Thus, the alignment with the 'oppressed masses' simultaneously legitimizes his revolt against his father, allegorizes anti-colonial struggle and reveals how blinded Driss is by his own feelings of pain, disbelief, hatred and contempt. He is so self-absorbed that he fails to see that he is seizing the cause of the 'oppressed masses' to legitimize his own revolt against everything and everyone.

In addition to this, the psychological, the ritual, the political, the social and the economic intertwine in the father–son conflict. On one level, the Oedipus conflict is aligned with regicide. As argued by McLarney, the protagonist blasphemously imagines his father as both godlike[72] and king,[73] and his fantasies about assassinating him to take his place assume connotations of regicide, alluding to a French model of revolution that implies overthrow of the monarchy and its associates.[74] On another level, *le Seigneur* is in a seemingly paradoxical manner simultaneously depicted as king, makhzan, God, feudal landlord and neo-bourgeois merchant.[75] As such, Chraïbi aligns the national elite with colonial power in the father figure and, as argued by Hayes, points to how the national elite both served and profited economically from colonialism.[76]

That Driss's revolt is somehow predetermined by his father's oppression is reflected in four 'confrontation' scenes. Whereas the first three scenes stage direct confrontations between father and son, the father is suspiciously absent in the fourth scene, which concludes the book with Driss's final act of defiance.

The first scene of confrontation, in which Driss supposedly is free to kill his father – if he has the courage – is the knife scene in chapter one. However, despite the fact that it is Driss who has stolen the knife from his father, it is the father who provokes the confrontation between the two: by turning his back on Driss and demanding that he throws the knife at him on the count of ten, he manifests his power over the entire family.[77] The brothers are paralysed by the situation, and before the mother interrupts at the count of ten, Driss has already closed the knife. On the one hand, this act signals that Driss refuses to succumb to his father's dictates, but on the other it reveals that he is trapped: if he throws the knife at his father's neck, he follows his father's command; if he does not, he proves his father's assumption that he is afraid. The knife scene is concluded with Driss referring to his father as the 'family god'[78] and, as such, the scene is central to the establishment of the autocracy of *le Seigneur*, around whom all the other characters are constructed.

The spitting scene in chapter three mirrors the knife scene of chapter one. When, shortly after Hamid's funeral, *le Seigneur* leaves for Aïn Bordja to buy cereal grain for almsgiving (*zakāt*),[79] Driss stages what is supposed to be his final act of revolt – a coup d'état, with *le Seigneur* absent. With reluctantly given help from two friends and his brother Nagib, Driss succeeds in emptying his father's storeroom. This act of rebellion is supposed to function as the final blow to a father who has been enfeebled by the ruination of his commercial enterprise and by the death of his youngest son. However, the spitting scene reverses this 'final blow', and even though Driss has already decided to leave the house, his father beats him to it by throwing him out. Two things about the events leading up to the spitting scene are particularly interesting. First, Driss articulates that his revolt is not simply a revolt against *le Seigneur*; it is also an act of defiance against his mother[80] – and in this, Driss is not all that different from his father. Second, when his father has returned from Aïn Bordja, Driss refers to himself as a 'puppet'[81] – underlining the immense power of *le Seigneur*. As in the knife scene, the whole family is gathered in the spitting scene, but this time *le Seigneur* punishes them collectively. In an act of self-abasement, he forces them all to spit him in the face, and, as Driss reasons himself, *le Seigneur*'s willingness to self-abase counters his own act of rebellion and emphasizes *le Seigneur*'s power.[82]

The gun scene in chapter five is part of a long dialogue between Driss and *le Seigneur*. For the first and only time in the novel, the voice of *le Seigneur* is the centre of attention: he is provided with space to articulate his point of view. Nevertheless, the dialogue remains a battle site, neither one seeing the other, and *le Seigneur* demonstrating once again that he is one step ahead of Driss. During the conversation Driss draws attention to the fact that they are both cheating each other.[83] On the one hand, *le Seigneur* has shifted from speaking in the majestic plural to an intimate 'I', but according to Driss, this is only to lure him in,[84] to have him believe that he is confiding in him, when in reality he is about to demonstrate his power once again. On the other hand, Driss has brought a gun to the conversation.[85] But rather than going through with his plan and committing 'regicide' with the bullet he claims is left in the magazine of the Luger, Driss reveals his intentions in order to demonstrate his power and that he has managed to convince his brothers to join him in his rebellion. Even *le Seigneur* acknowledges that Driss has succeeded in turning his sons against him,[86] but as his brothers have nowhere else to turn, it makes no difference. With the cheating out in the open, *le Seigneur* now reveals his hidden intentions – buying vacant land near Casablanca at a bargain with the plan of selling it at the highest price when the city needs to expand.[87] Knowing how to take advantage of a poor situation, *le Seigneur* demonstrates what he deems the nature of 'true' revolt. Whereas it may look as if *le Seigneur* is trapped in 'ossified' traditions, as Driss argues, he is in reality as 'modern' and as sly as Driss.

Driss's final act of defiance was, according to Salim Jay,[88] the most troublesome part of the book to many Moroccans at the time of publication, because Driss, in the toilet on the plane to France, says: 'Je pisse dans l'espoir que chaque goutte de mon urine tombera sur la tête de ceux que je connais bien, qui me connaissent bien, et qui me dégoûtent.' (I piss in the hope that every drop of my urine will fall on the heads of those whom I know well, who know me well, and who disgust me.)[89] From the perspective of the reception of the book, Chraïbi succeeded in pissing on everyone. But in his revolt, he failed, as he felt forced to renounce the book; and there is a conspicuous echo between the novel and its reception, as if the immediate reception of the novel had been as predetermined by the political situation as Driss Ferdi's revolt by the oppression of *le Seigneur* and the French protectorate. Moreover, as Hayes[90] has also pointed out, Driss's postponement of his revolt indefinitely came to mirror how the process of decolonization was thwarted by a monarch serving neocolonial interests.

Suicide as the ultimate revolt?

When Laâbi interviewed Chraïbi for *Souffles* 5 in 1967, Chraïbi began the interview by associating his revolt with his oppressed mother:

> La révolte qui couvait en moi était dirigée contre tout: contre le Protectorat, contre l'injustice sociale, contre notre immobilisme politique, culturel, social. Et puis, il y avait autre chose: ma mère. Rendez-vous compte: je lisais du Lamartine,

du Hugo, du Musset. La femme, dans les livres, dans l'autre monde, celui des Européens, était chantée, admirée, sublimée. Je rentrais chez moi et j'avais sous les yeux et dans ma sensibilité une autre femme, ma mère, qui pleurait jour et nuit, tant mon père lui faisait la vie dure.[91]

(The revolt brewing within me was directed against everything: against the protectorate, against social injustice, against our political, cultural, and social stagnation. And then there was something else: my mother. Be aware: I was reading Lamartine, Hugo, and Musset. Women, in these books, in this other world, that of the Europeans, were lyricized, admired, sublimated. I went home, and before my eyes and in my sensitivity was another woman, my mother, who wept all day and night because my father made her life so hard.)

Nearly twenty years later, in an interview with *CELFAN Review* in 1983, Chraïbi once again contended that *Le Passé simple* was a novel about his love for his mother, who in turn symbolized the homeland.[92] As the mother in *Le Passé simple* ends up committing suicide, the novel could thus be read as a radical loss of homeland, and consequently of one's past and identity – an interpretation supported by the title, which refers to a past radically divorced from the present. Chraïbi further underlines this link between the oppressed mother and the title of the novel in the *Souffles* interview:

S'il n'y avait eu *que* le Protectorat et le colonialisme, tout eût été simple. C'est du coup que mon passé, notre passé, eût été simple. Non, monsieur Sartre, l'enfer ce n'est pas les autres. Il est aussi en nous-mêmes. J'ai dit ce qu'il fallait dire sur ce passé, atrocement, et je ne regrette rien.[93]

(If the *only* [problems] were the protectorate and colonialism, everything would have been simple. Then suddenly, my past, our past, would have been simple. No, Monsieur Sartre, hell is not other people. It is also within us. I said what had to be said about our past, brutally, and I regret nothing.)

According to Chraïbi, the mother figure is a symptom of everything that is wrong in Moroccan society. Noticeably, however, the mother figure is more than a one-dimensional symbol of the homeland. As an objectified and 'voiceless' figure around whom everybody else is acting, she also reveals the multilayered nature of both Driss's and *le Seigneur*'s relation to her and to each other.

The mother's principal characteristic is that of a victimized and voiceless woman. The voice of the mother is reduced either to the sound of her weeping, day and night, or to her begging for help in order to die. This apart, her voice is almost completely absent from the novel. At the outset, she is represented as nothing but the possession of *le Seigneur*, who has the power to decide whether she should live or die[94] as she lives under the constant threat of repudiation.[95] Along the same lines, she is reduced to a prisoner of *le Seigneur*'s household: a house she supposedly has not left since she married *le Seigneur* at the age of fifteen. However, despite the fact that the narrator depicts his mother as someone to whom freedom no longer has any meaning,[96] she never comes to terms with being subjected to *le Seigneur*'s tyranny. Whenever she speaks, it is to ask either Driss[97] or the gods[98] to help her end her life. The relation between Driss's revolt and his mother's misery is further underlined in chapter three of the novel, when the narrator establishes that his urge to revolt was born at the sound of her weeping, which kept him awake at night when he was four.[99] Driss's revolt is thus the product of his mother's misery, and her representation as deprived of agency serves to legitimize that he acts and speaks on her behalf.

The mother has no identity except as mother and housewife; but even this role the narrator-protagonist accuses her of failing: 'Oui, ma mère était ainsi, faible, soumise, passive. Elle avait enfanté sept fois, à intervalles réguliers, deux ans. Dont un fils qui ne pouvait qu'être ivrogne et moi, qui la jugeais.' (Yes, my mother was thus weak, submissive, passive. She had given birth seven times, at regular intervals, two years. Including a son who could only be drunk and me who judged her.)[100] According to Driss, his mother is not simply a victim, but also a complete failure at raising her children – a failure emphasized by the fact that raising her children is portrayed as the only responsibility and dignity left to her. In chapter three, this is further exacerbated by the death of Hamid, to which her – according to Driss, undignified – response is to try to trick *le Seigneur* into impregnating her again.[101] At this point, however, Driss reveals that he is completely ignorant of his mother's situation or her point of view. In *Le Passé simple* the mother figure remains a caricature underlining her position as the true subaltern.

Moreover, even if the narrator-protagonist has taken upon himself to act and speak on his mother's behalf, he seems more resentful than protective of her. On the one hand, he rebels because she has been silenced and disempowered by *le Seigneur*; on the other, he resents her silence and failure to rebel (which, once again, reveals the impossibility of rebelling or of speaking up on behalf of someone you cannot understand). The mother is, however, not ignorant of her loss of dignity; but when she refuses to join Driss in his rebellion against *le Seigneur*, he interprets it as a sign of resignation:

Ah oui? Le reproche est dans tes yeux. Qui dit: 'Driss mon fils, toi que j'aime . . . etc . . . etc . . . laisse, cède, plie encore une fois; tu voudrais me défendre, me brandir comme un drapeau, tu te trompes, je n'en vaux pas la peine, vois, mes seins sont flasques et ma peau adipeuse, tu es absolu, trop absolu, la paume de mes mains s'est ratatinée comme une vieille figue et je ne sais plus sourire. Autrefois peut-être . . . mais maintenant? Je n'ai plus nulle envie, même pas d'un sursaut, en mon âme et conscience. Cède, Driss mon fils, cède encore une fois, cette fois-ci sera la dernière – et je te bénirai.'[102]

(Oh yes? Reproach is in your eyes. It says: 'Driss, my son, whom I love . . . etc . . . etc . . . let it go, give in, bend one more time; you want to defend me, wave me like a flag, you are wrong, I'm not worth it, see, my breasts are flabby and my skin is bloated, you are extreme, too extreme, the palms of my hands are wrinkled like

an old fig and I don't know how to smile any more. Once, maybe . . . but now? I
no longer have any desire, not even a spurt, in my soul and consciousness. Give
in, Driss, my son, give in one more time, this time will be the last – and I will
bless you.')

It is noteworthy that 'qui dit' (it says) indicates that it is not the mother speaking,
but Driss seizing her voice. The narrator-protagonist is positioning his mother as
someone who has given up and on whose behalf he consequently must revolt. The
voice of the mother is deliberately positioned as 'seized' by the men in the novel,
in order to counterpose Driss and *le Seigneur* in relation to one another and as
equally self-absorbed.

In his treatment of his mother, Driss is not all that different from *le Seigneur*,
as he himself admits: 'Pourtant, j'étais conscient: à moins d'un defaut d'optique, le
Seigneur s'était pleinement reproduit en moi.' (Nevertheless, I was aware: at least
by an optical default, *le Seigneur* had been completely reproduced in me.)[103] Driss
both revolts because of and against his mother, and in his revolt against her, he
is treating her as an imbecile,[104] and even her tenderness becomes monstrous to
him.[105] In contradistinction to this, *le Seigneur* reveals his affection for his wife
in the long dialogue with Driss in chapter five, after she has committed suicide.
Whereas he blames tradition and his upbringing for forcing him into maltreating
his wife,[106] *le Seigneur* insists that he – by not repudiating her or taking another
wife – has been good to her.[107] Despite their differences, father and son seem
equally hypocritical in relation to their wife/mother, and both of them assert their
masculinity and define themselves against the feminine.

Thus, on the one hand, the stereotypical depiction of the mother serves to display
Driss's blindness, confusion and pain. He is closer than anyone to his mother, but
he is so enmeshed in his own suffering that he does not see her. On the other hand,
however, and as a consequence of this, the mother only exists through the gazes of
Driss and *le Seigneur*, and as such she, as a novelistic character, serves to display the
hypocrisy of the two rather than provide a realistic picture of Moroccan women. In
this respect, her suicide forces Driss and *le Seigneur* to reconfigure their conflict as
they can no longer hide behind the idea of a conflict by proxy.

The mother's suicide has often been interpreted as the ultimate revolt against
le Seigneur, and her death as the precondition for Driss's emancipation.[108] The
narrator-protagonist himself argues that his act of rebellion inspired his mother
to throw herself from the roof and hit the ground like a sack of grain.[109] Internal
logic would then suggest that Driss has succeeded in winning his mother over and
that everything will now become simple: 'Si je gagnais ma mere à ma cause – et
nul n'est plus difficile à "dégonder" qu'un mediocre – le reste deviendrait aussi
simple qu'un simple d'esprit.' (If I could win my mother over to my cause – and
nobody is more difficult to 'unhinge' than a mediocre – the rest would be as simple
as a simple-minded person.)[110] However, the irony surrounding this proposition
contests such an interpretation and displays Driss's ignorance of his mother, and
there is a striking discrepancy between the proposition by the narrator that 'j'avais
gagné' (I had won)[111] and his unrelieved failure in his revolt.

Moreover, whereas the father contradicts Driss in accusing him of murdering his mother in a desperate attempt to prove a point and detach himself from his family, his arguments follow the same line of reasoning as Driss's: 'La poison, tu l'as injecté jusque dans l'extrême resignation de ta mère. L'idée d'une révolte ne lui fût jamais venue à l'esprit. Tu l'en as bourrée. Elle en est morte.' (The poison, you injected it until the extreme resignation of your mother. The idea of a revolt would never have entered her mind. You stuffed her full of it. She died of it.)[112] Just like Driss, however, *le Seigneur* is displayed as so self-absorbed that he is incapable of seeing his wife's suicide as anything but the disastrous outcome of Driss's stupidities, as well as a simple instrument for him to use in their conflict to prove his point.

However, I am neither convinced that the mother's suicide constitutes a revolt, nor that it effects any liberation for Driss. Constructed as the only act available to her, suicide represents less a choice of revolt than a last resort completely deprived of any hope of effecting societal change. To this extent, the novel orchestrates three contradictory representations of the mother. Did Driss win her over, as he argues himself? Did he lead her astray, as his father argues? Or did she commit suicide simply to escape an unbearable situation, without any intentions of setting an example or effecting Driss's emancipation? The novel nowhere suggests that Driss will succeed in his future revolt, nor that his father will not continue to be one step ahead of him and has, in reality, planned his future from the beginning. The ambivalence surrounding the father figure might actually indicate that his intention is for Driss to become the well-educated intellectual that he himself could not. Thus, the mother figure is both trapped in and seized by the father–son conflict. As there is no room for her, she is left with no other choice but to commit suicide. Paradoxically, however, Driss and *le Seigneur* even deprive her of this agency in attributing her suicide to Driss's revolt. Thus, if she symbolizes the homeland, it is a homeland struggling in vain to be seen and heard as more than a stereotype.

Simply living a life of 'deviance': Abdellah Taïa's L'Armée du salut[113]

Like *Le Passé simple*, Taïa's autobiographical novel *L'Armée du salut* functions as a parodic performance of the so-called ethnographic novel and its reception as a mimetic representation of 'authentic' reality through a genre 'borrowed' from the West. Whereas *L'Armée du salut* reflects an expressed wish to leave the question of acculturation behind and move on from the debate about cultural identity, it nevertheless directly engages in dismantling culturalist stereotypes about Morocco, women, homosexuals, Western freedom and so on.

L'Armée du salut is Taïa's first novel, written at the request of his publisher, Le Seuil, who wanted him to write a novel, as opposed to his earlier collections of short stories (*Mon Maroc* and *Le Rouge du tarbouche*). This venture into a new genre is reflected in the structure of the novel, and makes it very different from *Le Passé simple*, which is structured around a classical plot. The first version of

L'Armée du salut that Taïa submitted to his editor at Le Seuil was actually that of a 'mirror story', as he recounted in a conversation I had with him in March 2016: his childhood in the family home was mirrored in the story of his moving to Geneva as a young adult. His editor was not completely satisfied with the text, however, and expressed the feeling that something was missing. In their conversation the story of Taïa's relation to his older brother came up, and the idea of part two in *L'Armée du salut* was born. As the text was rewritten, part three became considerably longer, to the extent that the mirror effect disappeared. Thus the final text constitutes a negotiation between the expressed wishes of Taïa's editor and his own agenda with the text, and this is reflected in how *L'Armée du salut* subverts the classical structure of a coming-of-age novel.

In brief, *L'Armée du salut* is divided into three parts, each containing a fragment of Taïa's life. These fragments are linked together by the fact that each constitutes a transformation of his body and of him as a person discovering himself and becoming aware of the sexual contradictions that lie within him. The structuring element of Taïa's memories is thus the transformation of his body. Rather than narrating his life as a coherent whole, Taïa is depicting a few selected fragments that have shaped his sexual identity.

When set against the protagonist in *Le Passé simple*, the protagonist in *L'Armée du salut* stands out as both naive and credulous. Despite the fact that the society depicted is still permeated with social injustice, Abdellah is not angry at the world in the same way as Driss, and he only exceptionally expresses direct wishes to resist specific cultural, religious or sexual definitions imposed on him. How then is it possible to talk about *L'Armée du salut* as a narrative of commitment? At first sight, the protagonist is primarily preoccupied with a project of self-realization: coming to terms with his sexuality and becoming an intellectual in Paris. However, his search for identity is replete with resistance narratives: *L'Armée du salut* is essentially a resistance to any stereotypical depiction of the oppressed and marginalized – whether the protagonist himself, or any other character in the novel. In this respect, *L'Armée du salut* differs considerably from *Le Passé simple*. Rather than the protagonist himself revolting, his naivety and his 'self-absorbed' way of life indirectly subvert folkloric conceptions of so-called authentic Moroccan culture and sexuality simply by living a life 'deviating' from these stereotypes.

The impassioned father and the hysterical mother

In the first part of the novel, the narrator recalls the sexual texture of everyday life in the family home in Hay Salam in the town of Salé, just outside of Rabat. The house functions as a closed space where the narrator can explore the most intimate family relations. The family is relatively poor and lives in a small house with only three rooms: one for the father, one for the first-born son and one for the rest of the family, including Abdellah, his six sisters, his younger brother and his mother.[114] Thus Abdellah grows up with people all around him; and the passionate relationship between his parents is therefore not a private affair of the two, but an intimate part of family life. Living this close is something that shapes Abdellah's whole existence and sexuality, and writing the self, consequently, comes to imply revealing the nature of his parents' sex life as he imagined it when young. However, just as Driss in *Le Passé simple* is so blinded by his own feelings of pain, disbelief, hatred and contempt that he is incapable of really seeing and understanding the lives of anybody else, the point of view in *L'Armée du salut* is almost exclusively that of the 'self-absorbed' narrator: 'La nuit, mes rêves n'étaient pas sexuels. En revanche, certains jours, mon imagination s'aventurait facilement et avec une certains excitation sur ce terrain torride et légèrement incestueux. J'étais dans le lit avec mes parents.' (At night my dreams weren't sexual. In contrast, on certain days my imagination ventured easily, and with a certain level of arousal, onto this torrid and slightly incestuous ground. I was in bed with my parents.)[115]

By staying inside the head of the protagonist, the narrator creates a space where he can project his own sexual fantasies onto the sex life of his parents. That is, rather than actually disclosing anything about his parents to a supposedly voyeuristic French reader, the narrator seizes on their sex life to dramatize how family life has formed his own sexuality. What he does reveal, however, is his own forbidden sexual fantasies. And this is the catch-22 situation of authors such as Taïa. On the one hand, it is through being 'self-absorbed' that the narrator-protagonist of *L'Armée du salut* can both come into existence as the sexual being society so desperately wishes to hide from the public and thwart his own position as 'native informant'. But on the other, it is this excessive focus on the self and on clandestine sexuality that have attracted accusations of exhibitionism and of self-orientalization.

Unlike the rebellious and suspicious Driss of *Le Passé simple*, who sees violence and injustice everywhere, part one of *L'Armée du salut* is written almost as a eulogy to passionate sex and hysteria; the protagonist glorifies his parents' sexual desire as 'une parfaite harmonie sexuelle qui s'accomplissait naturellement. Ils avaient été faits l'un pour l'autre, de toute évidence le sexe était leur langage privilégié à travers lequel s'exprimait clairement l'image du couple qu'ils formaient' (a perfect sexual harmony, which was naturally achieved. They were made for each other, evidently sex was their preferred language through which the image of the couple they formed was clearly expressed).[116]

However, despite the apparent sexual harmony, the lovemaking nights of his parents often end with heated discussions leading to threats so brutal and violent that the mother's hysterical screams wake the whole family and the gossiping neighbours too. The picture perfect of an impassioned family not afraid of their own sexuality is disrupted when the neighbours knock on their door, demanding answers to the loaded question: 'Qu'a-t-elle, votre mère? Toujours aussi maltraitée par votre père?' (What's up with her, your mother? Is she still being mistreated by your father?)[117] To this the narrator responds with a passage of introspection. On the level of the story line, the neighbours' questions reveal how the passionate relationship of his parents is perceived outside the family home, whereas the internal monologue reflects how difficult it is for the protagonist to challenge the presumption that his father is abusive and his mother a defenceless victim.

The presence of the neighbours in the narrative reveals a discrepancy between the world view of the narrator-protagonist and that of the surrounding society. From this perspective, the narrator has failed in his effort to 'normalize' the sex life of his parents, in so far as the neighbours see nothing but domestic violence. In contradistinction with, for instance, Rachid O.'s *L'Enfant ébloui*, *L'Armée du salut*'s central theme is estrangement rather than normalization. The family house is permeated with sexual emotions, but as soon as these are transferred from the private space of the home to the public space of the surrounding community, they turn into 'les rumeurs les plus monstrueuses' (the most monstrous rumors),[118] exposing their passion as shameful and violent. It is noteworthy, however, that *L'Enfant ébloui* and *L'Armée du salut*, through 'normalization' and 'estrangement' respectively, paint the same picture: that it is not the sexual acts in and of themselves that are transgressive, but their movement from the private to the public, either by becoming visible to the neighbours in *L'Armée du salut* or through their public representation in a literary work.

Moreover, the neighbours in *L'Armée du salut* are depicted as hypocrites that act as saviours, only to pick up gossip to spread. According to the narrator, they do not grasp the nature of the relationship between his parents as they see nothing but the improper behaviour of an abusive husband. In contradistinction to the neighbours' perception of the father as abusive, the narrator depicts him as an inverted version of the downright violent father in Mohamed Choukri's *Al-khubz al-ḥāfī*:

أخي يبكي، يتلوى ألماً. يصغرني. أبكي معه. أراه يمشي أليه. الوحش يمشي أليه. الجنون في عينينه. يداه أخطبوط. لا أحد يقدر أن يمنعه. أستغيث في خيالي. وحش! مجنون! أمنعوه! يلوي اللعين عنقه بعنف. أخي يتلوى. الدم يتدفق من فمه. أهرب خارج بيتنا تاركاً إياه يسكت أمي. باللكم والرفس. اختفيت منتظراً نهاية المعركة.[119]

(My brother cries, he squirms in pain. He is younger than me. I cry with him. I see him walking toward him. The monster walking toward him. Madness in his eyes. His hands are an octopus. No one has the power to stop him. I call for help in my imagination. Monster! Insane! Stop him! The damned twists his neck violently. My brother squirms. Blood pours out of his mouth. I run away from our house leaving him to silence my mother. With punches and kicks. I hide and wait for the end of the battle.)

In *Al-khubz al-ḥāfī* the narrator-protagonist depicts his father as *majnūn* – mad, insane, possessed by *jinn* – and this madness is paired with his violent behaviour and strips him of his humanity. He is an irredeemable monster, who kills his own son with his bare hands and beats up his wife to silence her afterwards. In *L'Armée du salut* the father is also *majnūn* or *folle*, but in the sense of an impassioned lover. Here madness and monstrosity disrupt sociocultural norms and unsettle what it means to be sane or insane. Taïa turns Choukri's father figure upside down. He is now passionate and irrational, and if he symbolizes anything, it is a patriarch on the edge of breakdown. He might threaten with violence, but he is incapable of hitting his wife. Thus rather than being someone to revolt against, he is someone to feel sorry for. Moreover, whereas in *Al-khubz al-ḥāfi* the young Mohamed is a silent spectator of his father's violence and runs away from the house while the father silences his mother with punches and kicks, the children in *L'Armée du salut* reclaim their mother by crying, screaming, banging on the bedroom door and even breaking it down. In *L'Armée du salut* there are no clear victims, and while the children are afraid of what might happen to their mother, they are nevertheless free to act on their emotions without fear of their father.

By intertwining direct mention of Choukri as a source of inspiration to the protagonist in part two[120] with hypotextual references to the father figure in *Al-khubz al-ḥāfi* in part one, Taïa, on the one hand, underlines the autobiographical structure of the narrative. The fact that the book that opened the world of literature to the protagonist is also present between the lines in *L'Armée du salut* emphasizes the identity between author, narrator and protagonist. On the other hand, Taïa inscribes himself in a tradition of committed literature by recalling his literary affiliation with Choukri. *L'Armée du salut* is not simply an 'artistic' autobiography with the psychological state of the protagonist at the centre of the narrative; it is simultaneously part of a larger cultural memory and a literary testimony to life as a homosexual during the 1980s and 1990s.

The last aspect of the neighbours' intervention relates to the mother figure. Unlike *Le Passé simple*, *L'Armée du salut* is not a story about an oppressive patriarch and his submissive wife. Instead it challenges the stereotypical conception of Arab women as oppressed, by questioning what it means to be 'in power'. Noticeably, Taïa is neither denying nor ignoring existing gender inequalities in Morocco, but through the figure of the 'hysterical mother' he effectively dismantles stereotypical gender roles derived from a patriarchal gender hierarchy in which men are supposedly strong and in control of their emotions whereas women are weaker, both intellectually and physically, and controlled by emotion and instinct.

In medical discourse, hysteria was until 1980 a clinical disorder that described everything men found mysterious and unmanageable about women.[121] Hysteria was 'evidence' of the instability of the female mind. The only cure was marriage and pregnancy,[122] through which women – from Freud onwards – could regain their 'lost' phallus.[123] In this respect, hysteria became the condition of women who objected to patriarchy. The hysterical woman has since been reclaimed as the 'deviant other' in feminist theory as a possible site of resistance to patriarchal oppression, not dissimilarly to the recent evocation of shame as a possible site for queer resistance.

In *L'Armée du salut*, hysteria is simultaneously that which saves the narrator's mother from his father and that which reveals that she does not need to be saved after all. Whereas the father is driven by jealousy, the mother's calculated hysteria leaves him paralysed and unable to claim the position as head of household. In this respect, the hysterical mother destabilizes patriarchal gender roles. Moreover, by identifying with his mother's hysteria – 'L'hystérie est une maladie que je connais bien' (Hysteria is a disease I know well)[124] – the narrator claims space within this subversive discourse and aligns himself with the mother as simultaneously marginalized and dictator of the family house.

The sublime first-born son

In part two of *L'Armée du salut*, the narrator reveals his physical desire for his older brother, Abdelkébir. The main part of the second fragment is a recollection of the narrator's fascination with and physical attraction to his older brother as a young boy. This fragment opens with Abdelkébir's birth and the superstitions surrounding the celebration of the first-born son.[125] The opening sets the scene and underlines the special place of Abdelkébir in the family as a whole. In contrast with the older brother in *Le Passé simple*, whose drinking problem serves both to expose the mother's failure at raising her children and to undermine the control and authority of *le Seigneur*, Abdelkébir is depicted as almost superhuman. Compared to him, Abdellah shrinks to a parasite living his life through that of his brother: 'Comme un petit chien j'avais besoin de mon grand frère pour jouer avec lui, dormir contre lui, et parfois le lécher.' (Like a small dog I needed my big brother to play with him, sleep next to him and sometimes lick him.)[126]

The main part of the second fragment is a long diary passage. The time of narration is the summer of 1987. That summer, Abdelkébir takes Abdellah and his younger brother Mustafa on vacation to Tangier. Once again the narrative style reveals a 'self-absorbed' narrator who, seemingly, represents no one but himself: 'Est-ce que je vais écrire ici tout ce qui me passe par la tête? Tout ce qu'Abdelkébir m'inspire? Et ces fesses . . . Ses fesses. . . . Mon Dieu! C'est horrible! Quel bonheur! Je vais essayer de dormir moi aussi. Dors Abdellah, dors! C'est un ordre.' (Am I going to write down everything that goes through my head here? Everything about Abdelkébir that inspires me? And that ass . . . his ass. . . . My God! This is horrible! What a joy! I'll try to sleep too. Sleep, Abdellah, sleep! That's an order.)[127] Like the story about the sex life of his parents, his almost incestuous fascination with the body of his brother reveals less about the brother than about himself. The diary form in part two, essentially, functions as a parody of confessional literature by letting the narrator-protagonist blurt out about his blurting out of his innermost thoughts.

Nonetheless, Taïa exposes his family through this self-exposure. The narrative of physical attraction to his brother cost, for a period, Taïa his relationship with his brother, who did not approve of him writing about private family matters. In interviews Taïa has refused to talk about his brother and about what happened between them.[128] Even though it can seem as if nothing is too private to Taïa, here he draws a line between the private and the public, indicating that writing the self is not exhibitionist self-indulgence by an author obsessed with the scandalous. As the novel proceeds, the narrative about the brother turns out to serve another purpose than exposing himself and his family.

Behind the 'self-absorbed' style of writing, part two is also the story of a sensitive boy about to become a teenager. This transformation takes place when Abdellah finds out that his brother has met his wife-to-be and is happily in love. The closed space of family life is interrupted on the vacation to Tangier, when Abdelkébir goes missing one morning. He has left a note and has gone to Tétouan for the day. Even before he sees a hickey on Abdelkébir's neck, Abdellah suspects that his brother is in Tétouan to meet a girl. It is the feeling of being abandoned by his brother, whom he realizes that he is somehow in love with, that triggers his first homosexual experience with an older man. By interconnecting the special place of first-born sons in Moroccan families, homosocial desire, and homosexuality as an identity category, the novel simultaneously transgresses heteronormativity and places homosexuality at the heart of family life. Thus in contrast to *Le Passé simple*, where the resistance strategy lies in the brother's failure to live up to 'ossified' ideals, *L'Armée du salut* glorifies these ideals to the point where they undermine themselves by revealing their implicit queerness.

The day after his first homosexual experience, Abdellah feels sick for betraying his feelings for his brother, and, at the same time, he is tormented by the fact that he enjoyed being with a man:

> Je me sens mal, mal, mal.
>> Je suis un traître.
>> J'ai trahi Abdelkébir.
>> Au cinéma, avec Salim.
>> Et le pire, c'est que j'ai aimé ça, être entouré par les bras forts de cet homme de 40 ans qui sentait bon et qui me parlait dans l'oreille en français tout en essayant de trouver un chemin vers mon sexe, mes fesses. Je me suis donné à lui. Il ne m'a pas fait souffrir. Oui, j'ai aimé ça. Mon Dieu![129]

> (I feel sick, sick, sick.
>> I'm a traitor.
>> I've betrayed Abdelkébir.
>> At the movies, with Salim.
>> And the worst is, that I loved it, being embraced by the strong arms of this 40-year old man who smelled good and spoke French in my ear while he tried to get at my penis, my ass. And I gave myself to him. And he didn't hurt me. Yes, I loved it. My God!)

The initial feeling of sickness reveals that the protagonist is ashamed that he has failed to live up to the ideal embodied in his own image of his brother as the 'perfect man'. This particular scene functions as a rite of passage: Abdellah is in the process of detaching himself from the social norms, in particular the norms of sexual conduct. Taïa's literary narration of 'shameful' events both reflects the subject formation of the protagonist and functions as a queer resistance strategy. On the one hand, Abdellah is forced to redefine himself when Abdelkébir is removed from the centre of family life. Growing up, he realizes that the physical closeness and attraction that he has identified with family life are incompatible with the norms of public life. However, on the other hand, in coming to terms with his sexual desires and deciding that he will never do as his brother – he will never marry – part two simultaneously reads as a resistance narrative: a young boy resisting heteronormativity, as well as easily defined sexual categories. Moreover, by insisting that he will never marry, the protagonist does not just reject entering into a heterosexual relationship; he simultaneously resists homonormativity and the idea that marriage – as an essentially heteronormative standard of monogamous sexuality and family structure – is a desired goal for all.

Heading towards France

In the third and last fragment, the narrator recalls the story of his relationship with Jean, a Swiss man – a story that ends with him staying at the Salvation Army in Geneva. The narrative situation alternates between his present situation in Geneva and a flashback story of how he met Jean. Whereas the first two parts of the novel narrate the formation of the narrator's sexual identity, the third part depicts a homosexual protagonist in his first long-term relationship.

Part three opens with a 'crime of hospitality'. Abdellah is alone and helpless in Geneva airport. Jean's friend, Charles, has promised to pick him up, but he never arrives. Abdellah has no money and no place to go. He is lost and scared, but after three hours of waiting he decides to leave his luggage in a safe deposit box at the train station and go into the city. Fortunately, a kind taxi driver directs him to the Salvation Army, where he can stay while he waits to receive his scholarship. What happened before he arrived in Geneva is revealed to the reader gradually, through flashback stories about Abdellah's relationship with Jean.

The main theme in these flashback stories is sex tourism in Morocco and the stereotypical conception of homosexuality in this industry, where everyone is identified according to either an active/passive model or a transgenerational model or both. Without spelling it out, Taïa depicts how difficult it is to challenge this stereotype, which always depicts the relationship between an older Western man and a young Moroccan boy in terms of an unequal power relation in which the first has the purchasing power and the other is a helpless victim of exploitation. In part three, the narrator approaches this stereotype through his own experiences with Jean. Even though the narrator shies away from generalizations, the protagonist is constantly confronted with the cruel side of sex tourism. He is easily manipulated and easily exploited, and hidden behind his trusting nature there lies a complicated world in which clear victims are not easily identified.

The first time Abdellah meets Jean is at a seminar at Mohammed V University. On the last day of the seminar Abdellah approaches Jean, asks him out, and offers to show him around the city. Abdellah is the one taking the initiative, whereas Jean hesitates to begin with. Strolling around Salé and Rabat, Abdellah feels a connection between the two and starts to seduce Jean. Winning him over makes him feel proud. The narrator adds 'sans savoir de quoi exactement' (without knowing why exactly),[130] but the storyline indicates that it is because it is the protagonist who has agency. He is the self-creating subject in control of the situation.

On a trip to Marrakesh later the same year, Abdellah and Jean are stopped by two police officers who accuse Abdellah of bothering Jean, a tourist in Morocco. The police officers instantly assume that Abdellah is prostituting himself as a friendship or any equal relationship between a Moroccan boy and a Western man is inconceivable to them. The incident ends when the officers let Abdellah go with a warning, but they conclude by yelling in Arabic: 'N'oublie pas de te faire bien payer . . . et lave bien ton cul après, sale pédé.' (Make sure that you're paid well . . . and wash your ass well afterwards, dirty faggot.)[131] With one sentence, the exchange between Abdellah and the two police officers, which Jean does not understand because they are speaking Arabic, becomes a public scene. For the first time in his life, Abdellah is publicly stigmatized: the looks and smiles of passers-by stand in sharp contrast with the chapter's opening scene, where the narrator recalls how happily in love he was at the time. That night he does not sleep; he cries all night, without knowing if Jean has understood anything. The ending of the chapter reveals a distance between Abdellah and Jean. The fact that Jean can be mistaken for a sex tourist and Abdellah for a prostitute is something they do not talk about. Abdellah is alone; he has not only been stigmatized by the police officers but also been distanced from Jean. However, rather than depicting Jean as a stereotypical sex tourist disguising his power to purchase another human being under the cover of friendship, the narrator naively maintains the uniqueness of their relationship through the opening scene where the protagonist is happily in love and sharing his dreams and desires with Jean.

Six months later Abdellah and Jean go to Tangier. There, Jean introduces Abdellah to Mohamed, a Moroccan boy who dreams of leaving Morocco for the West. The depiction of Mohamed at the beginning of the chapter challenges the idea that young Moroccan boys who prostitute themselves necessarily are victims of exploitation:

> En attendant de trouver la bonne, celle qui serait douce, obéissante, respectueuse, généreuse et bandante, il s'était tourné depuis quelque temps, à peine un mois, vers les hommes. Ils étaient plus simples à satisfaire, à rendre heureux, il se contentait d'être là avec eux, à jouer avec eux, nu parfois mais pas forcément, il les laissait le sucer, il les pénétrait, il envisageait même de se laisser prendre lui aussi à son tour, une bite dans le cul, cela ne lui faisait pas peur, à partir du moment où ce don de ce qu'il avait de plus intime lui permettrait enfin de foutre le camp de ce pays de merde.[132]

> (While waiting to meet a good woman, someone who would be sweet, obedient, respectful, generous and sexy, he had, for some time, maybe about a month, turned toward men. They were much easier to satisfy, to make happy, he liked being with them, fooling around with them, sometimes naked, but not necessarily, he let them suck him off, he penetrated them, he even imagined letting them have a shot at him too, a dick in the ass, that didn't frighten him, as long as this most intimate gift would get him the fuck out of this shithole country.)

Mohamed is obsessed with the idea of leaving Morocco, and as a means to achieve this goal he has turned towards men. Rather than simply being exploited by Western sex tourists, he is using this industry as a door to the West. Sex in this case is all about money. But it reveals an imbalance of wealth that leads the reader to question whether Mohamed will succeed with his plan, or if he in reality is trapped in an industry where he is nothing but a commodity that can be bought with Swiss francs.

As the chapter proceeds, the narrator reveals that it is Jean who picked up Mohamed in the street, and that he is paying him to be with them. Jean's relationship with Mohamed leads Abdellah to question the nature of his own relationship with Jean.[133] Is Abdellah naive when he thinks that their relationship can be perceived as anything but prostitution? Jean is paying for everything, taking care of everything. Mohamed has no problem with being bought, but the unclear relationship between Jean and Abdellah once again indicates a distance between the two. Abdellah does not ask Jean if he is buying him as well, but concludes that they do not share the same values or doubts about their relationship.[134] The power imbalance between the two is further emphasized when the narrator notes that the protagonist has no experience with money, whereas Jean can buy everything he wanted with his Swiss francs in Morocco. But Abdellah's doubts and the distance between the two seem to have no consequences. The chapter concludes thus: 'À part ça, tout allait bien. À la fin de ce séjour de deux semaines à Tanger, Jean m'invita à venir chez lui en Suisse l'été suivant.' (Apart from that, everything was fine. At the end of this two-week stay in Tangier, Jean invited me to stay with him in Switzerland the following summer.)[135]

On his first trip to Europe, Abdellah goes to Geneva to stay with Jean for two months. Once there, he finds Jean difficult to live with. Switzerland turns out to be nothing like the Europe he had read about in books and seen on film. Switzerland is a strange and too-quiet place. It takes effort for Abdellah to adjust to Jean's world, and he never feels that he belongs.[136] Jean takes Abdellah to museums and art galleries, and the cultural horizon of this college professor fascinates Abdellah. He admires his knowledge, but at the same time increasingly comes to stand out as both young and naive. As he follows Jean, who pays for everything, a man suddenly approaches Abdellah and gives him a note with the message 'Je paie bien' (I pay well).[137] At this point, Abdellah realizes that he is nothing but a sex commodity in Jean's country, that he is being bought and that people around him see nothing but that.

But part three is also the story of a breakup – Abdellah breaking up with Jean and ending up at the Salvation Army in Geneva. The power balance between Abdellah and Jean shifts at the end of the novel. On his second trip to Geneva, Abdellah arrives a day later than planned because he has met two guys on the boat from Tangier to Algeciras. As soon as he arrives in Geneva he rushes to tell Jean all about his 'belle aventure' (beautiful adventure), where he rediscovered 'une certaine sexualité que j'avais eue durant mon enfance et le début de mon adolescence. Le sexe en groupe' (a certain sexuality that I experienced during my childhood and early adolescence. Group sex).[138] This is perhaps the scene where Abdellah appears most 'self-absorbed' and completely out of touch with Jean's feelings. However, as he is seen as nothing but a sex commodity, his only route to reclaim self-determination is by 'owning' his sexuality. In this respect, the protagonist's venture into group sex functions as a site of queer resistance. In all his naivety, Abdellah effectively dismantles the stronghold of the 'sex tourism' stereotypes by revealing that his and Jean's relationship is untenable. Because Jean has the purchasing power, he is free to invite Mohamed into their relationship without asking Abdellah; but when Abdellah interprets their relationship as 'open' and with room for exploring group sex, he is accused of being a whore who is using Jean to fuck his way up the social ladder, as Jean writes himself to a common friend of theirs: 'Abdellah n'était finalement qu'une petite pute, comme il y en a tant au Maroc, un arriviste sans scrupule, un mal élevé, un con, un ingrate. Un être noir. Un briseur de cœur. Un pauvre type égoïste qui ne méritait pas qu'on s'intéresse à lui. Un monstre.' (In the end Abdellah was nothing but a little whore, like the many there are in Morocco, an unscrupulous social climber, ill-mannered, a cunt, an ungrateful. A black being. A heartbreaker. A poor selfish type who does not deserve to be shown an interest. A monster.)[139]

Paradoxically, Abdellah is accused of exploiting sex tourism to gain something he wants at the very moment he effectively frees himself of its hold. This in turn displays the exploitative role of Western sex tourists such as Jean who, knowingly or not, are offering a prison disguised as 'Western freedom': 'J'étais dans une prison, de plus en plus dans une prison. La liberté en Occident? Quelle liberté?' (I was in a prison, more and more in a prison. Freedom in the West? What freedom?)[140] As Jean becomes more and more controlling, Abdellah decides to leave him one morning, before he is awake. He writes him a letter and returns to Morocco. But though Charles has promised to pick him up at the airport when he returns to Geneva two months later to pursue his studies, he never arrives.

However, the lost boy on his own in Geneva turns out to be a young man about to embark upon a European adventure and rediscover the meaning of love, freedom and humanity. Tellingly, his first glimpses of humanity and intimacy in Geneva are in the least expected places – at the Salvation Army, where people only come if they have nowhere else to go, and in a dirty public toilet, usually associated with promiscuity and one-night stands. Echoing how Driss Ferdi in *Le Passé simple* deconstructs the French slogan 'Freedom, Equality, Fraternity' through a parodic performance of the 'irrational Arab mind', Abdellah unsettles the conception of the 'West' as a place of freedom for all by assigning the humanity of the Swiss to a scene of masturbation and blowjobs in a public toilet.[141]

On the street in Geneva a forty-year-old man approaches Abdellah demanding: 'suis-moi!' (follow me!).[142] Abdellah assumes that he is once again mistaken for a prostitute, but this time he decides to explore the role and follows the man to the urinals close to la Placette. However, in these urinals he rediscovers a sexuality that he finds is missing in the rest of Geneva: 'la sexualité débordante et poétique' (the overflowing and poetic sexuality).[143] Significantly, this sexuality is clandestine and public at the same time, and similarly to his venture into group sex with Matthias and Rafaël, the narrator-protagonist pairs the scene of group masturbation with old friends and youth life in Morocco; that is, the intimacy between the men in the urinals is hidden from the public eye, but nevertheless accessible to all. This comparison could, on the one hand, be read as an exoticization of Arab sexuality and of clandestine sex between young boys in Morocco. But on the other hand, it could also be read as a literary play with the relationship between being out and being free. Abdellah finds freedom and intimacy on the margins of both Morocco and Switzerland and thus displaces the stereotypic narrative of emancipation where 'being queer' presupposes coming out in public, arriving in a city centre in the West and leaving one's religion, culture and family behind. For the first time in Geneva, Abdellah is not mistaken for a prostitute, a commodity that can be bought with Swiss francs. He is part of a fair exchange of casual sex, but importantly this exchange takes place in silence and he is neither really seen nor known by the older man.

The 'emancipated' Arab boy

Considering Taïa's career as an academic, author and cineaste living in Paris, the ending of *L'Armée du salut* is easily read as a simple happy ending to a coming-of-age story – that is, as a 'narrative of arrival' where the protagonist leaves his religion, culture, family and community behind in order to arrive in Paris, gain his freedom and assume his sexuality. Similarly, *Le Passé simple* has been read as a 'narrative of emancipation' – young Driss freeing himself from his oppressive father and becoming a man in his own right. However, just as there is something internally ambiguous to the ending of *Le Passé simple*, Abdellah's excitement about the future and the prospects of becoming an intellectual in Paris one day must be read in light of both his naivety and his redefinition of 'freedom' in Geneva. Whereas *Le Passé simple* testifies to the impossible location of French-educated Moroccans during the struggle for independence, *L'Armée du salut* testifies to the impossible location of Arab-Muslim queers within an international rhetoric of a 'sexual clash of civilizations'. In this respect, the ending of *L'Armée du salut* invites the reader to reflect on the difficult path upon which the protagonist is about to embark.

L'Armée du salut was published shortly after Taïa came out publicly in 2006, and the novel has therefore naturally been read as a confessional novel about life as a homosexual in Morocco. But despite the fact that the protagonist moves from Salé to Rabat, then to Geneva and aspires to go to Paris one day, his coming-into-existence as a Moroccan homosexual subject is neither an effect of this movement nor of a revolt against his family and origin. In this respect, *L'Armée du salut* is significantly different from the Oedipal revolt of *Le Passé simple*. In mirroring the narrator in his mother and hysteria, Taïa displaces the Oedipal narrative altogether and the idea that emancipation is achieved through a revolt against one's origins.

In *Le Passé simple* Driss desperately seeks to claim the position as a man of agency. That is, an active male subject as opposed to his passive and submissive mother and in place of his authoritarian father. In his revolt against his father he therefore reproduces the same masculinity and structures of domination that he seeks to overthrow. But *Le Passé simple* is not a simple story about a Moroccan youth whose mother's suicide effects his emancipation from his father and 'ossified' traditions. On the contrary. *Le Passé simple* both parodies stereotypic conceptions of the 'emancipated Arab boy', such as in Driss's baccalaureate exam, and questions how free this so-called emancipated boy in reality is. Moreover, Driss is not rebelling against Moroccan culture and tradition but against hypocrisy, both Moroccan and French.

Whereas *Le Passé simple* develops as an ironic tragedy, dominated by feelings of pain, disbelief, hatred and contempt that quickly suffocate any voice or glimpse of affection and love, *L'Armée du salut* is written as a eulogy to passionate sex and hysteria. Through naivety and an excessive focus on the self Taïa creates a space where Abdellah can live and express his queer identity. Even when this space is only in his own mind or in his diary, it nevertheless allows love, passion and excitement to triumph over discrimination, loneliness and shame. In this respect, *L'Armée du salut* parodies the confessional novel through an emotionally vulnerable protagonist whose disclosures draw the reader in and plays with her thirst for sexual storytelling and autobiographical disclosures. Thus in *L'Armée du salut* the 'self-absorbed' is neither an expression of exhibitionism nor of self-orientalization, but functions as a performative strategy through which Abdellah comes into existence as a queer subject.

Chapter 4

WRITING TRANSIDENTITY IN THE LANGUAGE OF THE 'OTHER'

THE *SOUFFLES* MOVEMENT, ABDELKÉBIR KHATIBI'S *AMOUR BILINGUE* AND ABDELLAH TAÏA'S *UN PAYS POUR MOURIR*

The choice of language in which to write has since independence been inextricably linked to questions of how to define the relation between language, culture, nation and identity. The literary recreation of a 'lost' cultural identity, a task upon which many post-independence Maghrebin authors embarked, was inseparable from 'the problem of the *medium* through which all of this could come about'.[1] Critical reflections on the effects of colonialism on language have been a central concern for many postcolonial Maghrebin intellectuals, such as Albert Memmi, Malek Haddad, Abdellatif Laâbi and Abdelkébir Khatibi, to name but a few. But the question 'Why do you write in French?' continues to haunt Maghrebin francophone authors. Even though the hegemonic relation between colonizer and colonized has been transferred in Adellah Taïa's life and career to the relation between rich and poor, his narrative strategy of writing 'poor' French – in order to resist the norms and conventions of 'rich' French and in order to force this 'powerful' language to speak for those rendered silent and invisible – is reminiscent of the 'textual violence' pursued by earlier generations of Moroccan authors. That is, Taïa's simple vocabulary, the particular rhythm of his prose, his straightforward writing style reminiscent of film manuscripts and the omnipresent emotional vulnerability of his characters draw the reader into a world where linguistic, cultural and sexual binaries are displaced.

As the 'problem' of language choice is confined neither to writing in French nor to writing fiction, the chapter begins by outlining the rich field of cultural journals since the beginning of anti-colonial resistance in pre-independence Morocco in order to discuss how the changing political reality of postcolonial Morocco affected the position of Arabic and French as languages of resistance and of literary expression. The focus of the first part of the chapter will, however, be the literary avant-gardism and leftist political thoughts of the *Souffles* movement during the 1960s and Laâbi's call for a 'decolonized' use of French.

Then the chapter proceeds with an analysis of how Khatibi, in his novel *Amour bilingue* (1983), addresses the question of writing in French through narrations of eroticism and 'transgressive' sexuality. In *Amour bilingue* Khatibi has articulated the bilingual experience through the story of an erotic relationship ruled by an associative madness in which the two lovers are both subject to violent erasure and haunted by their spectralized 'self'. In this respect, *Amour bilingue* embodies a rupture with the conception of bilingualism as a dualistic conflict between two languages and two cultures.

The last part of the chapter focuses on how Taïa's conception of the French language as a language of the rich, which can only be subverted by writing it 'poorly', is reminiscent of the thoughts of Laâbi and the *Souffles* movement. Taïa's narrative strategy of writing 'poor' French is, like Laâbi's textual violence, precisely meant to resist the norms and conventions of 'rich' French, and to force this powerful language to speak for those who are otherwise rendered silent and invisible. Unlike Khatibi's *Amour bilingue*, *Un Pays pour mourir* is not a novel about the bilingual experience told through transgressive sexuality but a novel about queer sexualities, told through the language of the rich and powerful. However, like Khatibi, Taïa reconfigures the relation between fiction and fact through a style of writing where layers of stories infect, affect and inhabit one another. That is, Taïa's use of 'poor' French interconnects his literary representations of queer identities with his own experiences with French as a language of separation, as well as with forcible erasure and invisibility. Thus when life and death interpenetrate while simultaneously taking on new meaning in *Un Pays pour mourir*, they embody an effort of space making similar to Khatibi's *bi-langue* – that is, an autobiographical gesture, staking out through layers of stories an experimental nation for Taïa's younger self, as well as for all other queer lives that have been subjected to the violence of public erasure.

French as language of resistance: The Souffles-Anfās *movement*

As argued by both Khatibi[2] and Réda Bensmaïa,[3] an increasing number of Maghrebin authors actively entered into the field of French literature after the Second World War in order to tell *their* version of *their* stories in opposition to the exotic portraits of Maghrebins in French literature. The novel as an established genre in French literature provided them with a new narrative form through which to express themselves and make themselves heard outside of their country. However, Maghrebin francophone authors were painfully aware of this forced 'acculturation', and at the time of independence, the idea of a new 'national' literature written in French was by many conceived as a contradiction in terms. Like the Tunisian author Memmi, who in *Portrait du colonisé* (1957) declared that 'la littérature colonisée de langue européenne semble condamnée à mourir jeune' (colonized literature in European languages seems condemned to die young),[4] many Maghrebin authors were convinced that political independence would be followed by both cultural and linguistic independence.[5]

However, counter to these expectations, the number of Maghrebin novels written in French continued to multiply. In his study of post-independence

Maghrebin literature (with focus on Algeria), Bensmaïa has identified the profound linguistic pluralism and the low literacy rates as the main reasons for this.[6] However, the choice of French as language of literary expression also had cultural and ideological underpinnings. Laâbi, for instance, took a clear stance against Memmi and the framework of acculturation,[7] and in *Souffles* 4 he argued for a 'decolonized' use of French and that 'il faut absolument entretenir au départ une méfiance vis-à-vis de la langue d'expression qu'on emploie. Que cette langue soit le français, l'arabe ou n'importe quelle autre' (it is absolutely necessary from the outset to remain suspicious of one's language of expression. Whether this language is French, Arabic, or any other).[8] However, the cultural and ideological underpinnings of the use of French as language of resistance ultimately forced Laâbi to opt to use Arabic when he launched *Souffles'* Arabic counterpart, *Anfās*, in 1971.[9] This ambiguous relation to the French language is one of the main reasons why the discussion about language choice has haunted generations of Maghrebin authors, and is still a subject of discussion today in relation to, for instance, Taïa's writing.

To return to Bensmaïa, linguistic pluralism and low literacy rates unquestionably posed problems for Maghrebin post-independence authors. As Khatibi argued,

Maintenant qu'on se trouve devant de grands problèmes d'édification nationale il faut poser franchement et sans détours la question de la littérature: dans des pays en grande partie analphabètes, c'est-à-dire où le mot écrit a peu de chances pour le moment, de transformer les choses, peut-on libérer un peuple avec une langue qu'il ne comprend pas?[10]

(Now that we face the great problems of nation building, the question of literature must be posed frankly and straightforwardly: in largely illiterate countries, that is to say where the written word at the moment has very little chance of transforming things, can we liberate a people with a language it does not understand?)

On the one hand, these authors faced the problem of writing in only *one* language while living within several.[11] Whether writing in French or Arabic, Maghrebin authors faced a language that was deterritorialized, 'without any deep cultural or social roots',[12] as neither of the languages could adequately translate the idiosyncratic traits of culture that were articulated in the vernacular languages (for instance Amazigh and *dārija*). On the other hand, low literacy rates compelled many Maghrebin authors to write in French (and publish in France) to find readers. With a limited reading public in the Maghreb, the question of language choice was inextricably linked to the question 'for whom to write'. These cultural and political conditions of literature forced Maghrebin authors to develop experimental representational strategies that did not simply address multiple readers (both Moroccans and French), but also constituted an act of subversion – a subversion of monological conceptions of languages, cultures and literary genres.

From anti-colonial resistance to institutionalization

While the novel entered the literary scene in Morocco in the 1950s, the Moroccan cultural journals and the short story had a slightly longer history and were to become just as vital a platform as the novel for the development of the post-independence literary scene in Morocco. Among pre–Second World War literary production, Khatibi has identified two dominant tendencies:[13] a reformist and arabizing tendency devoted to the traditional Arabic literary genre, *al-qasīdah* (the long poem), with the nationalist leader Allal al-Fassi (1910–74) as the archetypical poet-leader; and a modernist trend, 'oriented toward journalistic writing and in particular the short story which emerged as a dominant genre in the Arab world. In fact, mediated by the press that has brought it to a wider public, the short story evolved to become the most important narrative genre in Moroccan postcolonial literature.'[14]

As the French authorities banned many regular newspapers during the protectorate period (1912–56) and in general made it difficult to publish political information, cultural journals flourished in Morocco in the 1930s.[15] During this period they provided an alternative space for nationalist activities and political action as demonstrated by Gonzalo Fernández Parrilla.[16] The most influential journal during this period was *Risālat al-Maghrib* (Morocco's message), which was launched in 1942 and continued to appear until 1952, although its publication was often interrupted due to censorship and economic troubles.[17] From the appearance of its first issue on 1 October 1942, the journal was an integral part both of the nationalist milieu and of the early stages of the Independence Party (*hizb al-Istiqlāl*, founded in 1944), and it 'became an intellectual and literary school for nationalists'.[18] According to Fernández Parrilla, the cultural journals before independence were characterized by nationalist and salafi vocations, and one of their main goals was to confront the growing presence of French culture and language in Morocco.[19] It is, however, important to note that the journalistic initiatives of the nationalist movement (*al-ḥarakah al-waṭaniyyah*), while primarily in Arabic, also included French-language magazines such as *Maghreb* (1932) in Paris and *L'Action du Peuple* (1932) in Fes.[20] But, in Morocco, anti-colonial resistance was primarily articulated in Arabic.

Following independence, the nationalists continued to dominate the cultural field, and as they saw the Arabic language and Arabic literature, along with Islam, as key features of Moroccan national identity, new journals were primarily published in Arabic.[21] Moreover, as most of the intellectuals who had been involved in the Independence Party and the nationalist movement assumed duties in the new administration and institutions, the first journals published after independence were supported by the state. One of the most important among these was *Da'wat al-Ḥaqq* (The call for truth), which was first published in 1957 and is still published today. Supported by the new Ministry of Islamic Affairs, *Da'wat al-Ḥaqq* was directed by 'prominent figures related to the Nationalist Movement and the *salafiyyah*'.[22] It has been described as 'gardienne des valeurs arabo-islamiques mais conservatrice sur le plan littéraire' (guardian of Arab-Islamic values, but conservative in the literary field) by Khatibi,[23] and Fernández Parrilla points to how the journal reveals the relationship between state, monarchy and religious establishment.[24]

Common to these post-independence institutional journals was their combination of patriotism and religiosity with journalism and literature; but as these now official and institutional initiatives prioritized the political agenda and were saturated by patriotic and religious attitudes, 'Moroccan culture suffered a backlash during the early years of independence',[25] and with a growing disillusionment with the new state, the nationalist-salafi ideology lost touch with the younger generation.[26]

A new avant-gardist literary trend

In the 1960s a new generation of intellectuals who had been too young to participate in the independence struggle founded several independent cultural journals that contested the official and institutional model.[27] In 1964, *Aqlām* (Pens), *Majallah li-l-Qiṣṣah wa-l-Masraḥ* (Journal of narrative and theatre) and *al-Mawqif* (The stance) were founded. The first editorial manifesto of *Majallah li-l-Qiṣṣah wa-l-Masraḥ*, for instance, described the earlier generation of authors as guards and servile dogs, in opposition to the 'authentic committed intellectual' of the 'avant-garde'.[28] On the one hand, the manifesto stated that the goal of the journal was to establish a meeting place for the 'young generation', which according to the manifesto was an 'inevitable political generation' preoccupied with the realities of society.[29] On the other hand, it 'called for a break with the literature predominant up to that moment'.[30] The short story and the theatre, as indicated in the title of the journal, were at the time considered 'the most efficient literary instruments for establishing connections with the public and achieving these young intellectuals' unambiguous aspirations of "reaching the masses"'.[31]

Until this time, only a few journals, such as *Maghreb* and *L'Action du Peuple*, and authors, such as Sefrioui and Chraïbi, had opted for the French language. As such, the use of French was a 'new' phenomenon, and as it was still associated with the colonial powers, the publication of French-language cultural journals incited heated debate.[32] Like the founders of the cultural journals in Arabic, these young authors (mainly poets) aspired 'to play an active role in the redefinition of national culture'.[33] In choosing French as their language of literary expression, they launched an open clash with the nationalist-salafi ideology, as well as a break with the cultural initiatives promoted by or linked to neocolonial institutions.[34] In 1964 Mostapha Nissaboury and Mohammed Khaïr-Eddine launched *Poésie toute* (All Poetry), and, in the same year, Nissaboury supported the creation of the poetic journal, *Eaux vives* (Living Waters).

However, it was the experimental journal *Souffles* (literally 'Breaths', figuratively 'Inspirations') – founded by Laâbi along with Nissaboury and Khaïr-Eddine in 1966 – that was to become the most influential cultural journal in French. *Souffles* was launched at a crucial time in Morocco, just one year after the 23 March 1965 student protests in Casablanca, which were violently repressed and came to mark the beginning of the Years of Lead. Under the leadership of Mehdi Ben Barka, the *Union nationale des forces populaires* (UNFP) openly opposed King Hassan II, and it was the allied student group *Union nationale des étudiants au Maroc* (UNEM) that organized the student demonstrations in protest against a circular by the minister of education, Youssef Belabbès, that banned young people over the age of sixteen from attending the second cycle of lycée.[35] In June 1965, King Hassan II declared a state of emergency, and on 29 October that same year Mehdi Ben Barka was abducted in Paris and 'disappeared'.[36]

As with *Aqlām*, it was within this leftist opposition to the regime of King Hassan II that *Souffles* emerged, and 'while the first issues of *Souffles* primarily published experimental poetry and essays on Moroccan literature, popular culture, art, and film, the journal gradually expanded its focus to cultural production and political developments across the Third World'.[37] As a literary journal, *Souffles* was the first publication to feature the work of some of the most important Moroccan poets and novelists, such as Laâbi, Nissaboury, Khaïr-Eddine, Khatibi and Tahar Ben Jelloun.[38]

When the engineer and leftist militant Abraham Serfaty joined the editorial board in 1968, *Souffles* was gradually transformed from a literary to a political journal. In 1970, Laâbi and Serfaty along with other radical leftists founded the Marxist-Leninist political movement *Ilā al-ʾamām* (Forward),[39] and *Souffles* became a de facto mouthpiece of the radical left in Morocco and a textbook for discussion and debate among young political activists. Aware of the fact that the French language was limiting the scope of their readership, the *Souffles* group launched the Arabic monthly *Anfās* (Breaths) in 1971. The larger print run (5,000 copies) of *Anfās* made the journal a greater threat to the regime and precipitated the violent crackdown on the editorial team in 1972.[40]

On 27 January 1972 Laâbi and Serfaty were singled out as the driving force behind the revolutionary student movements and arrested and tortured by the Moroccan police.[41] On 25 February 1972 they were released, thanks to student protests, according to Serfaty.[42] Laâbi was rearrested on 14 March 1972 and sentenced to ten years of imprisonment for crimes of opinion. He was released in 1980 after a long solidarity campaign, but in 1985 he was forced into exile in France, where he is still living today. He was later rehabilitated by King Mohammed VI, and now lives part time in Paris and part time back in Morocco. Serfaty went underground shortly after their release and remained hidden for two years before he was imprisoned and sentenced to life in prison on a charge of plotting against the state. He was released in 1991 after seventeen years of imprisonment and, like Laâbi, exiled to France until the death of King Hassan II in 1999.

As argued by Laâbi in his preface to Kenza Sefrioui's *La revue Souffles 1966-1973: Espoirs de revolution culturelle au Maroc* (2013), *Souffles* was a revolutionary avant-gardist project which operated both in the cultural-aesthetic and the political field:

> *Souffles* avait un projet culturel, celui de la décolonisation des esprits, de la reconstruction de l'identité nationale revendiquée dans la diversité de ses

composantes, de l'insertion de la creation littéraire et artistique dans l'aventure de la modernité. Sur ce plan-là, elle a honorablement rempli son contrat. Mais elle avait, inscrite dans ses gènes si l'on permet l'expression, une dimension éminemment politique, compte tenu du traumatisme colonial, de l'archaïsme et du despotisme du régime en place, ainsi que du conservatisme de la société.[43]

(*Souffles* had a cultural project, that of decolonizing the mind, reconstructing a national identity claimed in the diversity of its components, inserting literary and artistic creation into the adventure of modernity. In that regard, it has honourably fulfilled its contract. But it had, inscribed in its genes, if that expression is permitted, an eminently political dimension, given the colonial trauma, the archaism and despotism of the state regime, as well as the conservatism of society.)

This bi-directionality made *Souffles-Anfâs* an important archive of experimental literature as well as of 'global Marxist and Third-Worldist thought and an early example of opposition to authoritarian regimes in the formerly colonized world'.[44] In this respect, the political commitment of the *Souffles* movement is significantly different from the way in which Taïa's 'poor' French resists the norms and conventions of 'rich' French, forcing the French language to speak for those who are otherwise rendered silent and invisible. However, Third Worldism and the call by the *Souffles* movement for a 'textual violence' that would shatter the original logic of the French language on all levels are the indispensable historical backdrops against which Taïa has reconfigured his 'battle' with the French language.

Abdellatif Laâbi and the call for a 'decolonized' use of French

It was within the context of *Souffles* that some of the most significant discussions about the use of French as language of literary expression evolved in Morocco. Out of frustration with the current state of affairs in the publishing field, Laâbi, Nissaboury and Khaïr-Eddine decided to create a journal that could function as a platform for a new generation of authors who, despite the abundance of new journals, did not recognize themselves in any of them.[45] Moreover, these young intellectuals faced an almost complete dearth of publishing houses, mediocre quality at the small existing houses, limited print runs, expensive distribution and hardly any literary criticism.[46] In a number of articles in *Souffles* (1, 2 and 4), Laâbi addressed this particular problem and lamented that the current Moroccan journals only rarely had a clear purpose, even the simple struggle for 'la dignité de la presse' (the dignity of the press).[47] *Souffles* was intended to make up for this.

In the editorial of the first issue of *Souffles*, Laâbi outlined the purpose of the journal and stated that writing in *Souffles* was an engaged enterprise: 'Les poètes qui ont signé les textes de ce numéro-manifeste de la Revue "SOUFFLES" sont unanimement conscients qu'une telle publication est un acte de prise de position de leur part dans un moment où les problèmes de notre culture nationale ont atteint un degré extrême de tension.' (The poets who have signed the texts of this manifesto-issue of the journal *Souffles* are unanimously aware that this publication is an act on their part of taking a stand at a moment when the problems of our national culture have attained a degree of extreme tension.)[48] As argued by Kenza Sefrioui, these authors were convinced that culture is political; they were conscious of the fact that literary creation and research are a matter of taking a position in the public space.[49]

While arguing that the purpose of *Souffles* was to become 'l'organe de la nouvelle génération poétique et littéraire' (the mouthpiece of a new poetic and literary generation) and 'un lieu névralgique de débats autour des problèmes de notre culture' (a nerve centre of debates about the problems in our culture),[50] Laâbi simultaneously located this new generation within a broader frame of reference: 'Quelque chose se prépare en Afrique et dans les autres pays du Tiers-Monde. L'exotisme et le folklore basculent.' (Something is up in Africa and the other Third World countries. Exoticism and folklore are tilting.)[51] The discussion about language is closely intertwined with Laâbi's demand for 'cultural decolonization' and his rejection of acculturation and the related folkloric and ethnographic depictions of Morocco. According to Laâbi, the priority for the poet is to arrive at a correspondence between written language and inner world, and this is not necessarily more easily achieved in one's mother tongue: 'La langue d'un poète est d'abord "*sa propre langue*", celle qu'il crée et élabore au sein du chaos linguistique, la manière aussi dont il recompose les placages de mondes et de dynamismes qui coexistent en lui.' (A poet's language is first of all '*his own language*', the one that he creates and elaborates within linguistic chaos, and the manner by which he recomposes the veneers of worlds and dynamisms coexisting in him.)[52]

The 'linguistic drama' of the colonized, which Memmi spoke of as a tangible effect of depersonalization and self-mutilation,[53] needed, according to Laâbi, to be reformulated within a framework of 'décolonisation *post-coloniale*'.[54] That is, rather than conceptualizing the linguistic situation in the Maghreb as a dualistic conflict between two tongues, two cultures and two worlds,[55] Laâbi proposed that linguistic dualism should be conceived as a creative potential:

> Or l'écrivain de race est celui qui fait un usage singulier et irremplaçable de la langue. C'est celui qui nous propose et impose un langage nouveau, marqué du sceau de son univers créateur. A l'écrivain de chez nous de désarticuler cette langue qui est sienne, de la violenter pour lui extirper toutes ses possibilités. [. . .] En définitive, le dualisme linguistique doit être posé à l'heure actuelle dans le vaste contexte de la décolonisation, non plus comme frustration coloniale mais comme usage particulier, comme conquête sur la désorganisation. C'est finalement un problème d'écrivains.[56]

> (But the ethnic writer is someone who makes a singular and irreplaceable use of language. It is someone who proposes and imposes on us a new language, marked with the seal of his creative universe. A writer who is one of us must disarticulate this language, which is his, do violence to it in order to extract all its possibilities. [. . .] Ultimately, the question of linguistic dualism must be raised

today within the broader context of decolonization, no longer as a colonial frustration but as a particular practice, as a conquest over disorganization. It is ultimately the writers' problem.)

This idea of a 'linguistic and textual violence' became a hallmark of the *Souffles* movement and of post-*Souffles* literary production in Morocco. As argued by Marc Gontard in *La violence du texte* (1981), authors such as Laâbi, Nissaboury, Khaïr-Eddine, Khatibi and Ben Jelloun each in their way pursued this textual violence. As early as in 1964, Khaïr-Eddine called in *Poésie toute* for a 'poetics of violence' against all established conventions, whether in relation to language, society or religion.[57] The *Souffles* movement was, however, not limited to francophone authors. Authors such as Mohamed Berrada and Muhammad Zafzaf, both of whom contributed to *Souffles*,[58] pursued a similar linguistic and poetic guerrilla in Arabic.

To return to Laâbi, he defined his literary practice as 'itinéraire' (itinerary) in *L'Œil et la nuit* (1969) to describe 'ce va-et-vient, dans un même texte, entre le poétique, le narratif et le discursif. . . . "L'itinéraire", c'est la traversée, inscrite dans le langage et l'écriture, d'un champ socio-culturel soumis à la violence' (this moving back and forth, in the same text, between the poetic, the narrative and the discursive. . . . 'The itinerary' is the crossing, inscribed in language and writing, of a sociocultural field subjected to violence).[59] In *Souffles*, Laâbi theorized this literary practice in terms of 'transculturation' and argued that Maghrebin literature in French should be 'une littérature terroriste, c'est-à-dire une littérature brisant à tous les niveaux (syntaxe, phonétique, morphologie, graphie, symbolique, etc.) la logique originelle de la langue française' (a terrorist literature, i.e. a literature that on all levels (syntax, phonetics, morphology, graphic, symbolic, etc.) shatters the original logic of the French language).[60] Thus transculturation and textual violence go hand in hand, as it is precisely through a deconstruction of the French language and literary genres that acculturation is resisted.

During the *Souffles* period Laâbi's poetry was revolutionary and challenged the forms of literary and political expression. His poetry was infused with 'verbal aggression, syntactic disrupture, and tonal decomposition'[61] to both capture and resist the experience of French cultural domination and authoritarian oppression. As in his poem *Marasmes* (Doldrums) (1966), which appeared in the first issue of *Souffles*, chaos and rebirth[62] are confronted in a poetic rage: 'A la poubelle poème / A la poubelle rythme / A la poubelle silence // le mot tonne / j'en suis la première victime / cependant je l'extrais / et le propulse / vers vous.' (Into the trash can poem / Into the trash can rhythm / Into the trash can silence // the word thunders / I am its first victim / but I pull it out / and propel it / towards you.)[63] In *Marasmes* the poet is battling with the French language in order to pull out a new literary language.

However, Laâbi's relation to the French language remained ambiguous during the *Souffles* period, and this ambiguity reveals an unfinished project of postcolonial critique. In *Souffles* 18 (1970), Laâbi argued that it is necessary to overcome 'bilingualism' if the project of decolonization is to succeed in liberating

Moroccan culture. In this respect, writing in French can only be provisional. It is, according to Laâbi, an integral part of the current stage of decolonization and anti-imperialist struggle on the cultural level; but in the long term, cultural liberation can only be achieved in 'nos langues nationales et populaires' (our national and popular languages).[64] In what was to become the last issue of *Souffles*, Laâbi went even further:

> Il est certain qu'une des graves ambiguïtés qui pesait sur notre expérience dès le départ, et qui devenait de plus en plus insoutenable au fur et à mesure que la revue s'engageait dans un combat plus large que celui de la culture, s'exprimait dans le fait que, tout en prenant position aux avant-postes de la lutte anti-impérialiste sur les plans idéologique et culturel!, nous tombions du simple fait d'exprimer ce combat en langue étrangère sous le coup de la contradiction la plus flagrante. Nous le disions bien (mais en le contredisant dans les faits) que le combat contre la culture impérialiste et bourgeoise au Maroc et dans le reste du Maghreb passe inéluctablement et obligatoirement par la reprise en main de notre culture, ce qui n'est possible en définitive que par la suppression de l'aliénation fondamentale à savoir l'aliénation linguistique.
>
> Aujourd'hui plus que jamais, et concernant un pays comme le nôtre dont le destin historique, le destin de lutte et de libération sont indéfectiblement liés à ceux de l'ensemble de la nation arabe, la lutte contre la francophonie impérialiste, l'usage de la langue arabe dans tous les domaines de la réflexion et de l'expression est une des conditions fondamentales de notre désaliénation et de notre engagement véritable dans le combat libérateur.
>
> C'est pour cela que nous n'avions pas attendu d'aboutir inconsciemment au cul-de-sac inévitable et à ses conséquences désastreuses, qu'elles soient l'aphasie ou la complaisance et la mauvaise foi. Nous avons œuvré de longue date pour que cette ambiguïté soit supprimée et la seule voie était de réaliser un instrument d'expression et de lutte en langue arabe.
>
> Aujourd'hui cet outil existe: 'Anfas' a vu le jour en mai dernier.[65]

(Certainly, one of the grave ambiguities that weighed in on our experience from the beginning, and which became increasingly unbearable as the journal incrementally engaged in a combat beyond culture, was that we, while assuming the position as outposts in the anti-imperialist struggle on the ideological and cultural plan!, fell under the most flagrant contradiction by the simple fact that we expressed this combat in a foreign language. We said it well (but contradicted it in practice) that the combat against imperialist and bourgeois culture in Morocco and in the rest of the Maghreb inevitably and necessarily involves taking possession of our culture, which ultimately is only possible through suppression of the fundamental alienation, namely linguistic alienation.

Today more than ever – and particularly in a country like ours where historical destiny, the destiny of struggle and liberation is unfailingly linked to that of the entire Arab nation, the struggle against imperialist *francophonie* – the use of the Arabic language in all domains of thought and expression is one of the fundamental conditions of our disalienation and of our true commitment to the liberating combat.

This is the reason why we have not waited to unconsciously reach an inevitable dead-end and its disastrous consequences, be they aphasia or complacency and bad faith. We have long worked toward eliminating this ambiguity and the only way is to create an instrument of expression and struggle in the Arabic language.

Today this instrument exists: *Anfas* saw the light of day last May.)

Laâbi and the *Souffles* movement had come to the conclusion that writing in French impeded complete decolonization, as the anti-imperialist struggle necessarily had to include a struggle against the neocolonial underpinnings of *la francophonie*. Whereas Laâbi earlier had argued for transculturation, textual violence and a 'decolonized' use of French as a means to resist neocolonialism, he argued in the last issue of the *Souffles* journal (without knowing that it was to be the last) that deconstructing the French language from within could only be a provisional goal. The continued relevance of the French-language journal *Souffles* was consequently defined in its being an instrument to communicate with and gain support from those who did not speak Arabic, whether French-educated Moroccans or foreign readers who would otherwise have no access to an inside perspective on the Arab world and progressive Arab militant thought.[66]

Towards an ethics of bilingualism: Abdelkébir Khatibi's Amour bilingue

Although Khatibi was not a part of the editorial board of *Souffles-Anfâs*, he contributed to *Souffles* (2, 3 and 15), and his *Le Roman maghrébin* was reviewed in *Souffles* by Ben Jelloun (13–14). Most importantly, his intellectual and aesthetic affinities with the *Souffles* movement are unmistakable. When he, in *Souffles* 3, asked 'peut-on libérer un peuple avec une langue qu'il ne comprend pas?' (can we liberate a people with a language it does not understand?),[67] he continued in a manner strikingly similar to Laâbi:

> Je suis peut-être pour la mort provisoire de la littérature et pour l'engagement de l'intellectuel dans la lutte politique. [. . .] En fait, j'exagère dans la mesure où je suis jusqu'au bout mon raisonnement. [. . .] A sa façon, l'écriture est une praxis, une action qui a à jouer pleinement son rôle. Il suffit que l'écrivain comprenne que la culture n'est pas la volonté d'hommes solitaires, mais construction d'un ensemble de valeurs et d'idées au service d'une plus grande libération de l'homme.[68]

> (I am perhaps for the temporary death of literature and for the intellectual's commitment to the political struggle. [. . .] In fact, I am exaggerating inasmuch as I am going all the way with my reasoning. [. . .] In its own way, writing is a praxis, an action that has to play its role fully. It is sufficient that a writer

understands that culture is not the will of solitary men, but the construction of a set of values and ideas serving a greater liberation of man.)

As this passage indicates, Khatibi was, in common with Laâbi and the *Souffles* movement in general, preoccupied with the relation between literature and society and with the author as a politically engaged intellectual. Thus to Khatibi the discussion of the role of French as language of literary expression in the Maghreb was as much a political as a cultural concern. In 1989, in a letter to the French minister of *la francophonie*, Alain Décaux, Khatibi, for instance, cautioned that it is important to distinguish between writing in the French language and affiliation with the French state: 'Il y a une confusion entretenue par les responsables français sur la notion de "francophonie". Ce n'est pas parce qu'on parle et qu'on écrit la langue française qu'on est politiquement du côté de la France. Ce sont deux ordres à séparer. La langue française est transnationale comme toute langue.' (French officials have upheld a confusion concerning the concept 'francophonie'. We are not siding politically with France, because we speak and write in the French language. These two orders should be separated. The French language is transnational like all languages.)[69] By dissociating the French language from the French nation state, Khatibi simultaneously questioned the relation between centre (France) and periphery (so-called francophone countries) and proposed that *la francophonie* should be reoriented according to a double strategy: 'celui du respect de la variété idiomatique et celui d'une universalité plurielle, à plusieurs pôles. Finie l'illusion d'un centre, d'un ethnocentre, générateur de la civilisation française, intégrée autour d'un territoire, d'un Etat et d'une idéologie' (that of respect for idiomatic variety and that of a plural universality, with several poles. Done with the illusion of a centre, an ethnocentre, generator of French civilization, integrated around a territory, a State, and an ideology).[70]

It is at the heart of this reorientation that we find Khatibi's *transnation* and *étranger professionnel*: 'On dit souvent que la nation de l'écrivain est la langue. Y aurait-il donc, au-delà des varieties idiomatiques de la francophonie, une nation littéraire ou plutôt une trans-nation qui serait le cœur meme de la francophonie?' (One often says that language is the writer's nation. Could it be then, beyond idiomatic varieties of *francophonie*, that it is a literary nation or rather a transnation which is at the very heart of *la francophonie*?)[71] The professional foreigner is precisely a writer inhabiting a transnation and performing a transidentity that effectively challenge any neatly distinct 'literary nationalities'.[72] In this respect, Khatibi's position was programmatic and his 'decolonial deconstruction'[73] reflects a clear political standpoint.

Amour bilingue

As *Amour bilingue* has been hailed as inaugurating a new period in modern Maghrebin literature in French, a few words about its relation to but difference from the works of the *Souffles* movement are required. I will begin with quoting Bensmaïa at length, because his appraisal of the book as an 'experimental nation' touches upon a number of interesting aspects about Maghrebin literature in French:

> What is striking in Khatibi's work in general, and in particular in *Love in Two Languages*, is that the sort of *Kampfplatz* represented by the question of (two) languages in the Maghreb suddenly appears to us as *history*. That is, with Khatibi – or, more precisely, *after* Khatibi – it seems that we are faced with something like a BEFORE and AFTER in the history and thinking of North African writing. The intervention or the inscription of *Love in Two Languages* in French-language Maghrebi literature is in this sense an *event* to which we must pay close attention if we hope to be in a position to understand the upheavals that have occurred on the contemporary Maghrebi cultural scene. On the eve of the euphoria that would turn into madness, Nietzsche said that his Zarathustra would 'split the history of humanity in two'. *Love in Two Languages* is the same kind of gesture; it splits the history of Maghrebi thinking and being *in two*. Not in two camps, or clans, or sides – that had already occurred and no doubt will continue to occur; rather, it splits history in two eras: BEFORE/AFTER. And not for the ever contingent reasons of (greater) beauty or artistic and stylistic genius, but essentially because this time the false transparency or obviousness of the bilingual problem itself is profoundly called into question.
>
> In other words, with Khatibi – and this is the originality of what is at stake in his book – the dilemma is no longer whether one *must* write in Arabic or in French, whether the choice is necessary or contingent, politically right or wrong. Rather, the point is to make visible another (infraliminal) level of writing and thinking that renders the dualistic opposition that has dominated Maghrebi literary production completely obsolete.[74]

With *Amour bilingue* Khatibi succeeded in 'the rendering (im)possible of (an)other narrative' as Gayatri Spivak later singled out as the most significant challenge of the subaltern: 'To steer ourselves through the Scylla of cultural relativism and the Charybdis of nativist culturalism regarding this period, we need a commitment not only to narrative and counternarrative, but also to the rendering (im)possible of (an)other narrative.'[75] That is, in creating this unsettling space of *Amour bilingue* in which Arabic and French can meet without merging, Khatibi simultaneously criticized the Moroccan policy of bilingualism and the French conception of *la francophonie*. On the one hand, he distinguished his conception of bilingualism from the monologic conception of language implicit in the French promotion of *la francophonie*, as described earlier. On the other hand, he effectively distinguished his own conception of bilingualism from the institutionalized Standard Arabic-French bilingualism in Morocco at the time. According to Khatibi, the whole idea of Standard Arabic representing Moroccan national identity and cultural authenticity while French was considered the language of science and technology reproduced monologic and ahistorical conceptions of languages – in addition to its complete disregard, at the time of Khatibi's writing in the 1980s, for the role of

Berber and Moroccan Arabic as mother tongues in Morocco. Thus Khatibi's call for what I would term 'an ethics of bilingualism'[76] was significantly different from the politics of bilingualism in Morocco at the time.

In *Amour bilingue*, Khatibi narrates the encounter between the languages of colonizer and colonized as an erotic bilingual love that 'begets a hybridized offspring, a language semantically infused by its Other, bearing the marks of linguistic and ideological contamination'.[77] This hybridized offspring is *bi-langue*, which signifies a space in which 'mother tongue' and 'foreign language' interact in a way that subverts hegemonic practices of linguistic and cultural domination. According to Khatibi, the other is present in every language, culture and subjectivity, as such, *bi-langue* is the embodiment of 'difference'; it is not a dialectical struggle but a constant movement between languages and cultures, as well as a movement between 'I' and 'non-I', as Khatibi set out as early as in his autobiography *La Mémoire tatouée* (1971). As argued by Lucy Stone McNeece, Khatibi challenges the whole idea that an autobiography offers access to the intimate world of the author's self,[78] and by writing an autobiography of the 'non-I', he simultaneously exposes the illusion that French should provide Maghrebin authors with a more privileged access to a self-conscious 'I' than, for instance, Arabic. In *La Mémoire tatouée*, self-knowledge requires self-abandonment – a dialectic between identity and difference – and, as such, it is, just as *Amour bilingue* is, closely intertwined with Khatibi's conceptualization of *bi-langue*, *pensée-autre* and *pensée en langues*.

'Folie de la langue'[79]

One of the most significant aspects of *Amour bilingue* is Khatibi's ability to make French and Arabic meet without merging, as Bensmaïa has also pointed out.[80] In the 'Exergue' (Epigraph) of *Amour bilingue*, this is reflected in an interplay of French and Arabic words:

> Il se calma d'un coup, lorsqu'apparut le 'mot' arabe *kalma* avec son équivalent savant *kalima* et toute la chaine des diminutifs, calembours de son enfance: *klima*. . . . La diglossie *kal(i)ma* revint sans que disparût ni s'effaçât le mot 'mot'. Tous deux s'observaient en lui, precedent l'émergence maintenant rapide de souvenirs, fragments de mots, onomatopées, phrases en guirlandes, enlaces à mort: indéchiffrables. Scène encore muette.[81]

> (He suddenly calmed down when the Arabic 'word', *kalma*, appeared, with its scholarly equivalent, *kalima*, and the whole chain of diminutives, puns of his childhood: *klima*. . . . The diglossal *kal(i)ma* returned without the word 'mot' having disappeared or faded. Both words observed each other within him, preceding the now rapid emergence of memories, fragments of words, onomatopoeias, garlands of phrases, entwined with death: indecipherable. Scene still silent.)

In creating a literary space in which the two languages haunt one another and reciprocally transfer meaning to one another without uniting in synthesis, Khatibi simultaneously subverts the relation between *signifié* (signified) and *signifiant* (signifier) in both languages. By associating the Arabic word *kal(i)ma* (word) with the French *calma* in the past tense *passé simple* (calmed down), *kal(i)ma* suddenly acquires a new meaning as the calming effect of childhood memories. However, the two words do not collapse into one: in the confrontation of *kal(i)ma* with *mot*, 'calma' disturbs the meaning of *kal(i)ma*, which no longer simply denotes 'word'. Moreover, the materialization of the two words observing one another triggers a chain of memories and associations in the mind of the narrator such that *mot* is replaced with *mort*, and suddenly memories are intertwined with death and become undecipherable and silent: 'Et en français – sa langue étrangère – le "mot" est près de la mort, il ne lui manque qu'une seule lettre: concision de sa frappe, une syllabe, extase d'un sanglot retenu. Pourquoi croyait-il que la langue est plus belle, plus terrible pour un étranger?' (And in French – his foreign language – 'word' [*mot*] is close to 'death' [*mort*], only one letter is missing: conciseness of his strike, a syllable, ecstasy of a restrained sob. Why did he think that the language is more beautiful, more terrible, for a foreigner?)[82]

As argued by Bensmaïa, this linguistic play with transference of meaning simultaneously enables Khatibi to 'translate' the untranslatable:

> It may indeed be more economical to say that Khatibi has switched languages, but he has done so in a breathtaking move that does not consist in either a reterritorializing return to Arabic or an Arabicization of French, but instead allows language to see double, making it 'loucher' in the active sense of that French word, which means 'to peer, to eye'. He subjects the French language to a system that enables it to translate the untranslatable, to express the inexpressible.[83]

The sequence *calma – kal(i)ma – mot – mort – souvenir*, which is additionally associated with riddles and the undecipherable, thus sets the scene of *Amour bilingue*, in which the story of a bilingual erotic relationship is ruled by an associative madness whereby both lovers are subject to violent erasure and haunted by their spectralized 'self'. One of the recurring associations is between *langue maternelle-mère-mer* (mother tongue-mother-sea). The narrator's relationship with the foreign language makes him reflect on the nature of *langue maternelle* and the sense of belonging implicit in its relation to mother, birth, roots and so on. This in turn directs his attention towards his relation to his mother and the intertwinement of her death with his relation to the foreign language:

> Je te tenais dans mes bras, sur mon ventre, et je t'avalais féeriquement par ma bouche pour t'engrosser en moi. Jalousie cannibale qui déchire les chairs, les blesse à coups de bistoury. Par cela, j'évoque les affres de ce récit obstétrical qui ne m'attachait, par la langue, qu'aux-belles-étrangères. Je ne sais pour quel conflit inavoué et dissimulé entre ma mère et ma naissance. Avec le temps, les doubles maternels me deviennent indispensables pour confirmer ma scénographie sans généalogie, non point, comme on dit, pour revenir au ventre de la Mère que

mon père mort et mon dieu invisible ont engrossée tout à la fois; mais pour accompagner ma mère réelle au terme de sa vieillesse et à son décès.[84]

(I held you in my arms, on my chest, and I swallowed you magically with my mouth in order to impregnate myself with you. Cannibal jealousy, which tears the flesh, wounds them with a bistoury. By this, I evoke the pangs of this obstetrical story which attached me, through language, only to-beautiful-foreigners. I don't know for what unavowed and concealed conflict between my mother and my birth. With time, the maternal doubles became indispensable to me in order to confirm my scenography without genealogy, not, as is said, to return to the belly of the Mother which my dead father and my invisible god had impregnated at the same time; but to accompany my real mother to the end of her old age and to her death.)

Here, the lover represents the embodiment of the foreign language. By devouring his lover in a simultaneous birth and rebirth – the birth of *bi-langue* and his rebirth as *bi-langue* – his mother (tongue) must at the same instant be put into the grave. Moreover, the illiterate mother is effectively divorced from this 'mother tongue' because of the diglossic difference between spoken and written Arabic.

Amour bilingue is not, however, a simple destruction of the idea of a mother tongue. In alternating between birth and death, between being and non-being, Khatibi displaces the whole idea of genealogy and of origin and root implicit in 'langue maternelle'. But 'scénographie sans généalogie' is not a rejection of historical perspective; rather, it is a reference to an 'origin-less' history. Just like Foucault's genealogy, Khatibi's *pensée-autre* is not a way of providing a counternarrative to an established and authoritative narrative – in this case about the nature and origin of language – but reflects an effort to think the relation between origin, knowledge and power in another way.

When the relation between death and birth, between being and non-being, becomes too intense, the narrator suddenly finds himself calm and back at the sea (*mer*)[85] in which he was swimming at the beginning of the story.[86] 'Rêvait-il?' (Was he dreaming?)[87] and 'Rêvait-je?' (Was I dreaming?)[88] further link the two scenes together, while questioning the relation between present story and memories, and underlining the indiscernibility of what is real and what is imagined in the story. Is the protagonist at the sea recalling memories of a past love affair (as depicted at the beginning of *Amour bilingue)*, or are both sea and memories a dream (as one gets the impression later in the text)? Moreover, the two scenes reveal another ambiguity to the story as it displaces the classical 'rules' of narratology. The transformation from 'il' to 'je' ('Rêvait-il?' – 'Revait-je?') is not simply a complex focalization strategy or a change in point of view. It constitutes an additional disturbance of the logic of the story. Are narrator and protagonist identical? The process of identification between the two takes place gradually: the story begins with an exclusive third-person point of view with internal focalization, but then suddenly begins jumping back and forth between third and first person, and towards the end of the story narrator and protagonist are identical, as if the narrator by narrating the story slowly becomes the protagonist himself. It is as if the novel on all levels questions the discernibility between identity and difference – whether between narrator and protagonist, language and speaker, man and woman, parent and child, *signifié* and *signifiant*, reality and fiction and so on.

Moreover, *Amour bilingue* simultaneously deconstructs the established literary genres as if it were a prototype of Laâbi's textual violence. In the epilogue of *Amour bilingue* the narrator directly touches upon the question of genre:

> Dire maintenant que ce récit est intouchable, qu'il est organisé dans la bi-langue par un double chiffre de lecture, serait très mystérieux. Aucun secret: seulement me laisser entendre dans cette langue qui ne m'entend qu'à moitié. Si l'on me demandait: 'Votre récit est-il un nouveau nouveau roman? Ou mieux, un bi-nouveau nouveau roman?' je répondrais que le roman n'a jamais voulu de moi. Nous ne sommes pas de la même historie.[89]

> (To say now that this story is untouchable, that it's organized in the *bi-langue* by a double figure of reading, would be very mysterious. No secret: just let me hear in this language that only half hears me. If I were asked: 'Your story, is it a *nouveau nouveau roman*? Or better, a bi-*nouveau nouveau roman*?' I'd reply that the novel never wanted me. We aren't of the same history.)

Arguing that *Amour bilingue* is neither a *nouveau nouveau roman* nor a *bi-nouveau nouveau roman*, the narrator displaces the genre 'novel' completely. These meta-reflections are important, because they reveal an implicit desire to distinguish Maghrebin literature in French from the development of the novelistic genre in France. While the avant-gardist style of writing in *Amour bilingue*, its rejection of plot, characters and omniscient narrator, resembles *le nouveau roman*, *Amour bilingue* is more than a mere imitation of a new genre in French literature. Significantly, this is not dissimilar to how *Le Passé simple* resembles the nineteenth-century French novel, while simultaneously displacing it as 'template' through a parodic performance of the Arab storyteller, as I have argued in Chapter 3. However, *Amour bilingue* is more radical in its quest for a new literary form. Similarly to Laâbi's itinerary Khatibi, in *Amour bilingue*, displaces established distinctions between prose and poetry, between the narrative and the discursive. As an example of linguistic and textual violence, *Amour bilingue* is a project of decolonization and, simultaneously, also an embodiment of Khatibi's double critique: it reveals the arbitrariness of binary oppositions such as that between 'mother tongue' and 'foreign language' through an other-thought (*pensée-autre*) which is neither inside nor outside, neither centre nor periphery.

Bi-langue: Between eroticism and bestiality

In *bi-langue* both lovers are subject to violent erasure and haunted by their spectralized 'self'; in this sense, *bi-langue* is a product both of their erotic love and of their breakup. Moreover, it is both something they give birth to and something they become inhabited by; 'le rêve parental assassin' ('the assassinated parental dream')[90] functions precisely to disturb any monolithic conception of *bi-langue*, as well as to underline the interpenetration of love and violence implicit in it. *Bi-langue* is thus an expression of *pensée-autre*, an other way of thinking the relation between identity and difference, being together and being apart, giving birth to and being born by. Consequently, *bi-langue* is not *a* new position, but *endlessly* new spaces where languages are continuously in the making.

In *Maghreb pluriel*, Khatibi links *bi-langue* to *pensée en langues*, which he defines as encompassing both a sense of alienation and a potential creativity.[91] To speak in languages (*parler en langues*) is always threatened by 'confusion' because of how the languages speak in and through one another; but it can nevertheless pave the way for something different, a different rhythm where innovation is the outcome of languages infecting, affecting and inhabiting one another. The bilingual author is, in Khatibi's words, a professional foreigner. By living between two languages, two borders and two cultures, the bilingual author no longer belongs to one history, one nation and one people. As Bensmaïa argues, Khatibi's texts

> are inscribed in a problematic that is attempting to redefine traditional boundaries of national, cultural, and ethnic belonging, and [. . .] they refer to one of the most actual political realities: the emergence of what certain contemporary sociologists have called 'global ethnoscapes', that is, those transnational spaces of identity that are becoming increasingly important in the politics of old nation-states.[92]

In this respect, *Amour bilingue* is inseparable from Khatibi's *transnation* and *étranger professionnel*, as well as his related double critique of the Moroccan policy of bilingualism and the French conception of *la francophonie*, as described earlier. However, despite his call for an ethics of bilingualism that can displace any hierarchical and hegemonic relation between languages, and indeed any essentialistic conception of language as unified in itself and dualistic in its relation to other languages, Khatibi has been perceived as less preoccupied with the forces of normativity and the realities of power than, for instance, Abdelfattah Kilito.

In his introduction to Kilito's *Thou Shalt Not Speak My language* (2008), Waïl S. Hassan, for instance, describes Khatibi's *Amour bilingue* as an example of 'utopianism' in opposition to Kilito's almost 'Darwinian fatalism'.[93] Hassan's description pinpoints some of the differences between Kilito's and Khatibi's approach to bilingualism, and the 'utopian' aspects of Khatibi's work are particularly clear in his ethics of bilingualism and his idealistic visions of what *la francophonie* ought to be. In this respect, Kilito's visualization of the relation between languages leaves the reader with a significantly different impression of bilingualism than *Amour bilingue*:

> When two languages live side by side, one or the other will always appear bestial. If you do not speak as I do, you are an animal. The 'I' in this case must occupy the dominant position; if I am the weaker party, it is I who am the animal. To call this situation a conflict is incorrect, because conflict requires adversaries of equal or

at least comparable strength. A lion may battle a tiger, but he simply devours a rabbit. Bilingualism does not evoke an image of two gladiators advancing upon each other armed with nets and tridents; rather, it suggests that one of the two combatants is already sprawled in the dust awaiting the fatal blow.[94]

Thus Kilito replaces Khatibi's eroticism with bestiality: bilingualism, according to him, does not represent 'the mutual enrichment of languages, but the annihilation of one by the other'.[95] As Kilito is preoccupied with the unequal power balance between colonizer and colonized, his conception of bilingualism as a relation of bestiality reflects the realities of power implicit in the colonial desire and ideology of conquest.[96]

However, eroticism does not, in Khatibi's depiction, represent peaceful love, neatly opposed to violent bestiality. The description of utopianism versus fatalism therefore glosses over some of the similarities between Khatibi and Kilito. *Bi-langue* is not a harmonious synthesis; it is as much a battlefield as Kilito's bestiality. First, it encompasses the protagonist's cannibalistic desire to devour his lover in order to impregnate himself with her (language). Second, the recurrent depiction of the conflict between mother and birth, the outcome of which is the death of the protagonist's mother (tongue), is anything but peaceful. And, last but not least, the feeling of mortification that permeates the life of the protagonist's lover upon her return home can only be overcome by her either obliterating herself or engaging in a battle with the incomprehensible. 'Mutual enrichment' is thus rather the outcome of annihilation than the opposition to it – just as self-knowledge requires self-abandonment in *La Mémoire tatouée*.

An important part of eroticism in *Amour bilingue* lies in the barely distinguishable sexes. Whereas the two lovers are narrated as a 'he' and a 'she', this gender difference is time and again disturbed by the narrator, who by 'whiting out the relationship to language (to languages in general), [. . .] simultaneously whites out the relationship to sexual difference'.[97] While Khatibi has not – like Taïa – portrayed LGBT lives in his works, *Amour bilingue* is nevertheless permeated with 'queer desire' and *bi-langue* is the embodiment of a queer subject position. Thus the representation of homosexuality and androgyny in *Amour bilingue* serves less to describe sexual acts in and of themselves than to signify a critical practice: that is, a subversion of the 'Hetero-Nation'. One example of this is the literary play with transsexuality and homosexuality as an act of transgression closely intertwined with the violent attraction of the foreign language:

Un jour – et c'est recent – il aima une femme, changea de sexe. Un sexe dans le sexe circoncis, sexe à double langue, comme un serpent. De son anus, émergeait la figure d'un dieu invisible. Il fut violé alors par sa langue étrangère. Jeté à terre, il souffrait atrocement. Mais – sensation bizarre – il était derrière son violeur, non pas à son tour le penetrant, mais il était pénétré par la jouissance de la langue – son homosexualité fiche dans les dictionnaires du monde entier.[98]

(One day – and it's recent – he loved a woman, changed sex. Sex in circumcised sex, two-tongued sex, like a snake. From his anus emerged the figure of an invisible god. He was then violated by his foreign tongue. Thrown to the ground, he suffered terribly. But – bizarre sensation – he was behind his violator, not in turn penetrating him, but he was penetrated by the enjoyment of language – his homosexuality filed in the dictionaries of the whole world.)

As this quote indicates, homosexuality – as well as transsexuality, prostitution, multiple partners and so on – functions as an instance of subversion; that is, they are not representations of queer identities, but exclusively a critical literary practice meant to disturb any normativity.

Another less violent example of 'transgressive sexuality' is the recurrent representation of the protagonist as androgynous and the narrator's obsession with androgyny. As argued by Bensmaïa, the figure of the androgyne in *Amour bilingue* is 'inseparable from the shifts brought about by the *bi-langue*'.[99] In this respect, it constitutes an adventure of travelling without belonging: 'Traduire l'impur dans le pur, la prostitution dans l'androgynie, était une aventure, qui exigeait d'être vécue sans aucune réserve. Il errait de pays en pays, de corps en corps, de langue en langue.' (To translate impurity into purity, prostitution into androgyny was an adventure that had to be lived without reservation. He wandered from country to country, from body to body, from language to language.)[100] The figure of the androgyne is precisely the 'other' of both sexes[101] – neither the one, nor the other, nor a synthesis – just as the professional foreigner neither belongs to nor possesses any language but is the 'other' of all the languages he speaks and writes.

Khatibi's androgyne body draws on a Sufi tradition of transcending normative gender categories, just as his hermetic avant-gardism relies on a literary tradition of mystical poetry. However, this is done without recourse to a narrative of mystical illumination or reunion with God. That is, at the heart of *Amour bilingue* is a permanent wandering between literary genres, languages and sexes that never reaches fulfilment through synthesis. Through the androgyne body male and female meet without merging just as French and Arabic does in *bi-langue* and just as the poetic, the narrative and the discursive does in *Amour bilingue*. Moreover, contrary to how Chraïbi in *Le Passé simple* and Taïa in *L'Armée du salut* parody stereotypic conceptions of the 'emancipated Arab boy' Khatibi displaces classical storytelling altogether. That is, while the associative madness of *Amour bilingue* draws the reader in, it does so through a deconstruction of the seductive narratives of the Orient in both Arab and Western imagination.

'Poor' French as a strategy of resistance: Abdellah Taïa's Un Pays pour mourir

Even if Bensmaïa has described Khatibi's *Amour bilingue* as marking a before and an after in the history of Maghrebin writing, plurilingualism and the accompanying questions of 'cultural alienation' are still central concerns for many contemporary Moroccan authors and critics. This is of course not because Khatibi's work lacks significance, but rather an effect of the cultural and political realities within and beyond the country's borders. Just as Khatibi wrote as a politically engaged intellectual against institutionalized bilingualism in Morocco and the neocolonial underpinnings of *la francophonie*, Taïa has been outspoken in his critique of both Moroccan 'bourgeoisie' French and *la francophonie*. However, Moroccan language policies have changed radically since Khatibi wrote *Amour bilingue*; and so, consequently, has the perception of what a 'national' language is.[102] Today Morocco is officially recognized as a plurilingual country,[103] and language has long been at the centre of cultural and political debates.[104] However, the recurring question 'What is Moroccan literature?' in Moroccan literary circles[105] reveals that the multifaceted nature of 'Moroccan literature' makes it difficult to define it in terms of national or linguistic borders.

Undoubtedly, the contemporary Moroccan literary landscape is plurilingual. Aside from creative writing in Arabic and French, it has witnessed the emergence of works written in both Amazigh and *dārija*, and it has come to include a number of diasporic languages.[106] Moreover, paying attention to the plurilingual literary production by Moroccans is important, because 'the predominant attention to Europhone literatures in postcolonial studies distorts the multiple reconfigurations of the narrations of identity that take place in the postcolonial world', as Ato Quayson has argued.[107] That is, reading francophone Moroccan (or Maghrebin) literature in isolation, as it has so often been read,[108] risks reinforcing the binary of, for instance, Arabic and French literary traditions by forcing Moroccan literature to fit into 'hegemonic single-language literary systems'.[109] Moreover, these reading practices tend to neglect not only that Moroccan literary works – independent of the languages in which they are written – have emerged from similar historical, cultural and political contexts but also that plurilingualism is an integrated part of them.

In *Fictions du réel*, Zekri names this insertion of multiple languages and idioms in the same text 'extraterritorialité de la langue' (extraterritoriality of language), and he points towards the incorporation of Moroccan Arabic into the written language and to the palimpsestic nature of Moroccan francophone writing as examples of this extraterritoriality.[110] Importantly, this is not a question of realism, but an effort to reveal the limits of monolingualism in a context marked by diglossia. That is, rather than convey an authentic picture of an ethnographic reality, the incorporation of dialect brings an aesthetic dimension to the Arabic text. Moreover, this heterolinguism is, as argued by Zekri, significant because the grammar of 'official' literary Arabic has been fixed by a sacralized historical heritage (pre-Islamic poetry and the Qur'an), which has been difficult for Arab-Muslim writers to transgress.[111] With Moroccan francophone writers the palimpsestic presence of Moroccan Arabic brings a strangeness to the text, which is different for arabophone and non-arabophone readers, but which creates a language 'entre-deux' that is neither French-French nor Moroccan Arabic but an other-langauge.[112] Seen within this perspective, Khatibi's conception of *bi-langue*, transnation and the professional foreigner are as valid today as when he first coined them, and Moroccan authors are still pursuing a 'textual violence', just as did the young generation of authors who were part of the *Souffles* movement.

French and la francophonie *in Morocco Today*

As noted by Zekri, not much knowledge of Moroccan literature is required to realize that Moroccan authors published in France are more known than those exclusively published in Morocco.[113] Moreover, efforts to establish an autonomous literary scene in Morocco face a number of challenges. First, only very few writers have managed to make a full-time profession from creative writing; many are forced to self-publish, at the expense of a critical editorial eye and, consequently, quality.[114] Second, Moroccan writers are still, in certain areas, restrained by juridical/political power and by censorship. The conjunction of these two aspects has, third, led to the dominance of French interests on the literary scene. That is, French cultural agencies have achieved a hegemonic position in the publishing field because no one else has successfully claimed this space.[115] For reasons of economic and cultural interests in promoting *la francophonie*, French institutions fund a number of Moroccan publishing houses, as well as a number of literary prizes, such as Prix Grand Atlas and Prix littéraire de la Mamounia.[116] As many scholars have pointed out,[117] it has, moreover, had an immense impact on the visibility and development of Moroccan francophone literature that Ben Jelloun won the Prix Goncourt for *La Nuit sacrée* (*The Sacred Night*) in 1987. The fact that Laïla Slimani won the same prize in 2016 for *Chanson douce* (*Lullaby*) unquestionably only adds to this. However, while all of this encourages Moroccans to write in French, it has simultaneously made them somewhat dependent on literary interests in France.

Moreover, the dominant position of francophone literature in Morocco is reinforced by the fact that the Moroccan reading public seem to prefer reading in French, as Moroccan author, Youssouf Amine Elalamy, explains:

> when you are publishing a book, we are not talking about literacy, we are talking about people who buy books and want to read books, which is a totally different thing. [Publishers] know from experience if you publish something in Arabic it doesn't sell, and if you publish in French it sells. [. . .] Do you want to publish in Arabic so that people say, 'Oh, that's politically correct,' or do you want to be read by Moroccans, actually?[118]

As both Zekri[119] and the authors interviewed by Megan C. MacDonald about publishing politics in Morocco in 2010–11[120] point out, all of this reveals a missing cultural politics supporting the creation of an autonomous literary scene in Morocco – be this supplied (or not) by the Moroccan political powers, the French literary centre in Paris or the Arabic literary centre in the Mashreq (or Beirut). Moreover, all of these challenges stemming from the mechanisms of the publishing industry reveal that Moroccan literature is dependent on, while it remains peripheral in relation to, the Arabic and the francophone literary fields. However, despite the continued presence of two monolingual literary systems – which Moroccan authors and critics have sought to dismantle since Chraïbi wrote *Le Passé simple* and which scholars have become increasingly aware of the need to challenge – Moroccan authors are not mere victims of hegemonic linguistic practices. That is, they are not simply caught in a catch-22 paradox in which they can choose between two equally horrific choices – either to become an 'arabe de service' for the French, or to subject themselves to tradition and censorship while remaining marginalized in Arabic literature. The Moroccan publishing field is far more vibrant than this, and what is interesting to explore is instead how Moroccan authors resist and subvert these hegemonic practices from within. The problem is neither bilingualism nor alienation nor acculturation; it is the coexistence of two hegemonic monolingualisms, or more precisely two hegemonic monolingual literary systems, which, as Kilito argues, split the bilingual experience in two.[121]

Kilito has, quite interestingly, described this situation as 'langue fourchue, littérature fourchue' (forked tongue, forked literature).[122] While the original Native American saying, 'Paleface speaks with a forked tongue', was used to signify lying, hypocrisy and the white man's deliberate deception of Native Americans, Kilito inverts the idiom 'forked tongue' in order to make it signify the bilingual experience. That is, by associating 'forked tongue' with the ability to speak two languages and by assuming that it was the Native American who learnt English rather than the 'white man' learning any of the indigenous Native American languages, he polemically concludes that it must be the Native American speaking with a forked tongue: 'il emprunte, pour s'exprimer, l'idiome de celui qu'il accuse d'avoir la langue fourchue' (he borrows, to express himself, the idiom of those whom he accuses of having a forked tongue).[123] Transferred to the split bilingual experience of Morocco, this 'forked tongue' becomes reminiscent of Laâbi's linguistic and textual violence, but as a subversive activity at play in Moroccan literature in both Arabic and French.

Not only colonial and postcolonial national history but also the neocolonial underpinnings of *la francophonie* and the continued presence of two hegemonic single-language literary systems have produced a situation where 'Moroccan literature' equals works written in Arabic (officially the national language), whereas works written in French require the addition *de langue/expression français.*[124] This has simultaneously naturalized Arabic as choice of literary language while requiring an explanation for the choice to write in French, as Kilito argues:

> Pourquoi écrivez-vous en français? Question posée rituellement à l'écrivain qui publie dans cette langue, question irritante et culpabilisante. Dans sa réponse, il se montre nuancé, subtil. Il invoque l'Histoire, la formation qu'il a reçue, il dira qu'il se sent relativement plus libre en français, qu'il ressent moins la pesanteur des tabous sexuels et politiques. Il avancera aussi qu'il est incapable d'écrire dans une autre langue, et parfois il parlera à mots couverts du plaisir que lui procure le français. Il ne reconnaîtra pas toujours qu'il y a un certain prestige à écrire dans cette langue, à avoir un double public (encore la langue fourchue!) et à bénéficier d'une large diffusion. Une autre hypothèse pourrait être envisagée: écrire, ce serait aller au-delà de soi-même, quitte à prendre ses distances, si cela s'impose, avec sa langue maternelle; il se pourrait qu'un écrivain choisisse, quand il en a

la possibilité, la langue lointaine, l'*étrangère*, pour être au plus proche de lui-même.[125]

(Why do you write in French? A question posed ritually to the writer who publishes in this language; an annoying and guilt-provoking question. In his response, he demonstrates that he is nuanced, subtle. He invokes History, the education he has received; he will say that he feels relatively freer in French, that he feels less burdened by sexual and political taboos. He will also advance that he is incapable of writing in another language, and sometimes he will speak covertly of the pleasure that French brings him. He does not always acknowledge that there is a certain prestige in writing in this language, in having a double audience (again forked tongue!), and in profiting from large distribution. Another hypothesis could be considered: to write, that would be going beyond oneself, even to distance oneself, if that is necessary, from one's mother tongue; it could be that a writer chooses, when he has the opportunity, the distant language, the *foreign*, to be closer to himself.)

Kilito originally wrote the essay 'Visage pâle' (Paleface) in 1998, but it does more than paraphrase answers previously given by Moroccan francophone authors; it also anticipates many of the explanations advanced by Taïa and other contemporary authors as the reasons for their choice of French as language of literary expression.

Displaced in the French language

Like Laâbi, Khatibi and Kilito, Taïa describes writing in French as a constant battle.[126] But Taïa's battle is, nevertheless, a different one; it is against other 'enemies' and pursued through different aesthetic means. Taïa did not grow up under colonial rule, and he therefore never experienced the odd bilingualism of speaking *dārija* at home while being taught to read and write French and *fuṣḥā* at school. Whereas, to Kilito and Khatibi, French was a language of separation insofar as it separated Moroccan children from their parents, who did not know French, the familiar from the foreign, daily life from school, and speaking from writing,[127] to Taïa, French is, first of all, a language that separates and put barriers between the rich and the poor in Morocco:

إنها اللغة التي يتحدث بها الأغنياء المغاربة بطريقة أنيقة, فقط ليعبروا عن تعاليهم علينا نحن الفقراء, ورغبتهم في إذلالنا.[128]

(It is the language that rich Moroccans speak in an elegant way, only to express that they look down on us, us the poor, and their desire to humiliate us.)

Quand j'étais petit, le simple fait d'entendre quelqu'un qui parlait français signifiait pour moi 'il veut m'écraser, il veut me dire que lui connaît ces grands écrivains français, qu'il est allé à Paris, que moi je ne suis qu'un pauvre et que jamais je n'arriverai à sa hauteur.'[129]

(As a child, simply hearing someone speaking French meant to me 'he wants to crush me, he wants to tell me that he knows these great French writers, that he has been in Paris, that I am nothing but a poor person and that I will never rise to his level'.)

Unlike Khatibi and Kilito, Taïa was a young adult before he learnt French; nevertheless, French was an omnipresent part of his daily life. Once admitted to Mohammed V University, his first encounter with the rich students from the French schools was an arrogance that constantly reminded him that he was nothing but a 'poor boy'. This provoked his desire to take revenge through the French language, which for so long had been used to 'crush' him:

> À côté d'eux, tout en moi disait le pauvre. J'ai alors pensé: je vais les écraser. Je voyais dans leur regard sur moi un apitoiement et un rabaissement que je refusais de tout mon être. Je me rappelle très bien leur ahurissement quand, au premier devoir, celui qui avait la meilleure note, c'était moi. Pour être meilleur qu'eux, je prenais une page d'un livre écrit en français, n'importe lequel, et je la recopiais. Je la regardais: c'est quoi? pourquoi cette langue a-t-elle une telle puissance? Je l'ai fait pendant des années: recopier, décortiquer, dominer. Un jour, j'ai commencé moi-même à écrire dans cette langue. C'est ce qui a fait de moi un écrivain.[130]

> (Next to them, everything about me said 'the poor'. So, I thought: I'll crush them. In the way they looked at me, I saw pity and belittlement which I refused with my whole being. I remember very well their amazement when the one who had the best score at the first assignment was me. To become better than them I picked out a page in a book written in French, no matter what page, and copied it. I looked at it: What is this? Why does this language have such power? I did it for years: copy, dissect, dominate. One day, I started to write in this language myself. That's what made me a writer.)

This urge to master the French language to escape the position of inferiority forced upon him by rich, French-speaking Moroccans is, quite interestingly, reminiscent of how many postcolonial intellectuals have reflected on their relation to the French language: a language that, as narrated by Chraïbi in *Le Passé simple*, was simultaneously promoted as the educational tool to 'civilize' the Moroccan population and effectively used to maintain Moroccans in an inferior position vis-à-vis the 'civilized' colonial power. In an echo of Kateb Yacine's well-known description of the French language as the Algerian's 'butin de guerre' (spoils of war) after the Algerian War of Independence, Taïa describes the French language as 'une arme de guerre' (a weapon of war),[131] something that can be turned against those who have used it to crush him and others like him:

> comment résister avec les éléments et les armes que les autres utilisent pour vous soumettre. Comment, moi, je vais utiliser cette langue qui n'a jamais été réellement la mienne, le français, langue maîtrisée seulement par les riches marocains et l'élite marocaine, comme un moyen d'exister socialement et de

me définir dans une guerre continuelle contre les autres. C'est ce qui pourrait expliquer le fait d'arriver à la littérature française. L'arme dirigée contre moi, le français, je la prends pour résister. Je n'ai jamais été amoureux de la langue française et je pense que je ne le serai jamais. Au Maroc, c'est la langue des riches, des frimeurs et des intellectuels aux pensées figées. Moi, j'avance dans cette langue avec mes origines premières, la pauvreté.[132]

(how to resist with elements and weapons that others use to subjugate you. How could I start using this language which was never really mine – French, a language mastered only by the rich Moroccans and the Moroccan elite – as a means to exist socially and to define myself in a continual war against the others. This might explain the fact that I discovered French literature. The weapon directed against me, French, I seize it to resist. I've never been in love with the French language and I don't think I ever will. In Morocco, it is the language of the rich, show-offs and intellectuals with rigid thoughts. Me, I proceed in this language with my first origins, poverty.)

This poverty is reflected in Taïa's literary style, which he himself has characterized as 'pauvre français' – not 'mauvais français' as in bad French, which some reviewers, both French and Moroccans, have accused him of,[133] but 'poor' French as in a language that reflects his poor background but simultaneously resists the norms and conventions of 'rich' or so-called 'good' French. As such, Taïa's style of writing is significantly different from Khatibi's writing. It is not simply an effort to have French and Arabic meet without merging as a deconstruction of French hegemonic literary practices (though this too is an important part of Taïa's creative writing); it is also an effort to force this powerful language to speak for those who are otherwise rendered both silent and invisible because they do not fit into 'bourgeoisie' norms or into literature as high culture.

As Taïa has often described in interviews, as a child he never dreamed of becoming an author because creative writing bored him and seemed to him to be written with an arrogance and complication that made it inaccessible to ordinary people. Instead he found his inspiration in Egyptian films and actresses, and his biggest dream was to become a filmmaker. Taïa's 'poor' French is, in this respect, reflected in his simple vocabulary, the particular rhythm of his prose, his straightforward writing style reminiscent of film manuscripts and popular art, and the omnipresent emotional vulnerability, which disarms the reader as Taïa's refusal to hide behind a complicated and elegant language simultaneously draws the reader in and facilitates an identification with the characters of his novels. Taïa's creative writing thus effectively dismantles the 'ivory tower' nature of art for art's sake, without succumbing to so-called documentary art.

Taïa is, like many other francophone authors, constantly confronted with the question, 'Why do you write in French?', and many of Taïa's answers are reminiscent of Kilito's paraphrase. First, he is not ignorant of the power and cultural capital of the French language: 'Je sais que je n'ai pas d'autre choix que d'aller vers Paris, là où

se situe le pouvoir culturel, là où il y a l'industrie du livre, la possibilité de devenir
cinéaste, la possibilité d'utiliser les droits de l'homme à bon escient, à mon profit.
Là où je pouvais arriver à quelque chose.' (I know that I have no other choice but
to go to Paris, where the cultural power lies, where the book industry is located,
the chance to become a filmmaker, the chance to use human rights wisely, for my
profit. The place where I could achieve something.)[134] Taïa is perfectly aware that
what he has achieved as author and filmmaker in Paris would probably never have
been possible if he had stayed in Morocco. However, this does not imply that what
he expresses in French cannot be expressed in Arabic, as Gibson Ncube argues,[135]
or in his 'native tongue', as Valérie K. Orlando argues in her review of the film
adaption of *L'Armée du salut*:

> Slimane – who is reading Nikos Kazantzakis's 1948 novel *Le Christ récrucifié*
> (Christ Recrucified) as they sit together on a bench – tells Abdellah in French (a
> language that Abdellah as a young boy can't understand) that 'learning French'
> will help him to 'leave Morocco' and escape. When Abdellah replies in Moroccan
> Arabic (Darija) that 'French is only for rich people,' his brother replies, 'power
> lies in knowledge. You shouldn't be afraid of French.' This scene is significant
> since it not only recasts the language of the former colonizer into something
> positive – as a means to arrive at another destiny – but it also marks a turning-
> point for young Abdellah, who sees the usefulness of an 'other' language as a tool
> to articulate what he cannot say in his native tongue and to express an alternative
> identity for himself.[136]

While I am unsure if 'native tongue' refers to Arabic 'broadly' speaking or
dārija in particular, I nevertheless disagree both with Orlando's statement that
French is 'a tool to articulate what he cannot say in' *fuṣḥā* or *dārija* and with her
interpretation that the film scene recasts French 'into something positive'. Instead
I would argue that the film scene (which is not a part of the novel) pinpoints the
powerful position of French in Morocco and that the only resistance strategy is
to take control of this language to subvert it from within (a practice reminiscent
of the textual violence of the *Souffles* movement). As I have outlined earlier, the
publishing industry is dominated by French cultural and economic interests that
make it more prestigious and profitable for Moroccan authors to write and publish
in French. Moreover, as Alalamy argues, the Moroccan reading public seems more
inclined to read in French than in Arabic. Taïa's choice of French as language of
literary expression is therefore strategic, as it brings with it a cultural capital which
he successfully has used to serve his agenda of addressing homosexuality and
LGBT rights publicly in Morocco.

Second, Taïa has argued that French guarantees him a certain distance from
himself and from Moroccan society.[137] Just as Kilito paraphrases, Taïa maintains
that he is incapable of writing in any other language: in other words, that it is
precisely by distancing himself from his own background – poverty, social norms,
taboos and so on – and through his confrontational relation with the French
language that he could become an author. However, when confronted with

culturalist conceptions of languages as monolithic carriers of particular cultural values, Taïa time and again has been forced to demonstrate that he has neither betrayed his own background nor in some magical way been liberated by writing in French:

أكتب بالفرنسية مجبراً! هذا يدفعني إلى الشعور بأنني خائن. خائن لعائلتي ولأصولي. إذن, لقد أخذت وضعية "العدو" بطريقة ما. هذا يؤرقني ويؤلمني أحياناً. لكن مع ذلك, فقد نقلت هذه العلاقة المركبة والصدامية مع الفرنسية والأصول إلى كتاباتي. أنا خائن . . . لكنني أجبر اللغة الفرنسية على تقبل العربية, بثقافتها و بناها اللغوية ومخيالها.[138]

(I am forced to write in French! This makes me feel like a traitor. A traitor to my family and my roots. Consequently, I have somehow assumed the status of 'the enemy'. This bothers me and pains me sometimes. Nevertheless, I have transferred this complex and confrontational relationship with French and my roots to my writings. I am a traitor . . . but I force the French language to accept Arabic, its culture, and its linguistic structure and imagination.)

Like Laâbi and Khatibi, he counters accusations of acculturation with arguments that he is pursuing a 'textual violence'. That is, by deconstructing the French language, his literary practices become an expression of transculturation – but transculturation in a multiple sense, as he is bridging the language of the rich and the language of the French with the reality of being poor, Moroccan and homosexual. Moreover, he insists that agency lies with him, not with the French language:

Le français ne m'a pas libéré, ne m'a pas aidé. Je le dis avec une arrogance presque assumée: c'est moi qui ai rempli cette chose qu'on appelle la langue française avec ma volonté et mon désir d'y arriver coûte que coûte. [. . .] je ne pourrai jamais dire que c'est le fait d'étudier le français et la littérature française qui m'a libéré en tant qu'homosexuel.[139]

(French has not freed me, it has not helped me. I say this with an almost assumed arrogance: it is I who has filled this thing called the French language with my will and my desire to achieve something at all costs. [. . .] I can never say that it is because I have studied French and French literature that I have liberated myself as homosexual.)

By reclaiming agency, Taïa insists that his creative writing – in spite of the hegemonic position of *la francophonie* – is his achievement; he filled this language with his stories, he paid the price for telling them and he, not the French language, is the one to be credited for the impact of his writing and activism. Moreover, Taïa has, in interviews, become very careful to underline that the fact that he cannot write in any other language does not imply that what he writes is impossible to express in, for instance, Arabic. Writing in French is his creative choice. Tellingly, this question of agency permeates his writing, as I have already demonstrated in my analysis of *L'Armée du salut* and as I will elaborate in my analysis of *Un Pays pour mourir*.

'Narrate or die'

'Je suis libre. À Paris et libre.' (I'm free. In Paris and free.)[140] These are the thoughts of the Moroccan prostitute Zahira at the beginning of *Un Pays pour mourir*. Just like her transgender friend Aziz from Algeria and the homosexual Mojtaba from Iran, Zahira has arrived in Paris driven by a desire for freedom, but she soon realizes that she is all alone: 'Ignorante j'étais. Malheureuse je suis. Et seule. Si seule à Paris. Au centre et pourtant comme au bout du monde.' (Ignorant I was. Unhappy I am. And alone. So alone in Paris. At the centre and yet as if at the end of the world.)[141] The three protagonists have all migrated to detach themselves from the taboos and laws of submission that permeate their home countries. But instead of finding freedom, they have ended up living marginalized lives, not much better than what they left behind. They are stranded in Paris without belonging; uprooted, but unable to let go of their roots because the only thing they have left is their dreams and their first memories.

In *Un Pays pour mourir* the stories of Zahira, Aziz and Mojtaba are interwoven while competing with and being infiltrated by other stories in the form of memories of past lives, letters, broken dreams and hopes for the future. Of interest is, thus, not simply how Taïa has given stories and voices to illegal immigrants in Paris, but how these voices infiltrate one another and dominant historical narratives, while simultaneously disturbing the relation between autobiography and fiction. In *Un Pays pour mourir*, stories and voices intermingle to fight off oblivion and indifference and thereby to force the French language, the language of power, to speak for the silent and invisible, who in turn come to haunt French language and literature.

Like Scheherazade in *A Thousand and One Nights*, the protagonists in *Un Pays pour mourir* struggle to keep death at arm's length by narrating and dreaming. 'Narrate or die', which is Scheherazade's condition of life, must in this context be understood both literally and metaphorically: the only way for them to exist – as woman, prostitute, homosexual, transgender and Muslim immigrant – is by narrating their stories. As Fatema Mernissi notes in *Scheherazade Goes West* (2001), Scheherazade has become the symbol of human rights in the Arab world. She is the political heroine who keeps a tyrant at bay through the power of intellect and imagination, and as a storyteller, she represents the triumph of reason and dialogue over violence. With their voices as their only weapon, storytelling becomes a site of resistance for the marginalized and unrecognized in *Un Pays pour mourir*. In this respect, *Un Pays pour mourir* is significantly different from *Amour bilingue*. Contrary to Khatibi, Taïa's simple vocabulary and the emotional vulnerability of his characters are meant to spellbind the reader in order to bring the characters to life. That is, Taïa plays with classical storytelling in a completely different manner than Khatibi's metafictional wandering.

Un Pays pour mourir is moreover an autobiographical gesture, staking out an experimental nation for Taïa's younger self – the innocent, naive and spontaneous effeminate boy who was lost forever when he became a teenager – and for all other queer lives that have been subjected to the violence of public erasure. Significantly, the novel opens with Zahira recalling the death of her father, and how he was tucked away and ignored for two years before he died. As Jean-Pierre Boulé[142] has also argued, this story mirrors Taïa's narration in *Lettres à un jeune marocain* (2009) of the death of his own father after four years of illness.[143] Moreover, the gentle but furious father of *Un Pays pour mourir* is reminiscent of the impassioned and irrational father of *L'Armée du salut*. In both novels Taïa displaces normative gender roles through a father figure who has been deprived of authority and a mother figure who is the dictator of the family house.

'Mais lui, mon petit papa doux et furieux, il n'a eu le temps pour rien. Ni pour bien vivre ni pour bien mourir. C'est arrivé vite. Deux ans à peine.' (But he, my gentle and furious little father, had no time for anything. Neither to live well nor to die well. It happened quickly. Barely two years.)[144] There is something ironic about the sentence 'c'est arrivé vite', as two years of dying is not only long in itself but incredibly long in the novel, because the family withers along with him:

> Chez nous, personne n'a changé, n'a bougé. On se regarde comme avant. On se frôle. On en a marre d'être ensemble. Il faut partir, c'est urgent. Mais nous n'avons nulle part où aller rêver autrement. Alors: on s'aveugle. On ne chante plus. On mange, on pisse, on chie, on dort. Personne ne jouit ici. Surtout pas la mère.[145]

> (At our place, no one has changed, no one has moved. We look at each other as before. We brush against each other. We're tired of being together. We have to leave, it's urgent. But we have nowhere to go, to dream otherwise. So: we blind ourselves. We no longer sing. We eat, we piss, we shit, we sleep. No one enjoys here. Especially not the mother.)

It is precisely the insistence that 'no one has changed' that reveals that everything has changed. Everyone in the house is trying to continue his or her daily life, but all are haunted by the steps of their sick father, whom their mother has installed on the first floor of the house and forbidden the children to see. Exiled in his own house, Zahira's father is ignored and slowly forgotten, but the sound of his footsteps – 'boum-boum, boum-boum. Boum-boum'[146] – becomes the rhythm of Zahira's life. When he was living upstairs and she lay in bed frightened that she might die while sleeping, his footsteps would mirror a calm heartbeat and gently helped her fall asleep as she gradually ceased to be conscious of him. But the footsteps are also what prevent her from forgetting him: as an adult, it is the sound of his footsteps in her head that makes her remember him; and it is his footsteps that haunt her, because she feels guilty for accepting her mother's decision.[147] Moreover, the sound of his footsteps becomes the rhythm of the novel which is dominated by main clauses and sentence fragments, such as 'Je suis libre. À Paris et libre.', 'C'est arrive vite. Deux ans à peine.' or 'Personne ne jouit ici. Surtout pas la mère.' Contrary to Khatibi Taïa uses rhetorical devices of spoken language and of oral storytelling, which provide rhythm to the narrative and intensify the narrative voices.

Just as Taïa, in his letter to his nephew, Adnane, in *Lettres à un jeune marocain*, writes 'mon père, Adnane, je l'ai tué' (my father, Adnane, I've killed him)[148] to confess that he and his siblings were turned into 'criminels insensibles' (insensible criminals)[149] the moment they accepted being barred from seeing their father, Zahira confesses to murdering her father by neither questioning nor resisting her mother's decision to 'protect' her children from their father's illness.[150] However, by not only remembering her father's story but also retelling it *to* her dead father, Zahira reverses his erasure and death. The story of her father reveals that nothing can truly die, but lives on as an instance of cryptic haunting. However, the story of Zahira and her father is ambiguous. The father might live on in her, but she died along with him.[151]

This ambiguity sets the frame of *Un Pays pour mourir*. While the dead might haunt the living, the forgotten our common history, there is no reconciliation in *Un Pays pour mourir*. As an experimental nation, the novel itself becomes a site of reconciliation where death and self-destruction constitute new beginnings. The ambiguous relationship between life and death is also reflected in the title of the novel, which is inspired by the expression 'Ce n'est pas un pays pour vivre, le Maroc, c'est un pays pour mourir' (It is not a country to live in, Morocco, it is a country to die in),[152] spoken by someone struck by social injustice. But in the novel, it is not only Morocco that is 'un pays pour mourir' – or France, for that matter. With nowhere to belong, everywhere becomes a place to die. Tellingly, death in the novel is something that happens 'out of place', whether in the exile of your own home (the suicide of Zahira's father), as an implication of gender reassignment surgery (Aziz), or as a murder in your haunted dreams (Zahira). Accordingly, the novel itself is a place to die and live on as an instance of cryptic haunting.

Oblivious foreigners

In an interview with *Al Huffington Post Maghreb-Maroc*, Taïa has described the intermingling of voices in the novel as reflecting what could be described as a polyphonic song of resistance: 'Quand il n'y a que le noir dans ce monde, il reste le chant libre pour survivre, aller jusqu'à la mort. Ecrire, c'est chanter pour moi. Oser chanter encore et encore, malgré les critiques et les ricanements incessants.' (When there is nothing but darkness in this world, what is left is the free song to survive, until death. To write, that is to sing to me. To dare to sing again and again, in spite of criticism and incessant sneers.)[153] To the characters in *Un Pays pour mourir*, daring to speak and scream – either to one another or, deliriously, to themselves and to the dead – equals singing to survive. Beyond their despair and their desire for death, they dream of freedom. It is this dream that makes them 'sing' in spite of everything, and this 'singing' is what distinguishes Taïa's 'oblivious foreigners' (my designation) from Khatibi's professional foreigner. That is, while Khatibi plays with the overflow of meaning present in *bi-langue*, Taïa's language is cut to the bone. The transparency of the thoughts of the characters in *Un Pays pour mourir* contrasts the opacity of Khatibi's writing in *Amour bilingue*. However, both transparency and opacity play with the French language. Taïa's minimalistic writing is not mere colloquialism, but his literary technique of writing in main clauses and sentence fragments adds a sense of obliviousness and naivity to the thoughts of the characters.

In *Un Pays pour mourir*, narratives and voices alternate between melancholy and madness, between desiring and deferring death, as in the story of Aziz/ Zannouba. Two long monologues – one by Aziz before his gender reassignment surgery, one by Zannouba after her surgery – form the story of Aziz/Zannouba. In part one, chapter two, Aziz's monologue is addressed to Zahira, who is almost completely silent – even when he poses direct questions Aziz answers himself. Significantly, only the passage where Aziz asks her to choose his new name forms a dialogue; the rest of the chapter is Aziz rambling associatively as in a stream of consciousness rather than as words spoken to someone else. This blurring of dialogue and internal monologue underlines the coming together of euphoria, madness and despair, now that Aziz's gender reassignment surgery is finally a reality: 'Demain, je la coupe' (Tomorrow, I cut it off).[154] Aziz is excited to 'quitter enfin ce territoire maudit des hommes!' (finally leave this damned territory of men!),[155] but the long monologue simultaneously reveals the unfathomable nature of the transformation he is about to undergo. Significantly, the story of Aziz/ Zannouba is not about sexuality but gender identity. Nevertheless, his gender performance simultaneously subverts sexual norms, whether heteronormativity or homonormativity. Aziz/Zannouba's sexual orientation is unclear, but because Aziz identifies as female, society has turned him into the passive object of (closet) gay men's desire and, in turn, made him hate men.[156]

With his gender reassignment surgery, Aziz is resisting not just heteronormativity but also homonormativity. On the one hand, his surgery constitutes a reversal of society's demand that he enters into the world of men at the age of thirteen. Tellingly, he himself defines this 'rite of passage' as a transformation that forced him to start wearing the mask of man, rather than leave behind the mask of childhood femininity: 'Mon Malheur a commence à ce moment-là, quand on m'a dit que l'enfance était terminée et qu'il était temps de porter le masque de l'homme. Ce n'était pas un conseil. C'était un ordre répété chaque jour et chaque nuit.' (My Misfortune began at that time, when I was told that childhood was over and that it was time to wear the mask of man. It was not advice. It was a repeated order every day and every night.)[157] Like Zekri's identification of circumcision and expulsion from the female hammam as two markers of heteronormativity which exert a symbolic violence on the homosexual body, separation from his sisters, with whom Aziz was free to cross-dress, destroyed him. Suddenly, all meaning of life was lost. One night he decided to 'ne plus exister. Je n'allais plus être un Algérien. Ni un Arabe. Ni musulman. Ni un Africain. Rien de tout cela. Je suis devenu dur. Un monstre. Un dégénéré. Sans but, sans guerre à mener' (no longer exist. I was no longer going to be Algerian. Nor Arab. Nor Muslim. Nor African. Nothing of all this. I turned hard. Became a monster. A degenerate. Without purpose, without a war to wage).[158] The story of Aziz is, in this respect, reminiscent of how Taïa was forced to annihilate himself and withdraw into silence when he was thirteen.[159]

By contrast with the 'manhood' that Aziz was forced to assume, childhood was a space of obliviousness towards social norms and conduct, where Aziz(a) could be girl and boy at the same time: 'Aziz. Aziza. Je pense les deux. Tout en continuant à chanter et à danser, je les mélange.' (Aziz. Aziza. I think both. While continuing to sing and dance, I mix them.)[160] It is this childhood happiness that Aziz wants to revive with his gender reassignment surgery. Rediscovering oblivious happiness is his way of resisting oppressive social norms and regulations:

> Quitter mon sexe, mon genre, les hommes, être une femme. Être une de mes sœurs. Avec elles. Loin d'elles. Couper tout ce qui est masculine en moi pour le devenir. Me réconcilier avec le petit enfant en gloire que j'avais été. L'écouter. Réaliser son rêve. Sa vrai nature. L'aimer de nouveau, enfin.[161]

> (Leave my sex, my gender, men, be a woman. Be one of my sisters. With them. Far from them. Cut all that is masculine in me to become it. Reconcile myself with the glorious little child I had been. Listen to it. Realize its dream. Its true nature. Love it again, at last.)

In contrast to Khatibi's whiting out of gender differences as a simultaneous whiting out of language differences embodied in *bi-langue* and the professional foreigner, the story of Aziz represents a desire for whiting out gender differences so as to return to obliviousness. However, while the storyline reveals the impossibility of a return to this childhood happiness because of the sociocultural norms that continue to haunt the life of Zannouba, it is nevertheless the obliviousness of the characters that subverts the same sociocultural norms, and it is through a deliberately naive and transparent language that they reinvent themselves.

On the other hand, Aziz's gender reassignment surgery reflects a resistance to the (closet) gay milieu; that is, both those Arabs who are afraid of coming out and therefore need him to be the effeminate, passive other, and his French customers, who desire him as effeminate, exoticized other. His surgery is thus a reaction against homonormativity and its heterosexual mimicking, which stigmatizes effeminate men and the trans-community as much as heteronormativity does. Trapped in this stereotype as effeminate, passive and exoticized other, Aziz nevertheless claims his freedom: by parodying the role he is expected to play, he reveals that those who are afraid of coming out because of the accompanying stigmatization are the ones who are not free:

> Encore un Arabe gay incapable de s'assumer. Franchement, de quoi ont-ils peur? Tu le sais, toi? Ce n'est que du cul. Deux sexes qui se rencontrent, se touchent, jouissent ensemble, reviennent à l'enfance ensemble. C'est facile à admettre, à comprendre, non? On veut tous baiser. Enfin, pas tous. Moi, j'aspire à autre chose.[162]

> (Another gay Arab incapable of coming out. Frankly, what are they afraid of? Do you know? It's just ass. Two sexes that meet, touch, enjoy together, return to childhood together. It's easy to admit, to understand, right? We all want to fuck. Well, not all of us. I aspire to something else.)

Unlike his customers, Aziz is out in the open; he cross-dresses, and while his clothes and makeup make his customers see him as an effeminate, passive other whom they can penetrate, his drag performance subverts the passive = feminine/ active = masculine relation: he is as virile as them, whereas they turn out to be unable to come unless he sticks a finger or two up their ass.

Moreover, it is his French gay customers who advise him not to go through with his surgery. While this concern might be justified given Zannouba's emotional reaction after her surgery, Aziz nevertheless depicts them as trapped by a hegemonic order not all that different from his closet-gay Arab customers. However, both his rambling before surgery and her reaction after surgery reveal an ambiguity as s/he is governed by the same normativity s/he is trying to subvert. While Aziz mocks the closet-gay Arabs for their hypocrisy, Zannouba is unable to call her sisters after surgery, because she is afraid that even those s/he was closest to when s/he was a child may have been enslaved by 'tradition'. Once again, this solitude and the distance between Zannouba and her sisters mirror Taïa's own solitude and the distance between him and his sisters and brothers when he first came out.

In part two, chapter one, Zannouba has locked herself up in her apartment after her surgery: 'Je ne vois personne. Je ne veux pas voir dans les yeux des autres le monstre que je suis devenue. Leur fausse compréhension. Leur pitié. Leur malaise. Leur gentillesse forcée. Alors, je mets tout le monde à l'écart.' (I don't see anyone. I don't want to see in the eyes of others the monster that I've become. Their false understanding. Their pity. Their discomfort. Their forced kindness. So I held everyone at bay.)[163] The happiness s/he thought s/he would find after surgery failed to appear:

> Je devrais me sentir femme. Être heureuse. Joyeuse. Faire une fête. Être légère, comme avant. Comme dans mes rêves d'avant.
> C'est l'inverse qui m'arrive.
> Je pleure jour et nuit. Nuit et jour.[164]

> (I should feel like a woman. Be happy. Joyful. Throw a party. Be gentle, like before. Like in my dreams before.
> It is the opposite that has happened to me.
> I cry day and night. Night and day.)

Identifying as the 'monster' she thinks everyone sees her as – just as Taïa identified as 'monster' in 'L'Homosexualité expliquée à ma mère'[165] – she is ashamed of not feeling as 'feminine' as she thought she would become.[166] Her solitude and desperation then turn into a delirious conversation between her former 'I', Aziz, and his new 'I', Zannouba; a last conversation permeated by fear of letting go of the little boy who, with the gender reassignment surgery, is gone forever, and desperation at not knowing how to be the girl s/he has always felt herself to be. Paradoxically, Aziz/Zannouba's effort to reverse growing up through gender reassignment surgery turns out to kill the little boy, Aziz, forever, and instead of returning to childhood happiness Zannouba finds herself at the edge of an abyss.

There is thus no reconciliation in the story of Aziz/Zannouba. Aziz is dead, and Zannouba is nothing without him. However, Zannouba is nevertheless, in all her desperation, Aziz's reinvention of himself. Zannouba becomes for Aziz both a place to die and a place to live on. She is his last combat and his last effort to resist oppressive sociocultural norms. But she does not know what to do, and the story ends with her desperately calling out for Aziz: 'Reviens. Reviens. Reviens.' (Come back. Come back. Come back.)[167]

Reinventing the 'self'

The day Zahira's father fell ill and was hospitalized (before being installed on the first floor) was the same day Zahira – as a lycée student – got paid for sex for the first time. While the two events are unconnected insofar as Zahira did not know her father had been hospitalized until she returned home later in the afternoon, they are narrated as if they – together – constitute a rite of passage from innocent childhood to acceptance of the unkind reality of adulthood. From that day, Zahira's profession is prostitution, and it is this profession she wants to display in Paris.[168]

However, as an illegal immigrant, her love for this 'city of freedom' is unreturned; she remains invisible, and her sense of belonging is contested not only by her status as illegal immigrant but also by the fact that not even her friends recognize her effort to find her true place in this world. Tellingly, the chapter is entitled 'au centre'; but while it narrates the life of Zahira at the centre of Paris, it simultaneously reveals her marginalized position. In her own way, however, Zahira resists this position by reinventing the purpose of her profession. In Paris, she is not *any* kind of prostitute; she is a prostitute to her fellow Muslim and Arab immigrants:

> C'est devenu ma spécialité. Les hommes arabes ou musulmanes de Paris. La plupart sans papiers. La plupart usés par cette ville qui les maltraite sans remords et par des patrons français blancs qui les exploitent au noir sans éprouver aucune culpabilité.
>
> Des Turcs. Des Égyptiens. Des Tunisiens. Des Algériens. Des Indiens. Des Marocains aussi, mais rarement. Quelques hommes déchus des pays du Golfe.
>
> Ma préférence, de loin, va aux pakistanais. Iqbal ne ressemble pas aux hommes sri lankais. Il fait plutôt pakistanais. Un peu plus dur qu'eux, pourtant.[169]

(It has become my specialty. Arab or Muslim men in Paris. Most of them undocumented. Most of them worn out by this city, which mistreats them without remorse, and by white French patrons who exploit them on the black market without feeling any guilt.

Turks. Egyptians. Tunisians. Algerians. Indians. Moroccans too, but rarely. Some fallen men from the Gulf countries.

My preference, by far, goes to the Pakistanis. Iqbal doesn't look like Sri Lankan men. He's rather Pakistani. A little harder than them, though.)

Feeling like a sister to these Arab and Muslim men, she lets them have her, even though they cannot pay what she charges. Sometimes she even offers herself for free, because she feels a certain affection for these men and cannot bear sending them home frustrated. In this respect, she turns prostitution into charity work, but paradoxically her generosity stands in the way of her own dream of becoming Iqbal's wife. On the one hand, she argues that she is working day and night to marry Iqbal; on the other hand, satisfying her poorly paying customers seems to have a purpose in itself. Moreover, while she claims that Paris is the place where she will be a prostitute out in the open, she keeps her profession a secret from Iqbal, and when he finds out that two of his friends have paid her for sex, he loses all respect for her. Not even her Sri Lankan boyfriend acknowledges her place and purpose in this world. Significantly, Zahira's description of Iqbal as 'he's rather Pakistani' reveals a hierarchy among immigrants where Sri Lankans are placed at the bottom of the ladder; but even at this 'bottom', there is no room for the dreams of a prostitute. In the end, Zahira ends up being nothing but a sexual object of Iqbal's desire. Despite her effort to have her sorcerers turn Iqbal towards her, nothing will likely change.

Another attempt to reinvent Paris is related to the story of Mojtaba and Zahira. Mojtaba and Zahira's first encounter is at Couronnes metro. Once again, Zahira, without knowing why, finds herself drawn to help this lost boy, and when he passes out, she is already holding him.[170] But instead of taking Mojtaba to a hospital, she takes him home and watches over him until he wakes up. They become friends and end up observing Ramadan together, but without knowing anything about each other. Zahira does not tell Mojtaba that she works as a prostitute. Mojtaba does not tell Zahira that he is homosexual, and that in fear of his life he had to flee Iran because of his involvement in the 2009 revolution. Being nobody together, they live an uncomplicated month. Towards the end of Ramadan, they go out to discover Paris and the tourist attractions that Zahira had always thought were not for her. The climax of their tour around the city is the Jardin du Luxembourg, which Mojtaba has always dreamed of visiting. They arrive just one hour before the garden is closing, but instead of leaving after an hour, they hide, and for one night they have the garden all to themselves.[171] For a fleeting moment, they conquer a part of Paris that was never meant for them. But while Zahira wishes for this moment with Mojtaba to last, she simultaneously wants to go back to her Paris. The Jardin du Luxembourg is not hers and never will be, and significantly her moment with Mojtaba ends without her having a say in it.[172] Ultimately, the story of Mojtaba and the Jardin du Luxembourg becomes another story of how difficult it is to reinvent oneself: the Jardin du Luxembourg is conquered and lost in the glimpse of a moment, and the next chapter opens with the words: 'Elle doit mourir' (She must die).[173]

The story of Zahira is concluded through the story of Allal, her boyfriend when she was young, and whom her parents would not accept as her husband because he was black. With the help of *jinn*s, Allal comes to kill Zahira in her dreams in Paris. As the invisible among the invisibles, he wants to revenge the humiliation Zahira inflicted on him: first by not standing up for him in front of her parents, and second by becoming a prostitute. Like all the characters in the novel, Zahira cannot escape her past. But these characters are not mere victims. All of them reclaim agency, and while they might not effect the changes they dream of, they nevertheless manage to reinvent themselves in the midst of their marginalization. Zannouba is Aziz's reinvention of himself, the Arab and Muslim customers are Zahira's, and death as two lovers' final reunion is Allal's. But as they do not effect any changes in their surroundings, this reinvention is inextricably linked to death. Zannouba becomes both a place to die and a place to live on for Aziz, just as Zahira's dreams do for her. As in Khatibi's *Amour bilingue*, where love and violence interpenetrate, in *Un Pays pour mourir* life and death go hand in hand; but as both life and death take on new meaning in the novel, their reinvention embodies an effort of space making similar to *bi-langue*.

The professional foreigner

While Khatibi's androgynous body draw on a Sufi tradition of transcending normative gender categories, Taïa's bodies are possessed by *jinns*, and their noises, voices and screams provide rhythm to his prose just as the haunting footsteps of Zahira's father. In this respect, the question of writing in French is symbiotically linked to the narrations of queer subject positions in both novels.

As a love story that sees double *Amour bilingue* is an autobiography of the bilingual experience, and the protagonist's incessant wandering between languages, sexes and cultures mirrors the text's back-and-forth movement between poetry, narrative and philosophical reflections. In all aspects, *Amour bilingue* is a literary play with identity and difference and thus an early story both by and about what Khatibi later termed 'the professional foreigner'. As Zekri argues, the professional foreigner, as he was first depicted in *Un été à Stockholm* (1990), is precisely someone who is neither one with his 'origin' nor completely cut off from it:

> Le fait de concevoir une étrangété opératoire permet de déjouer les fixations identitaires en leur donnant de nouvelles configurations générées par processus. La figure de l'étranger est éclairante à cet égard puisqu'elle nous rappelle la double exigence de ne pas assimiler l'étranger à son origine, mais aussi de ne pas éradiquer son passé, c'est-à-dire sa généalogie identitaire.[174]

> (The fact of conceiving an operational foreignness enables a thwarting of identity fixations by giving them new configurations generated by the process. The figure of the foreigner is illuminating in this regard since it reminds us of the double requirement not to assimilate the foreigner with his origin, but also not to eradicate his past, that is to say his identity genealogy.)

The professional foreigner is in this respect not a static figure, just as the transnation is not a set space. Both can take on any appearance, depending on the linguistic, cultural or social experiences of this professional foreigner:

Une expérience, mon expérience de la langue d'écriture tissée à une double, multiple langue m'a appris au moins ceci: toute œuvre réside, habite dans son unicité solitaire. À cette unicité si singulière, je donne depuis quelques années le nom d'étranger professionnel.[175]

(An experience, my experience of written language woven with a double, multiple language has at least taught me this: every work resides or lives in its own solitary uniqueness. To this so singular uniqueness I have for some years given the name professional foreigner.)

In this respect, Taïa is a professional foreigner, and his 'poor' French is the literary outcome of his personal experience with bilingualism and the written language. Moreover, though the difference between Khatibi's hermetic avant-gardism and Taïa's 'poor' French is significant, one should not mistake it for a difference between an intellectual and a non-intellectual author. Taïa is well educated with a PhD from Sorbonne on Fragonard and the libertine novel of the eighteenth century, and the naive rambling of his narrators is as much a literary play with identity and difference as Khatibi's *bi-langue*. That is, while Taïa's literary language appears stripped of ambiguity, it nevertheless enhances his characters' refusal to fit into any fixed identity categories – whether cultural, ethnic or sexual identities.

Just as Khatibi whites out the difference between languages and sexes through *bi-langue* and the androgyne body, Taïa whites out the difference between knowledge and ignorance, madness and sanity, hysteria and control through characters speaking and screaming in 'poor' French. That is, through a simple but intense language, which mirrors the emotional vulnerability of the characters, the reader is drawn into a world where linguistic, cultural and sexual binaries are subverted. In *Un Pays our mourir* none of the characters effect any changes, but by narrating their stories to themselves and to one another, they infiltrate dominant narratives by reinventing themselves as the heroes they were never allowed to be.

Chapter 5

SHAME, SILENCE AND NATION BUILDING

FATNA EL BOUIH'S *ḤADĪTH AL-ʿATMAH*
AND ABDELLAH TAÏA'S *INFIDÈLES*

Since the 1990s, and increasingly since the death of King Hassan II in 1999, the proliferation of Moroccan prison testimonies, written by political prisoners incarcerated during the Years of Lead, has contributed significantly to the restoration of Moroccan historical memory. As Susan Slyomovics argues in *The Performance of Human Rights in Morocco* (2005), the literary documentation of human rights abuses has, along with other public performance strategies, ensured the visibility of an otherwise suppressed memory.[1] Moreover, a new historiographical tradition encompassing gendered memories has been and still is challenging dominant patriarchal historiography in Morocco. However, this (re-)construction of national history and cultural memory remains ambivalent. Whereas women are still often stereotypically gendered and identified with the passive and 'helping hand' roles, Abdellah Taïa's novel *Infidèles* (2012) reveals that new efforts to include women in national historiography still exclude many others who remain silenced and marginalized – be they prostitutes, homosexuals, transgenders or others. Though *Infidèles* is significantly different from testimonial literature written by former political prisoners, Taïa's transformation of his childhood memories into a fictional narrative nevertheless provides a significant testimony of the Years of Lead. Similarly to *L'Armée du salut* and *Un Pays pour mourir*, *Infidèles* constitutes an effort to call queer identities into existence while simultaneously engaging in a larger effort to rewrite Moroccan history in order to include the stories of those who were not considered part of national recovery.

Like the silence to which Taïa turned to protect himself as a teenager,[2] the silence of women victims of political violence has the double function of protecting them from social stigmatization and upholding hegemonic narrations of the 'nation'. In this respect, the characterization of women as 'silent keepers of memory' – and their testimonies as too horrific to be voiced in public – has excluded women from the public sphere by transforming them into untouchable and silent representatives of 'national purity'. But the long and arduous struggle by Moroccan women to secure the recognition of women's rights as human rights has reappropriated and reconfigured Moroccan history and communal solidarity; and women's testimonies have effectively challenged their sociocultural positioning as silent witnesses. Along this line, women's testimonies have become a significant part of feminist politics. By making public women's experiences of violence and suffering, testimonial writing effectively disturbs the conception of politics as a masculine space and the nation as a feminine ideal transcending politics.

In her testimony *Ḥadīth al-ʿatmah* (2001) former political prisoner Fatna El Bouih narrates prison space as a 'dialogue of suffering' in order to reappropriate and reconfigure Moroccan history, language and community through the heterogeneous voices of women. Since the end of the Cold War, human rights have become the predominant moral narrative of international politics. Consequently, bearing witness to human rights abuses has become part of a transnational public sphere. Importantly in this respect, El Bouih's testimony orchestrates a multiplicity of voices, which dismantle the idea that the category 'woman' denotes a common identity and that the oppression of women has a singular form while it simultaneously forms part of a collective struggle to secure women's rights. In this sense, El Bouih's locally grounded approach to human rights and gendered violence mirrors Taïa's narration of sexuality, violence and social stigmatization in *Infidèles*.

Thus, this chapter explores how Moroccan authors have (re)articulated the role of shame and silence in the process of national reconciliation and the healing of past wounds. In Chapter 2, I explored how the question of silence that surrounds homosexuality in Morocco relates to a larger debate about 'authentic' Moroccan culture. In this chapter, I will investigate how the same cultural practices are at work in the process of national reconciliation and in the characterization of women as 'silent keepers of memory'. I will begin the chapter with outlining the context of women's activism and gendered memories of political violence because it is within this opening towards gendered memory work that El Bouih's and Taïa's disturbance of the relationship between 'monstrosity' and cultural and religious norms must be understood. Then I will provide an analysis of El Bouih's *Ḥadīth al-ʿatmah* with a focus on how social constructions of masculinity and femininity shape the way in which prison violence is exerted, experienced and narrated. That is, how the torturers perform masculinity in their exertion of power; how gender is reflected in women prisoners' experiences of violence, both political and criminal prisoners; and how El Bouih both depicts and resists these social constructions of gender in her representation of her prison experiences. I will conclude the chapter with an analysis of Taïa's *Infidèles*, with a focus on how he subverts the relation between 'normality' and 'monstrosity' in his narration of the stories of Saâdia, Slima and Jallal. That is, I will analyse how Taïa's interconnection of the Years of Lead, a xenophobic Europe and Islamic terrorism disturbs our conception of love and violence, good and evil, right and wrong.

Gendered memories of political violence during the Years of Lead

Moroccan feminist activists have, since the 1990s, successfully pushed for the recognition of women's rights as human rights. With the officially recognized gender approach of the Moroccan Equity and Reconciliation Commission (ERC) from 2004, women's experiences of violence during the Years of Lead have received political and legal recognition.[3] As Nadia Guessous argues in the ERC study, 'Women and Political Violence during the Years of Lead' (2009),[4] the gendered effects of political violence are numerous, and women have suffered in multiple ways from the effects of violence during the Years of Lead.[5] But until recently, the suffering of women has been more or less invisible and unacknowledged in collective memory work. Because the public sphere of politics and conflict usually is associated with men, women's suffering has been held secret and confined to the private sphere because of the risk of social stigmatization.

With ERC's gender approach, this has changed significantly in Morocco. But, as Bettina Dennerlein argues, the official discourse on women and political violence remains ambiguous.[6] Women's activism is still often de-politicized, and women are stereotypically gendered and identified with the passive and 'helping hand' roles, as well as reduced to indirect and accidental victims of violence and repression. Thus even studies dedicated to documenting women victims of political violence, at times, reproduce stereotypes and social roles that ultimately reinforce structural violence against women. However, the oral testimonies collected through the ERC study nevertheless contribute significantly to the documentation of the multiple configurations of women's roles in political resistance, as well as their suffering from state violence.

According to the study, women targeted by the state during the Years of Lead can be divided into four main groups: (1) women relatives of political activists, living in rural and marginalized areas; (2) women from rural and marginalized communities targeted for collective punishment; (3) women relatives of political activists, living in urban centres; and (4) politically active women.[7] Thus while the study 'highlights the fact that political violence is gendered and that being a woman made a difference in the experience of violence, it also suggests that not all women experienced political violence in the same ways'.[8] Class, culture, region, generation, family status, educational level and relationship to politics all had an effect on women's experiences of state-sponsored political violence.

Focusing on gendered experiences of political violence requires paying attention to the risk of essentializing gender differences, while simultaneously acknowledging that women, because of a gendered social system, have experienced political violence differently from men. Particularly in rural areas, women were often kept in the dark about the political activism of male relatives and were therefore completely unprepared for the violence they encountered. Because of gendered divisions of labour and space, illiterate rural women in particular had limited access to the public sphere and the world of politics, and often their husbands did not inform them about their activism.[9] While this might have been out of a desire to protect their wives, it nevertheless deprived the women of the possibility of taking precautions and preparing for state retaliation, which only heightened their sense of injustice and betrayal.[10] But despite their lack of knowledge, these women were not spared. With respect to violence and torture, women and men were, in many respects, treated equally horrifically:

> Like their male counterparts, they were illegally detained in inhumane conditions; interrogations of women often involved cruelty and torture; they were deprived of their most basic rights while in detention; and were kept under surveillance and repeatedly harassed by state authorities after their release. This was as true for politically active women as it was for female relatives of political activists and members of their community. [. . .] Women, like their male counterparts were tortured. Being female did not exempt them from torture nor did it seem to elicit any sympathy or lenience from prison guards. Women were beaten all over their bodies, sometimes with sticks and belts; they were kicked, punched, electrocuted, and suffocated; they were submerged in water, made to drink dirty or salty water, and hung from their legs; they were emotionally tortured, threatened with death, humiliated, verbally abused and emotionally tormented.[11]

Gendered and sexualized forms of abuse were multifold. As a deliberate technique of shaming, women were often left naked despite the presence of male guards or male prisoners.[12] During menstruation they were deprived of sanitary napkins and left to bleed and soil themselves, and many women suffered from increased menstrual cramps because of the poor conditions in prison.[13] Women were forcibly separated from their children (down to six-month-old babies), tortured in front of their children, or forced to watch their children being tortured.[14] Body searches in the street were often performed to 'identify' their gender as a form of sexual harassment that served to isolate victims of political violence from other members of their community, who would keep their distance out of fear of harassment.[15] Rape and sexual assault occurred frequently, and women prisoners lived in constant fear of sexual violence.

It is, however, worth mentioning, as Laura Menin has demonstrated,[16] that sexualized violence was not confined to women. It was also directed against male prisoners to reinforce their 'feelings of powerlessness by unsettling their sense of masculinity'.[17] Just as a gendered social system prescribes specific roles for women, it imposes a norm of 'masculinity' on men, but male prisoners were systematically deprived of the ability to live up to this normativity. The same heteronormative social system that ostracizes LGBT persons was thus turned against male prisoners during the Years of Lead as a means of shaming. As Nour-Eddine Saoudi, a former political prisoner, explains in an interview with Menin in 2013:

> In their system of violence the macho dimension was part of their way to destabilize and break the male prisoners' morale by addressing them with the

most abject terms – 'faggot', 'I will fuck you', 'son of a bitch' – and by the agony of the bottle, when prisoners were forced to sit on a bottle.[18]

Prisoners in Derb Moulay Cherif, where both Saoudi and El Bouih were incarcerated and tortured, had their heads shaved and were given a number instead of a name[19] as a means of systematically destroying their subjectivity. Moreover, whereas women were re-gendered as male and thereby denied the status of women political activists, men experienced being 'feminized' through sexualized violence and rape. Thus both men and women were victims of sexual violence, and for both men and women it has been surrounded by silence, because sexual abuse is considered shameful and a taboo, because it disturbs the social constructions of a 'proper woman' and a 'proper man'.

Nevertheless, women's experiences of sexual violence differed from those of men, because they were often punished simultaneously by the state and society.[20] Rumours about what happened to women in prison stigmatized them and placed them in a position as 'fallen', and consequently in constant need of proving their 'moral integrity' and 'respectability'.[21] Women victim-survivors have experienced people from their community pointing fingers at them, spitting and insulting them and their children. In some cases, husbands have divorced their wives after finding out that they were raped in prison, or on the mere suspicion that they had been 'tainted' by sexual violence. Other women lived with the secret of rape out of shame and fear of being stigmatized. All in all, women victims of sexual violence were further victimized by a society that considered them guilty and impure, and in effect punished them for the crimes of others.[22] Thus, just like Taïa turned to silence to protect himself as a teenager, the silence of these women had the double function of protecting them and upholding cultural and religious norms.

Fatna El Bouih's gendered memory work

It is as a precursor to and integral part of these recent efforts to include gendered memories in contemporary Moroccan historiography that El Bouih's political activism, testimonial writing, social work and museum-based memorial work must be understood. El Bouih was born in Ben Ahmed, a village in the Settat province, in 1955. In 1971 she left the village on a boarder's scholarship for Lycée Chawqi, a prestigious girl's high school in Casablanca, where she soon became active in the National Union of High School Students, formed by an underground Marxist movement and labelled illegal by the regime of King Hassan II.[23] Thus El Bouih plunged into political and feminist activism at a crucial time in Morocco's turbulent political history, merely a year before the violent crackdown on the editorial team of *Souffles*.[24]

The beginning of the Years of Lead is generally associated with the violent repressions of the student protests in Casablanca on 23 March 1965. The brutality of the security forces, led by General Oufkir, was followed by Hassan II directing his anger against young, educated Moroccans in a public address on national television on 29 March 1965: 'Allow me to tell you, there is no greater danger to the state than so-called intellectuals; it would have been better for you to be illiterate.[25] Afterwards schools and university campuses were shut down, and on 7 June 1965, Hassan II dismissed the parliament, suspended the constitution of 1962 and declared a state of emergency that was to last more than five years.[26] As a consequence of this, the arena for political dialogue moved to informal settings – in the universities, in the salons of the educated elite, among students and emigrants in Paris, and within the trade unions, which were closely allied with the left.[27] It was out of this milieu that the 'New Left' (*al-yasār al-jadīd*) sprang, with the outlawed Marxist-Leninist movements, *Ilā al-ʾamām* and 'March 23 Movement' (named to commemorate the March 23 Casablanca uprisings) in the forefront.

However, with the failed military coups against Hassan II in 1971 and 1972, the number of political activists who were forcibly disappeared increased considerably. After the attempted coup at Skhirat Palace on 10 July 1971, the coup leaders were executed and sixty-one military officers were tried and sentenced to prison terms ranging from one year to life and incarcerated in Kenitra central prison.[28] In 1972, after the second failed coup, known as the Boeing Royal Affair and thought to have been led by General Oufkir,[29] Tazmamart, a French-built military barracks in the remote regions of southern Morocco, was converted into one of the most brutal secret detention centres. In 1973, fifty-eight men from the two coups were kidnapped from Kenitra central prison and 'disappeared' into Tazmamart until 1991.[30] The year 1973 marked a further change in the history of Morocco's human rights abuses when the main torture centre at Dar El Mokri in Rabat was transferred to Derb Moulay Cherif in Casablanca, which had space to torture large numbers of individuals and thus enabled mass secret detentions.[31]

It was during this heated time in Moroccan history that El Bouih became politically active in the National Union of High School Students. The first time she was arrested was on 25 January 1974 as the leader of a high school student protest about the conditions in Morocco's secondary schools, held the day before.[32] She was detained overnight at the Maarif police station in Casablanca, and during the night she was raped by one of her torturers. Her courageous public testimony immediately after her release gained her widespread sympathy and recognition. When she was brought to the police station and interrogated again a week later – trying to force her to denounce her own confession about being raped – high school students protested, went on hunger strikes and boycotted classes. After a week, the police were forced to release her, and later they announced that the case was closed.[33]

Her membership in the March 23 Movement resulted in her second arrest when, on 17 May 1977, she was forcibly disappeared into Derb Moulay Cherif along with five other women activists – Latifa Jbabdi, Widad Bouab, Khadija Boukhari, Maria Ezzaouini and Nguia Boudaa.[34] After seven months of torture in Derb Moulay Cherif, she was transferred first to Casablanca civil prison, popularly known as 'Ghbila' (the cemetery), and then to Meknes prison, where she was held in preventive detention until 1980, when she was finally brought to trial and sentenced to five years in prison for 'conspiring against the security of the state' and for distributing political tracts and posters.[35] While completing her sentence in Kenitra central prison from 1980 to 1982, she earned her *licence* (BA degree) and began her MA in sociology.[36] Her acclaimed literary testimony of 2001, *Ḥadīth al-ʿatmah*, covers the period from her arbitrary arrest and forcible disappearance to her release in 1982.

During the last decade of his rule, Hassan II made an unforeseen turnaround that simultaneously made it easier for the women's movement to campaign for women's rights. With the fall of the Soviet Union, Morocco's role as a pro-Western ally became geopolitically irrelevant, and international pressure forced Hassan II to accede to changes, particularly with respect to the practice of human rights.[37] These demands by the West, combined with an opening towards the world through satellite television and internet as well as a growing number of educated people and an increase in Islamist propaganda, led Hassan II to revise his repressive methods. Morocco therefore experienced a slow but notable improvement in its political climate and human rights situation in the early 1990s.

Within this changing political climate, El Bouih has been a significant voice in the women's movement. Her work for women's rights includes co-founding Morocco's first shelter for battered women, initiating the creation of special centres for victims of domestic violence in hospitals and through the courts system, conducting regular visits to women prisoners, and establishing a nursery in Oukacha prison for children of women detainees.[38] In 1991, she became a member of the coordinating council for the then-existing women's groups in Morocco, and along with Union d'action feminine (UAF), of which Latifa Jbabdi was president, she began a campaign to collect one million signatures to change the *Moudawana* (the Moroccan Family Code governing women's status). In 1992, they presented their suggestions to Hassan II, and in 1993 a number of these changes were implemented.[39]

When the liberal-minded Mohammed VI ascended the throne in 1999, the pace of reform accelerated considerably, and El Bouih came to play a significant role in the post-1999 truth and equity work. On 17 August 1999, a few weeks after the death of Hassan II, Mohammed VI ordered the ACHR (Advisory Committee on Human Rights, created by Hassan II in 1990) to create an independent Indemnity Commission, and in response to this, the non-governmental association for Morocco's victims of human rights abuses, al-Muntadā al-Maghribī min Ajl al-Ḥaqīqah wa-al-Inṣāf (the Moroccan Forum for Truth and Equity), was formed.[40] But Morocco's ruling elite nevertheless argued for the necessity of 'turning the page' (*ṭayy al-safḥah*).[41] There were no public hearings or attempts to provide the nation with an account of the past, and blanket amnesties were part of the creation of the Indemnity Commission. For this reason, a number of former political prisoners, including El Bouih, refused to request money from the commission.[42]

Moreover, since 1999, El Bouih has been active in an association calling for the transformation of Morocco's secret detention centres into museums.[43] On 4 May 2000, she participated in a sit-in around Derb Moulay Cherif, organized by the Moroccan Forum for Truth and Equity. Over 1,000 participants formed a human chain around Derb Moulay Cherif, which they were barred from entering, and told their stories of political violence and torture.[44] From outside, the participants demanded that the building be turned into a museum and a documentation centre for the Years of Lead.[45] With the official ERC in 2004–5, El Bouih was elected member of a 'Committee on Memory'.[46] In marked contrast to the Indemnity Commission, this commission was charged with collecting testimonies. With this new victim-centred commission El Bouih chose to file for reparations, and '[i]n 2005, she was accorded a small lump sum payment as reparations. More importantly to El Bouih, the state formally and officially acknowledged that her arrest, forcible disappearance, torture, and detention were illegal and unwarranted.'[47] In 2007, the next phase of reparations was launched to rehabilitate geographical regions that had been targeted by the regime, and El Bouih was appointed head of the Derb Moulay Cherif initiative.[48] In June 2009, she returned to Derb Moulay Cherif to tour the inside as an observer, and since then her task has been 'to illuminate the black enclosure of Derb Moulay Cherif, and to make it readable and knowable'.[49]

Women's testimonial writing

Testimonial writing has been an indispensable part of securing a collective memory of the Years of Lead. Political prisoners began to write already during their incarceration. The most famous among these early testimonies are probably Abdelaziz Mouride's graphic novel *On affame bien les rats!* (They Even Starve Rats!), which was originally written in Arabic, smuggled out of prison page by page and published pseudonymously in France as *Fī 'aḥshā baladī* (In the Bowles of My Country) in 1982;[50] Abdellatif Laâbi's poetic memoir *Le Chemin des ordailes* (*Rue du Retour*), published in Paris in 1982, two years after his release, and, like Mouride's graphic novel, not available in Morocco before 2000; and Abdelkader Chaoui's *Kāna wa-akhawātuha* (Kana and Her Sisters), which he wrote during the early 1980s and which was published in Morocco in 1986 while he was still incarcerated in Kenitra central prison, but after a week was seized and forbidden by the authorities.[51]

However, as during the Years of Lead anything resembling political activism could lead to arbitrary arrest, forcible disappearance and torture, many Moroccans were forced into silence, both in prison and after their release. Testimonial writing was therefore rare before the 1990s.[52] With the death of King Hassan II in 1999, Morocco witnessed a massive outpouring of publications that have contributed to uncovering the truth about Morocco's dark years. Among these publications, a significant few were written by and about women political prisoners.[53]

As a testimony *Ḥadīth al-'atmah* is significant because El Bouih situates her history within a collective history of women's political activism and suffering and in a remarkable solidarity with women criminal prisoners as well. In this respect, it reflects her activism and memory work undertaken before the publication of her own testimony. After her release, she found herself unable to speak about her own experiences, and her initial strategy, aimed at constructing a collective memory, was therefore to interview other women political prisoners:

> Remember that the model for all Moroccan females is the woman who lowers her eyes, never raises her voice, whose tongue 'does not go out of her mouth', as

in the Moroccan proverb 'into a closed mouth no flies can enter'. Girls are raised
with: 'Silence is wisdom and from it comes even greater wisdom.' It is part of my
society. This was the way I, my colleagues and friends were raised and I revolted
against this situation.[54]

Like the women interviewed in the ERC study, El Bouih and her fellow women
political prisoners were forced into silence after their release by fear of cultural
stigma and shame, because society regarded women's imprisonment, torture
and rape as a deprivation of their 'purity' and 'morality'; and because speaking
in public was considered a man's privilege. Moreover, former women political
prisoners have been viewed as martyrs and silent keepers of memory, and women's
testimonies as too horrific to be imparted to the general public:[55]

> Woman-as-the-sacred-heart-of-the-nation is still a prevalent theme in
> Moroccan culture. For a woman to admit that she was tortured, 'spoiled', and
> for her to reveal that some of her sisters were even killed by men who were
> supposed to cherish and protect them, would mean that Moroccans themselves
> had sought to annihilate their own being – their own mothers – and the life
> blood of the nation.[56]

Consequently, testifying became an act of defiance in the face of conservative social
and cultural norms that denied the sociality of women's pain by transforming them
into untouchable, silent representatives of 'national purity'. As El Bouih points out
in the foreword to *Ḥadīth al-ʿatmah* a testimony is dialogical:

> هناك جرح آخر في الذاكرة المغربية: جرح الاعتقال بناء التأنيث. ولعل آذانا كثيرة تتوق سماع صوت هذا
> الألم.[57]

> (There is another wound in Moroccan memory: a prison wound inflected in the
> feminine. Perhaps many ears are longing to hear this voice of pain.)

A testimony is not simply a voice speaking up; it requires ears that hear.[58] Thus
through testifying, El Bouih insists on the sociality of her pain, and through
witnessing, the reader gives her pain and suffering a life outside of her body. It is in
this dialogue between author and reader that women's experiences are brought into
the realm of politics, where they disturb the conception of politics as a masculine
space, and the conception of the nation as a feminine ideal transcending the
political.

Moreover, by giving voice to the untold stories of female victims of torture
and human rights abuses, El Bouih simultaneously challenges what Sara Ahmed
has termed 'the fetishization of the wound'.[59] The conception of women as silent
witnesses constitutes precisely a fetishization of the wound in which the wound
becomes a sign of a fixed identity that is idolized, rather than a means to rethink
the relation between present and past and ensure political transformation. As
such, women as silent witnesses imply a repetition of past violence rather than
a breaking of the seal of the past. When El Bouih writes 'there is another wound

in Moroccan memory', she points precisely to the fact that the past lives on in the present as long as women are kept silent. As Sara Ahmed and Jackie Stacey have pointed out, 'within feminism, the use of testimony has been significant as part of the making of feminist politics: it has been about women becoming subjects of their lives, and speaking rather than remaining silent about trauma, injustice or violence'.[60] Speaking up as a woman, then, becomes a performative speech act that works against the performative act of defining women as 'silent witnesses'.

Noticeably, then, attributing the label 'martyr' to women holds an implicit ambivalence, as the 'elevated' position as martyr simultaneously eliminates women from the political space. One of the most famous female martyrs in Morocco is Saïda Menebhi (1952–77), who died in Ghbila during a mass hunger strike launched to claim the right to the status of political prisoner. As the martyr is the epitome of the silent witness, Menebhi's death is easily fetishized – that is, turned into a symbol of Morocco's dark past with no further explanations. But the story of Menebhi as a female political activist and prisoner of conscience has been reinstated in the realm of political action, both through her own poetry and through the narrations of her life and activism by other former political prisoners.

In *Le Chemin des ordailes*, Laâbi, for instance, brings the story of Menebhi to life through a bedtime story.[61] Menebhi is often seen as a latter-day Scheherazade,[62] and the bedtime story in *Le Chemin des ordailes* mirrors both her life and death and the story of Scheherazade. However, by framing a seemingly traditional fairy tale with real-life events, Laâbi simultaneously turns the figure of Scheherazade upside down. Rather than stopping the tyrant through storytelling, as the traditional Scheherazade story goes, the little girl Saïda mobilizes the people by sacrificing herself. But the bedtime story is a sad story, one that reveals that even unbearable sacrifices only hint at transformation. Much is left to be desired.

Like Laâbi, El Bouih turns Menebhi's death into an event that generated more female political opposition inside the prison walls. But unlike Laâbi's parable, told to his daughter as a bedtime story, El Bouih depicts the brutal reality in prison after Menebhi's death. The women political prisoners were terrified by the fact that the prison authorities let Menebhi die. Her death made them even more aware that they were completely cut off from the outside world and that they had no means to communicate their version of the event. They were in the hands of 'a terrifying and murderous gang'[63] that they knew were quite capable of silencing them, as protest had been shown to be at risk of death. However, rather than being scared into silence, they realized that they could only survive and regain their basic rights if they risked their lives.[64] Thus, they drew strength from this horrific event and launched yet another hunger strike, and after two weeks their demands were met.[65]

Both Laâbi's parable and El Bouih's testimony depict the mobilizing power of Menebhi's death and show the strength and courage of women who were simultaneously deprived of the status of 'political activists' while they were imprisoned and tortured as such. As I will demonstrate in the following El Bouih's writing reveals that the mere presence of women political activists in prison disturbed the predominant patriarchal and misogynistic norms and in itself constituted an act of resistance.

Dialogue of suffering: Fatna El Bouih's Ḥadīth al-ʿatmah[66]

Ḥadīth al-ʿatmah opens with a dreamlike vision of the river Bou Regreg, which reminds the narrator of her morning bath. Both the bath and the river are coupled with water, purification and a peaceful silence – the one reviving body and soul and the other limitless and accompanied by an overwhelming feeling of freedom. But the dreamlike vision is limited by fear of the unknown. The feeling of freedom in the opening scene is soon replaced by the fear of a strong man who can alter the course of her boat with one stroke of the oar and kidnap her. Thus the dream turns into a nightmare, reminding the narrator of the tales in *A Thousand and One Nights* that her father would recount for her in the evenings when she was young, and of how the stories of kidnappings and abducted women and girls used to give her nightmares.

Both the reference to *A Thousand and One Nights* and the dreamlike vision of Bou Regreg that turns into a nightmare force the reader to hesitate between what is reality and what is a dream or a nightmare in the testimony as a whole while simultaneously associating nightmare with men assaulting women and reality and dreams with femininity. Immediately before depicting the day of her arrest, the narrator is woken from her fear of being kidnapped:

لقد وصلت الشط بأمان, وما زالت رائحة العطر المندسة في جسدي تؤكد لي أناقتي والرغبة المسيطرة
عليّ في التجدد, وتصلني بأحلام واعدة في المستقبل. [67]

(I had indeed reached the shore safely, and the scent of perfume that still permeated my body reassured me of my elegance and the desire for renewal that controlled me and connected me to dreams of a promising future.)

Connecting the feminine body with dreams of a promising future, this quote sets the scene of El Bouih's testimony and contrasts femininity with her kidnappers and torturers. However, while it is repeatedly underlined that all kidnappers and torturers were men, gender differences are displaced when it comes to torture as a means of breaking down body and soul of both men and women.

Moreover, coupled with the sentence, 'dreams are essential to those who do not possess power',[68] dreaming acquires a double meaning: it is both the necessary precondition for survival for the dispossessed – in the testimony, El Bouih herself and women prisoners in general – and a narrative means to subvert the relationship between what is imagined and what is real. Significantly, the latter is not meant to undermine the truth value of her testimony, but to accentuate the monstrosity of the world of Morocco's secret prisons. Whereas nightmares are something from which you can awake and which can be turned into dreams of hope, torture in Morocco's secret detention centres was an omnipresent nightmare from which there was only momentary escape by passing out from pain.[69]

At the beginning of Ḥadīth al-ʿatmah El Bouih's father tells her stories just as the vizier in *A Thousand and One Nights* tells his daughter, Scheherazade, two stories in an attempt to convince her not to marry King Shahryar and sacrifice herself to save the people. However, unlike the vizier, El Bouih's father is unaware of the similarities between his bedtime stories and his daughter's destiny. But El Bouih nevertheless sacrifices herself in a similar way when she is sentenced

خمس سنوات بتهمة ارتكاب جريمة التفكير في غد أفضل, التفكير في عالم تحترم فيه حقوق الإنسان, عالم يبعد المرأة عن الدونية.[70]

(five years for the crime of imagining a better tomorrow, imagining a world where human rights are respected, a world for women far removed from inferiority).

By mirroring her testimony in the story of Scheherazade, El Bouih's bearing witness to the atrocities committed during the Years of Lead becomes a means by which to create 'a better tomorrow'. Tellingly, Abderrahim Tafraout, the first critic to review *Ḥadīth al-ʿatmah*, headlined his article 'Shahryar was killed by Fatna'.[71] As the headline hints, El Bouih is not simply narrating stories to appease the king and have him pardon her as Scheherazade; she is speaking up against the authorities demanding justice and respect for human rights. Thus in parallel with Taïa's use of storytelling as a means to call the marginalized into existence and stake out an experimental nation for his younger self, El Bouih uses storytelling both as a strategy to secure a collective memory about women and gendered violence and to insist that women cannot and should not be forced into silence.

Significantly, the figure of Scheherazade further links together her childhood memories and the destiny of all women political prisoners. The Scheherazadian 'narrate or die' becomes a resistance strategy both for El Bouih in writing *Ḥadīth al-ʿatmah* and for her fellow women political prisoners:

لقد استطعت إلى جانب رفيقاتي, رغم الحراسة المشددة والرقابة المستمرة, أن أمد الجسور بيني وبينهن. لقد تعرفنا على بعضنا البعض في الصمت والظلام, وفي ظل منع الكلام والرقابة وعين الحارس اليقظة. لقد انطلقت أصابعنا في مهارة وحذر فائقين تخط فوق الضلوع أروع القصص والحكايات والأحداث والنكت. تحولت الأصابع إلى أقلام, وجنبات الصدور إلى صفحات. لقد اختزلت الحياة إذن في هذه اللحظات المختلسة إلى حركات وإشارات لا يفهمها إلا نحن, ولا يخلقها إلى نحن.[72]

(Together with my comrades I managed, despite the intense surveillance and constant control, to build bridges between us. We became acquainted with one another in silence and darkness, even though speaking was forbidden under the watchful eyes of the guards. Our fingers moved skillfully and with extraordinary caution to write on the ribs beautiful tales and stories, events and jokes. Fingers were transformed into pens, and the sides of chests into pages. In these stolen moments then, life was reduced to gestures and signs that we alone understood, and we alone created.)

Writing on each other's bodies is a strategy that men as well as women have used in prison to resist both the silence imposed on them and the torture their bodies endured. Already in prison they testified to one another and used storytelling as a survival strategy.

A woman named Rashid[73]

Contrary to the narrative constructed by the new king through the ERC, El Bouih's testimony, along with many other prison testimonies, reveals the identity of her torturers, who have never been prosecuted. The first time Youssfi Kaddour, the chief torturer at Derb Moulay Cherif, appears in *Ḥadīth al-ʿatmah*, his status as *muʿallim*, 'the teacher', the boss of those who are to 'educate' El Bouih, is contrasted with his harsh and 'uneducated' vocabulary:

هنا عمرك ما غادي تشوفي السماء .. هنا إلى هزيت البانضة نمحيك, وإذا تكلمت نقطع ليك اللسان.
اديوها فين تربى. كان هذا الرجل هو 'المعلم' اليوسفي قدور.[74]

('Here you will never see the sky . . . If you remove your blindfold, I erase you, and if you speak, I cut out your tongue. Take her to where she shall be educated.' This man was the 'muʿallim' Youssfi Kaddour.)

The indication of futurity through *ghādī*; the use of *ilā* instead of *idhā* in the first conditional sentence; the conjugation of the verbs *nimḥīk* and *naqṭaʿ* where the prefix *nūn* indicates first-person singular; and the use of *feen* instead of the conjunction *ḥaythu* are all markers of dialect. Together with the violent threats uttered by Youssfi Kaddour, his use of dialect underlines the irony of him being *muʿallim*, as this title of respect neither suits the way he speaks nor the way he acts.

Moreover, by incorporating dialect in her testimony, El Bouih reveals the limitations of *fuṣḥā*, which lacks the harshness of dialect, and therefore cannot capture the monstrousness of her prison experiences. Importantly, however, El Bouih's use of dialect also works as a form of embedded translation, which deconstructs the idea that literary memory belongs to the realm of *fuṣḥā* alone. Whereas her depiction of the torturers reproduces the common conception of *fuṣḥā* as high variety and *dārija* as low variety, her overall use of dialect in her testimony challenges this hierarchical relationship. By introducing dialect as a proper literary language, she positions herself and her experiences in opposition not only to the torturers and the regime of King Hassan II but also to the traditional conception of the function of literature and literary imagination. Similar to her intertextual references to *A Thousand and One Nights* the use of dialect places her testimony within the frame of a popular struggle to secure a national memory.

When El Bouih was kidnapped and imprisoned in 1977, she disappeared from the face of the earth along with many other political activists. Though she knew she had disappeared somewhere into Morocco, the feeling of being exiled was intensified by Youssfi Kaddour's terrifying words: 'Rānī nimḥīk' (I will erase you).[75]

كان الشعور بالمنفى قويا. حين قال لي الكوميسير: 'راني منحيك', قلت: لقد وقع هذا, لقد انمحيك من
خريطة الوطن, فلا أحد يعلم مكاني, لا وجود لي إلا في ذاكرة المقربين, بل لعل هؤلاء اعتبروني, بعد أن
أصناهم البحث, في عداد المفقودين أو الأموات.[76]

(The feeling of exile was powerful. When the police chief said: 'I will erase you,' I said: This is already reality, I have been erased from the country's map, no one knows where I am, I have no existence except in the memory of my close friends. Indeed, after conducting an exhaustive search, they may have already concluded that I am among the lost and dead.)

Being erased from the map of her country, with nobody but her captors knowing her whereabouts, El Bouih describes her situation as that of a displaced person who has doubly disappeared: first as a political activist, then as a female voice in the political sphere.[77] To silence women as political agents, all women political prisoners in Derb Moulay Cherif were re-gendered, and El Bouih was told to obey commands under the name Rashid.[78] Paradoxically, the need to re-gender women exposes that these women had already succeeded in disturbing patriarchal norms. As the literary critic Fatima Zahra Zryouil mentions in her introduction to *Ḥadīth al-ʿatmah*, the prison guards, by clinging to hegemonic patriarchy, in reality reveal their fear of the new women's movement:

لماذا لا يتخيّل الجلّاد إمكانية اعتقال امرأة من أجل أفكارها؟, هل نفسّر ذلك بالتأويل البيهي الذي يحيل مثل هذه المواقف إلى العقلية الذكورية السائدة المحقّرى للمرأة؟, أم أنّ هناك عوامل أخرى ـ خفية, ومنها مثلا الخوف الذي تستثيره لديه المقاومة الأنثوية الجديدة والمدهشة في المجال السياسي؟ فيحاول طمسها بكل الأساليب التي يتوفّر عليها.[79]

(Why is it impossible for the executioner to imagine arresting a woman for her ideas? Do we explain this with the self-evident interpretation that refers this kind of situations to the prevailing patriarchal mentality which despises women? Or are there other factors – hidden and among them, for instance, fear aroused in him by the new and astonishing feminist resistance in the political field? Then he attempts to eradicate her with all means available.)

Whereas the torturers showcased their masculinity by feminizing male political prisoners through sexualized violence and rape, as argued by Saoudi, when they were confronted with women, their stereotypical conception of gender relations was continuously disturbed. On the one hand, they needed to re-gender women to eliminate them as political activists and to subject them to the same torture methods as men; but on the other, they were incapable of ignoring women political prisoners as women whose political engagement threatened their masculinity. As Jbabdi, for instance, depicts in her testimony published in *Ḥadīth al-ʿatmah*:

مرة دعيت بمفردي للتحقيق, ركبت سيارة 'السطافيت' كالعادة, كانت مملوءة عن آخرها بالحراس والبوليس, كانوا محملين بالرشاشات, وأمامنا وخلفنا سيارتان بنفس الحمولة, ناهيك طبعا عن الدراجة النارية التي تشق لنا الطريق, عندما استويت في مكاني وأمروا بالإقلاع ثارت ثائرتهم, لم يرضهم أن يستنفروا بهذا الشكل المضحك من أجلنا أو بالأحرى من أجلي وأنا مجرد امرأة في نظرهم. احتجوا وصرخوا وجعلوا منها قضية كرامة ورجولة, واحترت هل أسخر من الوضع لأنه فعلا مضحك, أو ألعن الفكر الذكوري الذي يربط عدم خطورتي بجنسي لا بفكري واختياراتي وحدودي كإنسان.[80]

(Once when I was called on my own to investigation, I climbed into a car filled, as always, with guards and police. They were loaded with machine guns, and in front of us and behind us were two cars with the same load, not to mention the motorcycle that cleared the road for us. When I sat in my place and they were ordered to take off, they revolted, refusing to get up in this ridiculous way for us, or rather for me who was a mere woman in their eyes. They protested and screamed and made it a matter of dignity and manhood, and I was at a loss as to whether I should mock the situation because it was really funny, or curse the patriarchal thought that links my non-importance to my sexuality, not to my thoughts, my choices and my limits as a human being.)

As Slyomovics has also argued, Jbabdi's tone oscillates between bitterness and humour.[81] There is something tragicomic about the prison guards' inability to make these women fit into their misogynistic world. Tellingly, by exerting gendered violence the torturers both draw on a conservative cultural system in which women can be forced into silence out of shame and fear of being stigmatized and yet undermine this very system by indirectly acknowledging that these women have succeeded in their political activism to such a degree that they are now imprisoned and eligible for torture.

Screams of silence

The need to re-gender women political prisoners is what simultaneously aligns El Bouih with the women criminal prisoners (who are themselves victims of oppression and gendered violence) and what distinguishes her from them as she insists on claiming her place as a woman in the public realm of men and politics. It is therefore significant that *Ḥadīth al-ʿatmah* also include criminal women prisoners. The story of a woman called F.L. and her daughter Ilham, who was born in prison, is the tragic story of a woman who served thirty years in prison for drowning her two boys. This woman had been forced to marry an older man, then committed adultery with a youth her own age. Out of fear of the clan, she had killed her two boys to prevent them from tattling about her to her husband. Unable to free herself from the misogynistic norms of society, F.L. made a desperate choice and committed a horrible crime in order to avoid scandal and shame.

Significantly, the story of F.L. is as much a story about women's inferior position in Moroccan society. Reading El Bouih's account leaves the reader with the feeling that this whole situation could have been avoided if women had freedom of choice. El Bouih does not defend the acts of F.L., but in her narrative, it is not only F.L.'s acts that are monstrous. Society as a whole is. Her critique is directed at those cultural traditions that allow families to marry their young girls, against their will, to men who could have been their father or even grandfather, and at the cultural norms that – combined with fear of the state – force families to ostracize women who bring shame and dishonour to the family and clan. In this respect, F.L.'s acts come to haunt society. By infecting dominant moral narratives, her monstrosity becomes a mirror of society rather than a defining trait as 'monstrous other'.

Along this line, an important and recurrent narrative strategy in *Ḥadīth al-ʿatmah* is that of 'inversion'. Just as El Bouih plays with the relationship between nightmare, dream and reality at the beginning of her testimony, she disturbs the relationship between day and night, normality and monstrosity in her narration of prison space. Importantly, prison conventions are, in El Bouih's testimony, not simply opposed to the laws that rule Moroccan society. To a large extent they mirror and uphold the same cultural norms that Moroccan law is built upon. That is, the culture of impunity that permeates prison mirrors a lack of respect for women's right to equality.

With respect to F.L. and Ilham, this inversion of what is 'normal' and what is 'monstrous' is reflected in how the relationship between mother and daughter is both perceived and lived in prison. After F.L. has given birth, both prisoners and guards suspiciously watch her when she is with her newborn. Nobody believes that a woman who has thrown her two sons in a well is capable of having a natural relationship with her daughter. Consequently, the relationship between F.L. and Ilham can only be a mother-and-daughter relationship after nightfall, when the inmates are asleep and F.L. can embrace her baby away from their hostile eyes:

وفي الليل تكون من نصيب الأم الوالدة, ويسود القانون وكأن لليل سلطة جاصة.[82]

(At night she was allotted to her biological mother, and law ruled, as if the night had special powers.)

With F.L. and Ilham, the laws of nature are restored at night and suspended during the day. At night she is a loving mother, in the daytime a monstrous child murderer. Thus night, rather than a space of lawlessness, becomes a space of order in which F.L. and Ilham are temporarily out of sight and where F.L. for a fleeting moment can follow her maternal instincts.

However, when focus shifts from F.L. to Ilham, the sympathetic depiction of F.L. is simultaneously complicated as in a double critique of social norms and F.L.'s acts:

هل هناك أقسى من أن يكتب الإنسان بدمعه أولى صفحات تاريخه .. لقد كانت والدتها جد متذمرة من وجودها في السجن, في عالم لم تحلم به أبدا, تتضور جوعا وألما, يقهرها القيد وتستاء من ظلم الزمان وقهره فلا تجد أمامها إلا هذا الكائن الصغير الذي يرافقها في رحلتها اضطرارا, فتفجر فيه كل أحقادها كأنه سبب تعاستها .. كانت تضرب طفلتها ضربا مبرحا ولا تتوانى عن رميها مثل حشرة حقيرة مزعجة.[83]

(Is anything more cruel for a human being than to write the first pages of his life story with tears . . . Her mother complained bitterly about her presence in prison, in a world she had never dreamed of, where she suffered from hunger and pain, where the shackles had crushed her, and she resented the injustice of fate and its oppression. All she had before her was this small being, who was accompanying her on her involuntary journey, to direct her hatred against, as if she was the cause of her misery . . . She would beat the child violently and not hesitate to throw her like a despicable and annoying insect.)

Throughout the narrative of F.L. and Ilham, Ilham is the voice of innocence. But as the innocent child paying the price for society's infamy, her tears and her crying reflect the annihilation of this innocence. Her nanny, caretaker or 'second mother' in prison might be able to rescue her from her birthmother, but only temporarily. Nothing can remove the sadness on her face that mirrors the tears and distress of the women around her since her earliest childhood.

The chapter about F.L. and Ilham culminates in Ilham's release at the age of four, when F.L. grants custody of her child to her brother. Here, Ilham's voice is the voice of resistance and revolt against prison life, and her instinctive reaction to the prospect of freedom reveals the powerlessness of the women prisoners:

كانت صرختها صمتا .. كان صمتها الصرخة المكتومة بين أنفاس السجينات .. كانت فضحا لعجزنا ..
ثورة ضد جبننا, لأن الطبيعة تقتضي أن نصرخ ألف مرة, أن لا نطيق البقاء هناك لحظة واحدة, فأحرى
سنوات وأعمارا..
لعل إلهام كان لسان حال والدتها التي لم تستطع أن تصرخ بحقها في الحياة, سواء في مجتمع ظلمها,
أو سجن سيمتص نضارة زهرها ويحيلها إلى العدم.[84]

(Her screams were her silence . . . Her silence was the suppressed screams of women prisoners . . . It laid bare our powerlessness . . . It was a revolt against our cowardice, because nature required that we scream a thousand times, that we refuse to remain there a single moment, let alone years and lifetimes . . .

Perhaps Ilham voiced the predicament of her mother, who was unable to call for her right to life, whether in a society that was unjust to her or in a prison that sucked the bloom of her youth and turned her into nothing.)

The linkage of silence and screams – as if the two are interchangeable – both reflects that screams are a kind of silence in opposition to the articulated human word of a testimony and challenges the societal belief that women should be silent witnesses, as screams are a resounding revolt against silence. On the one hand, Ilham's screams are her silence, and as silent women are 'pure women', her screams come to reflect her purity and thus replace silence as the female guardian of memory. Rather than internalizing misogynistic societal norms, women should scream. On the other hand, screams are also the opposite of articulated protest; they are the last resort when words and arguments are ignored. In Ilham's case, screaming is her desperate reaction to end the farewell scene – she so eager to leave prison, the prisoners so silent and sad to part with her.

Similarly, screaming in protest is the last resort of the women political prisoners in Derb Moulay Cherif when one of their fellow inmates is threatened with rape. In this infamous detention centre, where men and women were perpetually tortured and insulted, they mobilized all their strength and broke the enforced silence in a desperate effort to protect their comrades and themselves:

لقد صرخنا عاليا. وكانت ليلة مشهودة, لعل جدران ذلك المعتقل تعرف في تاريخها أول أصوات
الاحتجاج, والعجيب في الأمر أنها أصوات نساء.[85]

(We screamed aloud. It was a memorable night, the prison walls learned, perhaps for the first time in its history, voices of protest, and remarkably it was women's voices.)

To the prisoners, screaming becomes an act of affirmative resistance to gendered violence and rape. Like the characters in Taïa's *Un Pays pour mourir*, to whom daring to speak and scream equals singing to survive, the women political prisoners in *Ḥadīth al-ʿatmah* scream in spite of everything – in spite of shame, fear and further violence.

Taking revenge through love: Abdellah Taïa's Infidèles

Taïa's novel *Infidèles* is not directly about political violence during the Years of Lead, but the torture scene in part two of the novel nevertheless depicts the brutality of gendered violence in Morocco's secret prisons during that period. Moreover, as the torture scene simultaneously mirrors the dehumanization faced by the protagonists – Jallal, Slima and Saâdia – in everyday life because of their public association with sex and shameful desire, the novel adds significant perspectives on the relationship between sexuality, violence and social stigmatization.

Infidèles follows Jallal, the queer son of a prostitute, Slima, from his childhood to his death. Slima is the daughter of Saâdia, an *introductrice* (introducer) who assists couples in having sex on their wedding night. Treated like outcasts, all three protagonists are, ironically, much needed in society, and thus foregrounds the hypocrisy of the conservative social, cultural and religious mores that control many people's lives.

As noted by Taïa in an interview with Jean Zaganiaris, it is no coincidence that the protagonist is called Jallal.[86] Named after the great Sufi poet, Jalal al-Din Rumi (1207–73), Jallal is the embodiment of the androgynous and transsexual Sufi body, and throughout the novel his sexuality is deliberately uncertain. Thus the character Jallal draws on a long history of disturbing gender and sexual normativity. In this respect, *Infidèles* is reminiscent of Khatibi's *Amour bilingue*, with its representation of queer sexualities as a critical practice to subvert the 'Hetero-Nation'. However, in a significant difference from *Amour bilingue*, *Infidèles* interconnects queer sexuality and spirituality that culminates in a suicide mission. That is, *Infidèles* is a troubling story of how the Years of Lead haunt generations of Moroccans and, in combination with a xenophobic Europe, create terrorists from sensitive and fragile men who, in turn, subvert the construction of masculinity within Islamic extremism.

Infidèles opens with a long monologue by Jallal, who at the age of ten is trying to convince his mother, Slima, to move from Hay Al-Inbiâth to Hay Salam (two neighbourhoods in Salé, the city across the river, Bou Regreg, from Rabat) to start a new life and to rewrite their story: 'Notre passé n'existera pas, à Hay Salam. On l'écrira comme on voudra. Une autre fiction.' (Our past won't exist in Hay Salam. We'll write it as we please. Another fiction.)[87] Tellingly, while Jallal is smart enough to know that rewriting their past will be a fiction, he is not asking his mother to change, or to hide her way of life and her profession. He simply wants to go somewhere else in the hope that the customers there will be less terrifying and less monstrous than the men they run into in Hay Al-Inbiâth.

Despite his young age and the naive undertone of his arguments, his monologue reveals a perceptive boy who can see through the double standards of many of his and his mother's clients. 'Tu seras lapidée un jour, maman, par ceux-là mêmes qui, chaque nuit, viennent discrètement chez nous demander ton pardon, un peu de plaisir.' (You'll be stoned one day, mom, by the very people who every night discreetly come to us to ask for your forgiveness, a little pleasure.)[88] But their position as pariah and the insults they have to put up with every day have also made him wish for revenge, and, tellingly, the novel opens with Jallal trying to convince his mother that he is old enough to stand up for her and himself and finally fight back – both by insisting that they stop subjecting themselves to degrading treatment and by declaring that he has learnt how to spit, and that he is not afraid of spitting back at everyone who despises them. This is an important scene, because Jallal as an adult in Brussels reconnects with this 'bad boy' by finally daring to spit, and by arguing that his suicide mission is his way of 'spitting back hard' at Morocco:

Je ne veux plus ce ritual. On attend depuis très longtemps. C'est fini. C'est fini. La dernière fois, on est tombés sur un monstre. Il voulait me manger. Il m'a fait des choses bizarres. Je te l'ai dit. Tu t'en souviens? Non? Vraiment? Allez, viens, on rentre. On rentre, maman. . . . On rentre. Les rues sont désertes, personne ne nous verra, ne nous insultera, ne nous jettera des pierres. Et si on crache sur toi, je me battrai pour toi. Je te défendrai. Je ne m'enfuirai pas. J'ai grandi. Je le vois, j'ai grandi. J'appris à cracher sur les gens moi aussi. Tout au fond de moi, je n'oublie rien. Je ne cherche pas le mal, mais si on me regarde avec des yeux mauvais, des yeux qui jettent des sorts, je sais désormais quoi faire. Je crache. Je fais face. Je ne baisse pas les yeux. J'affronte. Je crache. Je crache sur tout ce monde qui nous méprise, qui ne te reconnait pas, maman. Je crache. Je crache de tout mon cœur, de toute mon âme. Je crache le plus loin possible, aux pieds de mon agresseur, mon ennemi, le salaud qui ne me laches pas, qui me poursuit de ses remarques mesquines, de sa morale religieuse de frustré sexuel.[89]

(I don't want this ritual anymore. We've been waiting a very long time. It's over. It's over. The last time we came across a monster. He wanted to eat me. He did odd things to me. I told you. Do you remember? No? Really? Come on, we're going home. We're going home, mom. . . . We're going home. The streets are empty, no one will see us, insult us, or throw stones at us. And if anyone spits on you, I'll fight for you. I'll defend you. I won't run away. I've grown up. I can see it; I've grown up. I've learned to spit on people too. Deep inside, I forget nothing. I don't seek evil, but if someone looks at me with evil eyes, with eyes that cast spells, I know what to do. I spit. I face it. I don't lower my eyes. I face it. I spit. I spit on all the people who despises us, who doesn't recognize you, mom. I spit. I spit with all my heart, with all my soul. I spit as far as possible, at the feet of my aggressor, my enemy, the bastard who won't let me go, who follows me with his petty remarks, with his sexually frustrated religious morality.)

Just as in Driss Chraïbi's *Le Passé simple*, spitting represents the most despicable act of abasement, while simultaneously revealing the powerlessness of the characters in the two novels. While Driss's father, in an act of self-abasement, forces Driss to spit at him in order to emphasize his own power and control, Jallal's urge to spit back at the people who despise him and his mother collides with his self-image. His effort to convince his mother that he will not betray himself by spitting reveals that, in fact, he will: 'Cracher ne fait pas de moi un mauvais garçon. Un mal élevé. Je suis déjà à part. Laisse-moi cracher. Laisse-moi te prouver que j'ai grandi. Laisse-moi montrer comment je peux te protéger.' (Spitting doesn't turn me into a bad boy. Someone badly brought up. Besides I already am. Let me spit. Let me prove to you that I've grown up. Let me show that I can protect you.)[90]

This quote is significant because Jallal, in arguing against himself, simultaneously reveals the absurdity of the cultural and religious norms that judge him 'badly brought up'. On the one hand, he insists that he will not become a bad boy by standing up for his mother; but on the other, he argues that it makes no difference because he is already 'badly brought up'. Just like women who had been sexually assaulted or raped in prison are considered 'damaged goods' and socially stigmatized, ten-year-old Jallal is 'tainted' by his mother's profession and his alleged homosexuality, and this makes him a 'bad boy' despite the fact that he is well behaved, gentle and caring. This, contrasted with the violent behaviour of spitting, stone-throwing, verbal insults and sexual abuse that Jallal and Slima encounter on a daily basis, makes it almost laughable that Jallal and Slima are the ones considered 'abnormal' while everyone else's violent behaviour is justified by society's moral codes. This depiction of Jallal is, moreover, reminiscent of how Taïa in 'Homosexualité expliquée à ma mère' describes himself as someone who eludes his family because he is simultaneously 'monster' and 'gentle, bookish, and well-behaved'.[91]

The social constructions of masculinity and femininity that shape how violence is exerted and experienced in Morocco's secret prisons are the same that justify the social stigmatization of Saâdia, Slima and Jallal and the violence they encounter in *Infidèles*. In this respect, *Infidèles* is an exploration of 'everyday time', with its discontinuous and heterogeneous narratives that have been disavowed by official narratives of the 'nation'. Similarly to *Ḥadīth al-ʿatmah*, *Infidèles* subverts the relation between 'normality' and 'monstrosity', but unlike *Ḥadīth al-ʿatmah* it does so through a story devoid of 'good' and 'evil'.

The 'perverted' woman everyone needs

The story of Jallal's grandmother, Saâdia, is the story of a woman who has been cursed all her life because she gives young people guidance in their sex lives. As an introducer, her knowledge about how both men and women are sexually satisfied makes her both dangerous and powerful, because her know-how is simultaneously needed and feared. On the one hand, her strong femininity and sexuality threaten the conservative norms of society according to which sexual desire is shameful; on the other hand, it is through her profession that families are able to meet the social norms of female virginity, because she has the power to create a fiction of purity by making sure that blood appears on the sheets of newlywed couples.[92] Her profession thus simultaneously safeguards and subverts conservative norms of sexual conduct.

Saâdia's story is revealed through a long monologue which, like Jallal's in the first chapter, is addressed to a silent Slima. It is a final 'conversation'. Tellingly, it opens with Saâdia wishing to leave this world in a state of purification, she who has always been considered perverse and impure: 'Le monde m'a toujours donné une autre image de moi-même. Je suis perverse. La vieille perverse dont tout le monde a besoin. Un peu sorcière. Un peu médecin. Un peu pute. La spécialiste du sexe.' (The world has always provided another image of me. I'm perverted. The perverted old woman everyone needs. A bit of a witch. A bit of a doctor. A bit of a whore. The sex specialist.)[93] The literary play with the question 'what is purity?' relates Saâdia's story both to Taïa's biography and to El Bouih's testimony, where the subverted relation between silence and screams displaces 'female purity' altogether. As with the workings of shame, as described by Ahmed,[94] Saâdia's (im)purity both reveals a commitment to a communal ideal and disturbs the normativity of the community. That is, Saâdia's monologue is an expression not of anti-normative resistance, but of subversive love.

In an effort to resist hostility and rejection, Saâdia ends up living a life in constant movement. It is too painful for her to stay in the same place. Life in constant movement also characterizes the lives of Slima and Jallal, and their stories are bound together by the returning reference to the first scene of the film *River of No Return*, in which a man is cutting a tree. For Saâdia, moving is the culmination of a number of crucial events reflecting the hostility she has encountered throughout her life: the love of her life rejecting her, her sister disavowing her and her son's death. In her long monologue, Saâdia is asking Slima to bring her back to Azemmour and bury her at the same cemetery where she buried her son. Even if she felt forced to leave this place, it has nevertheless come to represent freedom and inclusion, a place that differs from everywhere else: 'Azemmour m'accueillie sans me juger, sans me traiter comme une mécréante. Azemmour est un territoire à part. Une cité d'un autre temps. Libre et sauvage.' (Azemmour welcomed me without judging me, without treating me like a miscreant. Azemmour is a unique territory. A city of another time. Free and wild.)[95] But the story of her son's death reveals cracks in this picture perfect. Just two months old, he died from what appears to be sudden infant death syndrome. One morning when Saâdia woke up, he had stopped breathing and his body was already cold. But instead of mourning in public, Saâdia kept his death a secret and buried him during the night at the local cemetery. Even in the city that is 'free and wild', reality catches up with Saâdia. Internalizing conservative cultural and religious norms that consider sex outside of marriage a sin, she is almost relieved that her son has escaped this cruel world before facing social stigmatization as 'the son of a whore'. Nevertheless, Saâdia's depiction of Azemmour and the insights she shares with Slima to encourage her to take up the 'introducer' profession herself reveal that nothing is black and white: Saâdia is both proud and self-loathing, in the same way that her surroundings both welcome and reject her. It has been her burden in life to keep the secret that society is anything but the mirror of cultural and religious norms.

The story of Saâdia functions as a double critique in the sense that the narrative subverts the relation and discernibility between centre and periphery. As a writing from the margin, *Infidèles* reveals the arbitrariness of specific hegemonic practices – not to reverse these established hierarchies but to think the relation between inside and outside differently. Butler has argued that there would be no heterosexuality *as* origin without homosexuality *as* copy. In a similar but slightly more complex dynamic, the norms of sexual conduct, purity and virginity presuppose the profession of the introducer, who in turn radically destabilizes the entire framework of 'norm' and 'deviance', making it impossible to locate any logical priority of either 'position'.

The prostitute and the Polisario

The Western *River of No Return* (1954), starring Robert Mitchum and Marilyn Monroe, is central to the story line of *Infidèles* and a key to understanding the novel as a whole. Similarly to how films were a space for Taïa to exist *in silence* as teenager and homosexual at the age of thirteen,[96] *River of No Return* makes Jallal wonder about the world and gives him a vocabulary to understand the hypocrisy surrounding him and his mother. The film is also intertwined with Jallal's image of his mother, and with the closest he comes to a father figure in his life: a soldier and one of his mother's regular clients. The film is thus simultaneously linked to his memories of loving and caring relationships and a key to understanding the meaninglessness of the cruelty in the world.

River of No Return opens with a scene where a man is cutting down a tree. Then three magnificent sceneries – the river, the mountains and the forest – appear. This opening lasts for about one minute before the theme song of the film begins, whereupon the man reappears on screen. What startles Jallal is the indifference with which the tree is severed from its roots. By focusing on the tree, he brings life and significance to something nobody else seems to acknowledge:

Mais, d'abord, il faut qu'il se détache de lui-même, du reste de son corps, de ses racines bien profondes dans la terre. Il le fait. Il va se décider à le faire. Il tombe. Il n'est plus droit, son corps long, sa racine au ciel, se précipite, chute, petit à petit, au ralenti, puis très très vite. Au même moment, la séparation se produit. Le détachement. Un corps avec deux racines. Un corps vieux, d'avant, qui allait vivre encore longtemps, des centaines d'années, plus qu'aucun homme, un corps éternel, au sens propre, est en train de mourir. On le coupe en deux. On le divise.[97]

(But, first of all, it must detach itself from itself, from the rest of its body, from its deep roots in the earth. It does. It will decide to do so. It falls. It is no longer straight, its long body, its root in the sky, rushes, falls, little by little, then very very quickly. At the same time, separation occurs. Detachment. A body with two roots. An old body, before, which would live for a long time, hundreds of years, more than any man, an eternal body, in the proper sense, is dying. It is cut in half. It is divided.)

Whereas Jallal wonders why the cowboy had to cut down the tree and why he leaves it behind without looking back, the opening scene of the film offers no explanation. While the magnificent scenery that follows is a celebration of the beauty of nature and life, Jallal finds it sad, cruel and frightening. He pictures the scenery as a scene of mourning, as a funeral for the tree:

> Les autres arbres se sont détournés. Ils ont peur de regarder. On les comprend. La mort est dure à regarder. On ferme les yeux. On les voit: les arbres sont tous en train de fermer lentement leurs yeux. Mais nous, on est fascinés, captives, et on continue de regarder. De regarder sans savoir quand on doit nous aussi fermer les yeux.[98]

> (The other trees have turned away. They are afraid to look. We understand them. Death is hard to look at. We close our eyes. We see them: All the trees are slowly closing their eyes. But we're fascinated, captivated, and we keep looking. Watching without knowing when we should also close our eyes.)

This scene of mourning Jallal imagines as a scene of fascination and fear. The fellow trees are paralysed, afraid to look, but the onlooker is fascinated by death as well as by the fear of the trees. Given the themes of stigmatization, radicalization and suicide bombing in *Infidèles*, it is difficult not to read Jallal's interpretation of the film scene as an analogy of how we (the media, readers, witnesses) often revel in suffering and death with disturbing indifference towards the underlying meaning(lessness) of it all. The scene, moreover, seems to mirror how Taïa himself was the uprooted object of both fascination and fear when he came out in public. But to Jallal, the opening scene of *River of No Return* remains enigmatic, and he keeps questioning its meaning.[99] In the film, the opening scene is devoid of meaning insofar as it is meaningless to cut down a tree in order to depict beauty, but later on it turns out that Matt, Kay and Mark use the tree to escape down the river. In *Infidèles*, the opening scene and the tree as raft come to mirror the indifference with which Jallal and his mother are treated. What is the purpose of the stigmatization and violence they encounter? What is the purpose of forcing them to live an uprooted life with no sense of belonging anywhere?

Almost paradoxically, the film simultaneously forms part of Jallal's loving memories both of his mother and of one of her regular clients. Not far from their new house in Hay Salam (where Jallal has convinced his mother to move) is a military base. Many of Slima's new clients are soldiers, and Jallal and Slima become particularly attached to one of them: 'Il était beau comme un père imaginaire. Il n'existait pas. Le métier de ma mère l'avait fait exister. Le rêve, le fantasme impossible, était devenu une réalité. Deux fois par semaine, ce soldat était notre père dans notre nouvelle maison.' (He was beautiful like an imaginary father. He didn't exist. My mother's profession had made him exist. The dream, the impossible fantasy, had become a reality. Twice a week, this soldier was our father in our new home.)[100]

For two years – from when Jallal is eleven until he is almost thirteen – the soldier comes to visit them twice a week, while Jallal visits the soldier four to five times a week. But the nature of their relationship remains ambiguous: Jallal is apparently as much the object of the soldier's desire as he is a boy the soldier cares for as if he were his son: 'Il ne s'est jamais plaint de ma presences trop envahissante, de mes chansons trop naïves et de mes fesses trop maigres. Pour me faire aimer un peu plus de lui, je me suis inventé un rôle. Sa bonne. Le bordel de sa chambre, c'était moi qui le rangeais.' (He never complained about my too invasive presences, my too naive songs and my too thin ass. To make me loved a little more by him, I invented a role for myself. His maid. The brothel of his room, it was me who tidied it up.)[101] For two years, Jallal sees no one but his mother and the soldier. For two years, the soldier is simultaneously father, lover and friend.

Living in this bubble, *River of No Return* – about a cowboy who has just completed a prison sentence, his son who ends up shooting a man in the back just like his father and a saloon singer who cared for the boy while his father was in prison – comes to bind Jallal's memory of his mother to his memory of the soldier. Shortly before the soldier's departure for the war – the novel is set in the 1980s during the Western Sahara War (1975–91) – Jallal and the soldier study the wording of the theme song to *River of No Return*. This is a song of lost love, and on the day of his departure the soldier asks Jallal to sing it to him as a farewell present. He is leaving, and he will probably never return from the war. Jallal, the soldier and Slima know that, and the song of the lost love on the river of no return mirrors what is about to come. But the relationship between Jallal and the soldier remains enigmatic. Is the soldier exploiting him, is he caring for him as a father for his son or is there a degree of mutual recognition between them that escapes a simple relationship of sexual exchange, friendship or father-to-son? The relationship even eludes Jallal; but although the soldier's intentions are unclear, his kindness and companionship bring love into Slima and Jallal's life.

Whereas Jallal naively links his mother's tears to her self-identification with the sad and beautiful Monroe, and he thinks the soldier's departure and journey towards death does not touch her, the relationship between Slima and the soldier turns out to be closer than Jallal ever imagined. But the twelve-year-old Jallal is so captivated by the film and his own relationship with the soldier that he fails to see their relationship. Instead his mother's fascination with Monroe becomes his own, and he imagines his mother as Marilyn and Marilyn's sadness as a mirror of his mother's:

Ma mère, cette nuit-là, s'appelait Marilyn. Elle était mécréante comme elle. Malheureuse comme elle. Une pute. Une servante. Une déesse. Elle se cachait. *River of No Return* me révélait ma mère autrement. Elle n'était pas seulement ma mère. Elle n'était pas qu'à moi. Elle était la mère des autres aussi. La mère, la sœur jumelle de Marilyn.

Le cinéma a été inventé pour cela. Nous faire voir nos mères sous un nouveau jour. Les avoir pour toujours. Les partager sans aucune réticence. Sans aucune jalousie.

Je m'appelle Jallal.

Je suis le fils de Marilyn Monroe.[102]

(My mother, that night, was called Marilyn. She was a disbeliever like her. Unhappy like her. A whore. A servant. A goddess. She was hiding. *River of No Return* showed me my mother differently. She was not only my mother. She was not just for me. She was the mother of others too. Marilyn's mother, twin sister.

Cinema was invented for that. To make us see our mothers in a new light. Have them forever. Share them without any reluctance. Without any jealousy.

My name is Jallal.

I'm the son of Marilyn Monroe.)

The amalgamation of Monroe and Slima simultaneously elevates Slima to an unrecognized goddess and reveals that Jallal is too young to understand her troubles. On the one hand, Jallal feels her misery, and through the figure of Monroe he captures her split existence as someone who simultaneously satisfies men and lives a marginalized life. On the other hand, he fails to see that her life is more complicated than that. The most brutal passage of *Infidèles* is when Slima tells Jallal how she was imprisoned and tortured because she was alleged to know about their soldier's involvement with the Polisario Front, the Sahrawi national liberation movement whose aim is to end the Moroccan presence in Western Sahara. In *Infidèles*, the soldier is associated with General Dlimi, Hassan II's right-hand man after General Oufkir, and who allegedly sought to overthrow Hassan II in a third coup in 1983 to put an end to the regime's corruption and human rights violations and to start negotiations with the Polisario. It turns out that Slima knows everything about their soldier, and about all the other soldiers who came to visit her regularly. At this point, real-life names pop up in the novel: in addition to General Dlimi, Slima faces Youssfi Kaddour, she questions the role of the interior minister, Driss Basri, in ordering her torture, and she is imprisoned somewhere in the desert in southern Morocco next to the Oufkir family.

Neither timeline nor places precisely match historical events, but the names nevertheless draw reality into the novel and turn it into a literary testimony of the Years of Lead from the point of view of a non-intellectual, non-activist prostitute. Slima self-defines as anti-intellectual,[103] and she is in no way active in political resistance, but her professional and intimate relationships with the soldiers make her a target of state-sponsored political violence. For three years she is imprisoned and tortured, only to realize that the soldier died well before her arbitrary arrest. As with the tree in *River of No Return*, meaninglessness resounds around Slima's torture, crushing, and the annihilation of her very being in order to extract from her information about soldiers who have already been killed and thrown into the sea. But just as the tree will probably live on in a new shape, Slima's time in prison functions as a rite of passage, mirroring a significant rite of passage in Taïa's own life.

Similarly to how former political prisoners have depicted the torture they endured in prison, Slima is subjected to brutal, sexualized violence. However, she soon realizes that her torturers are not sexually frustrated and hungry for sex; the only thing they desire is to see blood flowing, and this paralyses her: 'Résister aux hommes assoiffés de sexe, c'est mon métier. Ne leur donner ce que je veux. Peu. Très peu. Mais comment résister à la police secrète? Autant te le dire tout de suite, mon fils, je n'ai pas pu résister. Je n'ai pas su. Ce n'étaient pas des hommes. C'étaient des bouchers. Des monstres.' (To resist men who are thirsty for sex is my profession. To only give them what I want. Little. Very little. But how to resist the secret police? As much as I can tell you right away, my son, I couldn't resist. I didn't know. They weren't men. They were butchers. Monsters.)[104]

What is significant here is not so much how she is tortured, but what the torture scenes reveal about sex, power and violence. In her professional life as a prostitute, Slima was used to being in control. She held what men desired, and men respectfully and humbly obeyed her to have their thirst satisfied, whether her insistence that her house not be turned into a souk or her order that they should not scream at orgasm.[105] But in prison, she is deprived of this control. Her profession is reduced to 'legitimate rape' and it becomes a tool to crush her with: 'Ils disaient que, puisque j'étais une pute assumée, il fallait me traiter en pute. M'honorer ainsi. Me violer du matin au soir. Au milieu de la nuit. À tout moment.' (They said that, because I was a whore out in the open, they had to treat me like a whore. Honor me like that. Rape me from morning until evening. In the middle of the night. At any time.)[106]

In this respect, prison is the extreme mirror of the dehumanization Jallal and Slima faced in the hammams of Hay Al-Inbiâth. Inside as well as outside of prison, sex workers meet monsters in the form of men. They live with the risk of commodification, sexual violence and rape; they struggle to be respected as dignified human beings. Thus Slima is both in power and deprived of power. The torture scene represents the extreme case of deprivation, where sex is not a question of desire, but an instrument of humiliation and torture. The torturers are the monsters of monsters, and to Slima they come to represent exactly that: a mirror of the worst sides of Morocco, and what makes her leave her home country as soon as she is out of prison, never to come back. In this respect, *Infidèles* is not dissimilar to El Bouih's depiction of prison as simultaneously 'monstrous other' and 'distorted mirror' of society.

Rape and all sorts of torture in the end make Slima confess, but she never internalizes the misogynistic world view that a woman can be shamed into silence and destroyed by sexualized violence. She wishes to die, she regrets giving birth to Jallal in such a cruel world, but she never accepts the torturers' view on prostitutes, and she remains faithful to her and Jallal's soldier.

Tellingly, her confession functions as a multilayered rite of passage – from silence to speaking, from prison to freedom, from Morocco to Egypt. To save herself, she must let herself be destroyed. But through this destruction, she is constituted anew. One of the means of torture is the recurring sound of animals barking, blaring, screaming – all sorts of infernal noises that disrupt silence every five minutes, and horrify Slima. At first she is convinced that the animals are right above her, but after a couple of days she realizes that the torturers are replaying the same sounds again and again, day and night. Despite her conviction that she will never get used to these sounds, that she will never survive without sleep, the sounds end up rescuing her by transforming a life in silence into voiced resistance:

J'ai cru que je ne survivrais pas à ces bruits d'apocalypse. Et pourtant, dans mon effondrement physique total, dans ma déchéance, ma mort lente, un miracle s'est produit. Ne m'ayant pas tuée, ces bruits ont fini par devenir mes accompagnateurs. Mes repères. Mes amis. Je les reconnaissais tous, un par un, ces animaux fictifs, ces voix dans l'agonie. Je les appelais même, parfois. Je devenais, petit à petit, folle avec eux, avec et par eux.
Je parlais.
Ce sont elles, ces voix, qui m'ont permis de parler. Encouragée à le faire.
Parler. Parler. Parler. Enfin.
Tu m'as connue dans le silence, Jallal. Dans l'action sans paroles.
Là-bas, loin, entre deux mondes, près du bourreau El-Hadj Kaddour el-Yousfi, j'ai crié des mots. J'ai murmuré, chuchoté, caressé des mots.
Je parlais aux animaux.
Les animaux me parlaient.
Tu me crois, mon fils à moi? Tu me crois, petit Jallal?
Je ne pouvais rien faire d'autre. Je suis analphabète. Pas cultivée.
J'ai communiqué avec des animaux qui n'existaient pas. Ils me tuaient et me libéraient. Grâce à eux, j'ai finalement pu résister à la torture.[107]

(I thought that I wouldn't survive these sounds of apocalypse. And yet, in my total physical collapse, in my decline, my slow death, a miracle occurred. Not having killed me, these sounds ended up becoming my companions. My bearings. My friends. I recognized them all, one by one, these fictitious animals, these voices in agony. I even called them sometimes. I became, little by little, mad with them, with and by them.
I talked.
It was them, these voices, that allowed me to talk. Encouraged to do so.
Talk. Talk. Talk. Finally.
You've known me in silence, Jallal. In action without words.
There, far away, between two worlds, near the executioner El-Hadj Kaddour el-Yousfi, I shouted words. I murmured, whispered, caressed words.
I talked to the animals.
The animals talked to me.
You believe me, my son? You believe me, little Jallal?
I couldn't do anything else. I'm illiterate. Not cultivated.
I communicated with animals that didn't exist. They killed me and freed me.
Thanks to them, I could finally resist torture.)

Driving her mad, the animal voices end up breaking Slima down. But in her own way, she turns her confession into an act of resistance. That is, while the torturers kill silent Slima, she finds new ways to resist through the act of speaking. Torture makes Slima talk; not simply as a forced confession but as a dismantling of the power of the torturers. To the torturers she confesses everything she knows about General Dlimi and the other soldiers – their political discussions, their plan to assassinate Hassan II – but she exaggerates to protect their soldier. On the day of her release, El-Hadj Kaddour el-Yousfi believes that her and Jallal's soldier was faithful to Hassan II until his last breath. While it remains questionable whether this makes any difference in the end, Slima nevertheless finds a way to survive by not giving the torturers everything and by remaining faithful to their beloved soldier. And on her way out of prison, she does what Jallal wanted to do while they were living in Hay Al-Inbiâth. She spits El-Hadj Kaddour el-Yousfi in the face, twice. Outside the prison, Slima is suddenly sure that he is both self-loathing and exhausted from torturing so many people. Instead of turning angry, he sheds a tear, as if her act of abasement has done him good. He says: 'Pars, ma fille. Pars avant qu'il ne soit trop tard. Quitte ce pays. Quitte ce Maroc où il n'y a plus de place ni pour toi ni pour moi. Pars. Pars . . .' (Go, my girl. Go before it's too late. Leave this country. Leave this Morocco where there is no longer room for neither you nor me. Go. Go . . .)[108] Instead of Slima being completely destroyed by the torture, the focus shifts to El-Hadj Kaddour el-Yousfi's self-destruction through torturing. Slima is leaving, but he is still trapped. Thus her life in forced exile is simultaneously staged as a life of resistance.

While Slima's life is anything but an autobiographical depiction of Taïa's life, it nevertheless mirrors how Taïa's life transformed from one lived in silence to one of voiced resistance after years of 'killing the self' in order to prevent others from destroying him.[109] Just as the silent Slima is annihilated after years of torture, the effeminate Taïa disappeared forever when he became a teenager and forced himself to hide his sexuality for fear of sexual violence and rape. As a teenager, Taïa turned to silence to protect himself; whereas Slima's silence remains enigmatic, it nevertheless guards over a past that no one will ever know, neither Saâdia, who took her in at the age of six, nor Jallal, nor the reader.

In this respect, the passage from silence to voiced resistance is ambiguous. That is, voiced resistance grants agency to Slima, to Taïa and, in testimonial writing, to political prisoners; but speaking up will never reveal everything. Just as El Bouih points to the forgotten women criminal prisoners, *Infidèles* is the story of a mother and a son who suffered immensely during the Years of Lead, but whose stories have never been included in the narrative of national recovery. In this respect, El-Hadj Kaddour el-Yousfi is right: there is neither room for the torturers nor for women like Slima in the process of national reconciliation.

Queering extremism

Outside the prison it is spring, and in the heavenly beauty of a wadi in the south of Morocco, Slima mourns the death of the soldier while remembering the end of *River of No Return*, where Marilyn Monroe throws her red shoes from the carriage in which she, the cowboy and the boy are riding off together. But whereas Marilyn got her cowboy and will never go back to her old job of saloon singer, Slima's soldier is dead, so she is forced to go back to hers. She picks up Marilyn's shoes – her skin, her struggle, her sadness, her tragedy and, in spite of everything, her hope – and with her shoes she is determined to gather the means to go to Cairo to reunite with Jallal: 'Le voyage continue. Les larmes ne s'arrêteront jamais.' (The journey continues. The tears will never stop.)[110] Like the tree, she is violently uprooted, and her reinvention in exile is at a great cost.

When Slima and Jallal reunite in Cairo – where Slima, with the help of a rich client, managed to send Jallal before her imprisonment – Jallal has turned sixteen. After three years apart, they are estranged from one another.[111] As argued by Jean-Pierre Boulé, the distance between Slima and Jallal mirrors the distance created by Taïa's coming-out interview between him and his mother.[112] Tellingly, the novel is dedicated to Taïa's mother, M'Barka, who died in 2010. The loving relationship between Slima and Jallal, painfully disrupted by their forced separation, also ends with Slima's death. While Slima has been destroyed and forced to rebuild herself after three years of torture, not only has Jallal grown into a young man but teenage life without Slima and in complete solitude has changed him, and they never really reconnect: 'Je suis devenu ce monstre. Sans ma mère. Même quand elle est revenue, son absence a continué de m'habiter. C'était vraiment une autre femme. Dans un monde opaque.' (I became this monster. Without my mother. Even when she returned, her absence continued to inhabit me. It was really another woman. In an opaque world.)[113]

As in 'L'Homosexualité expliquée à ma mère' and *Un Pays pour mourir*,[114] Jallal's self-identification as monster functions as a literary figure which deconstructs the relation between what is 'normal' and what is 'deviant'. Separated from his mother, he is simultaneously separated from humanity. When the late husband of his mother brings him to Brussels, this cold and suffocating city leads him to reconnect with his childhood urge to spit.[115] But behind this 'bad boy', this 'monster', hides a sensitive man who is searching in vain for love, companionship and recognition. When he meets Mahmoud (a Belgian convert to Islam who is hospitalized with terminal cancer), he finds the final purpose of his life: a suicide mission, to revenge his mother through an act of love.

This is a troubling story of love and violence. The narrative strategy of depicting Jallal as exclusively sensitive and sympathetic simultaneously disturbs dominant narrations of Islamic extremism as monstrous and queers the idea of brotherhood and religious salvation through the suicide mission. Jallal's final mission intertwines his story with that of Saâdia and Slima. All three reinvent Islam in order to leave this world purified and reunite in heaven. These 'infidels' are the ones who are going to heaven, where Marilyn Monroe awaits them. Thus the whole question of what it means to be religious is disturbed. In marked contrast to *Un Pays pour mourir*, the characters in *Infidèles* find peace and recognition in the afterlife.

Entwined with the story of how Slima goes to Mecca and Medina on her first and last pilgrimage to unite with her prophet as simultaneous believer and non-believer, Muslim and non-Muslim,[116] the story of Jallal's haphazard shift to extremism is less about religious radicalization than about love, companionship and brotherhood. Jallal and Mahmoud become intimate friends, both physically and spiritually. Jallal sleeps in the hospital bed with Mahmoud, hiding from the world in his arms. They recite the ninety-nine names of Allah. Right before their suicide mission in Casablanca, they spend the night in the Hassan II mosque in an ecstatic dance, reminiscent of Sufi whirling. But Mahmoud's intention with the suicide mission remains enigmatic to Jallal. It is not until they put on their explosive belts at an internet café that Jallal realizes that their cause is not the same. Is Islam terrorism or love? Angry, disillusioned and distressed, Jallal is nevertheless soon convinced that Mahmoud also acts from love, and he ends up ashamed of his doubts.[117] Thus Jallal's naivety and insecurity bind love and terrorism together in a double critique of Moroccan human rights abuses, Islamic extremism and European xenophobia. To Jallal, the only way to leave a testament of his and his mother's suffering is through a suicide mission:

> Laisser un testament. Un message. Lequel?
> Je ne savais pas s'il avait raison de vouloir commetre un attentat. Je savais, en revanche, qu'on est obligé à un moment donné d'interpeller, de cracher fort, ne plus être bien élevé, ne plus être petit. Rendre service. Se sacrifier. Violemment, mourir pour les autres. Pour l'islam et sa gloire?[118]

> (Leave a testament. A message. Which?
> I didn't know if he was right in wanting to commit an attack. I knew, on the other hand, that we're obliged at a given moment to shout, to spit hard, no longer be well-behaved, no longer be a kid. To help. Sacrifice oneself. Violently, die for others. For Islam and its glory?)

Read as literature of testament, *Infidèles* is disturbing. When Taïa sent the manuscript to his publisher, Le Seuil, they were disconcerted that he did not condemn terrorism.[119] However, as Taïa himself argues, 'our monsters are like us.'[120] By whiting out the difference between good and evil, the novel challenges official narratives of 'right' and 'wrong' in both Morocco and Europe. In parallel with El Bouih's disturbance of the relation between 'monstrosity' and religious and cultural mores of society through her narration of prison space, Taïa depicts an 'enemy' who is as human, loving, and caring, like anyone.

Significantly, Mahmoud's terrorist mission fails, because the owner of the internet café realizes what they are about to do. Having alerted the police, he tries to hold them in the café, but they escape. In the street, the other internet café guests yell: 'Ce sont eux! Ce sont eux les terroristes! Les terroristes! Ils sont terroristes et pédés.' (They're the ones! They're the terrorists! The terrorists! They're terrorists and faggots.)[121] Significantly, Mahmoud's response is: 'Nous ne sommes pas des pédés. . . . Nous sommes des frères.' (We're not faggots. . . . We're brothers.)[122] The queer relationship between Jallal and Mahmoud exposes Mahmoud's hypocrisy, but he is neither less loved by Jallal nor barred from heaven.

Running away from the police, they end up hiding in a cinema, where Jallal shares his love for *River of No Return* with Mahmoud and they end up singing the theme song together before blowing themselves up. 'On pouvait partir. Maintenant. Rien que tous les deux. Mahmoud. Jallal. Mahmoud et Jallal. Sans prendre personne avec nous. Sauf nos souvenirs à deux. Échouer dans la mission terroriste de Mahmoud. Fous d'Amour, réussir la nôtre.' (We could leave. Now. Just the two of us. Mahmoud. Jallal. Mahmoud and Jallal. Without taking anyone with us. Except our memories of two. Fail in the terrorist mission of Mahmoud. Fools of Love, succeed in ours.)[123] Ultimately, Mahmoud's religiosity is replaced by Jallal's profanity, and instead of reuniting with God through ecstatic dancing in a mosque, they unite through the act of singing a profane love song in a cinema.

Jallal's suicide mission – which is narrated as a radical act of 'writing' a testimony of love and companionship in a world of violence and suffering – simultaneously queers extremism and constitutes the extreme case of the 'self-absorbed' as a site of queer commitment. The narrative strategy of combining terrorism and love cannot be reduced to a literary comment on terrorism. Instead, it functions as a literary technique of pushing the 'self-absorbed' to the extreme: only by blowing himself up can Jallal scream his existence to the world – but through this scream, he is in the same moment gone forever.

Ultimately, the message they send is a message of courage, faith, love and despair.[124] At the gate of heaven, Marilyn Monroe awaits them, beyond 'wordly categorizations': 'Je suis humaine. Extraterrestre. Partout. Nulle part. Homme. Femme. Ni l'un ni l'autre. Au-delà de toutes les frontiers. Toutes les langues.'[125] (I'm human. Extraterrestrial. Everywhere. Nowhere. Man. Woman. Neither the one nor the other. Beyond all borders. All languages.)[125] With Monroe, social constructions of masculinity and femininity, as well as their embodiment in political violence, are completely dismantled. Whereas life on earth in *Infidèles* is an exploration of 'everyday time', with its discontinuous and heterogeneous narratives that are disavowed by official narratives of the 'nation', life in heaven subverts these hegemonic regimes, but without whiting out identity or suffering. Jallal and Mahmoud can now be together as brothers, and Slima has found spirituality, has reunited with Saâdia and is awaiting Mouad. But the soldier still suffers from PTSD.

Screaming as queer resistance

Both *Ḥadīth al-ʿatmah* and *Infidèles* counter silence with the ambivalence of screaming. On the one hand, screaming is a collective expression of resistance as opposed to enforced silence. Contrary to crying, which is a more private expression, screaming is audible in the public sphere and constitutes an effort to escape oppression and violence – for instance women prisoners screaming to protect themselves and each other against rape. But on the other, screaming is also the last resort when words and arguments are ignored. As opposed to the articulated word of voiced resistance and testimony, screaming is an act of desperation.

In *Infidèles* talking, rambling, singing and blowing oneself up function as an effort to scream one's queer existence to the world. That is, similarly to how *Ḥadīth al-'atmah* disturbs the relation between normality and monstrosity, the stories of Saâdia, Slima and Jallal dismantle the regulatory regime of the 'Hetero-Nation' by deconstructing the relation between 'norm' and 'deviance'. In this respect, screaming is both a means to reappropriate and reconfigure Moroccan history and community and what reveals how difficult it is for queers to be seen and heard in their difference.

In contrast to *Ḥadīth al-'atmah*, *Infidèles* is full of monsters yet devoid of 'good' and 'evil'. Like *Ḥadīth al-'atmah*, however, by disturbing the relation between 'monstrosity' and cultural and religious norms, *Infidèles* challenges official narratives of 'right' and 'wrong'. That is, similarly to how the child murderer, F.L., comes to haunt society as a distorted image of dominant moral narratives about women's role in society, the *introductrice* Saâdia simultaneously safeguards and subverts conservative norms of sexual conduct. In this respect, both texts queer the 'nation' by narrating the stories of those who have been silenced by heteronormative narrations of the 'nation'.

Infidèles is significantly different from testimonial literature written by former political prisoners, but in situating the narrative in Morocco during the Years of Lead, it nevertheless relates to a larger effort to rewrite Moroccan history in order to include the stories of those who have not been considered part of national recovery. The testament Jallal leaves in *Infidèles* is a testament of suffering, of how the loss of his mother simultaneously is a loss of humanity. However, despite his feeling that this loss has turned him into a monster, Jallal is a sensitive boy in search of love and companionship. His suicide mission is thus not simply violent revenge but also an act love. It is both Jallal's way of spitting back hard at all the people who have mistreated him and his mother and his way of leaving a testimony of love for his mother.

The mother figure is perhaps the most important figure in Taïa's writing and the literary character that best captures the sense of being beyond 'worldy categorizations' as Marilyn Monroe in *Infidèles*. Significantly, *Infidèles* is dedicated to Taïa's mother, who died in 2010, and the question 'where does one turn for companionship in the absence of a mother?' is thus an autobiographical one. To Jallal the absence of his mother is replaced by the theme song of *River of No Return*, just as cinema and literature to Taïa is a space to resuscitate his mother and create an experimental nation for alternative ways of being in the world. But *Infidèles* is also a story of melancholy, sadness and despair. Because without a mother who understands the language of love, hysteria and tyranny, the desperate screams of a sensitive boy suddenly appear monstrous and in *Infidèles* takes the shape of a suicide mission.

CONCLUSION

HYSTERIA AS MASK AND THERAPY

Le monde n'est plus le monde, ma mère. Et ton coeur qui me portait et qui jamais ne m'a rejeté à cause de mon homosexualité, ce coeur dur, c'est vrai, ce coeur sauvage, c'est vrai, ce coeur est devenu mon coeur. Je suis comme toi. Exactement comme toi. Je vis pour moi et pour toi. Le devoir de mémoire? Peut-être. Mieux: l'impossibilité de ne pas voir l'évidence. La vie c'est la mort, la mort c'est la vie. Et entre ces deux étapes, il y a un tunnel. Et dans ce tunnel, on crie. On doit crier. Il ne faut jamais jamais s'arrêter crier.[1]

(The world is no longer the world, my mother. And your heart which carried me, and which never rejected me because of my homosexuality, this hard heart, it's true, this wild heart, it's true, this heart has become my heart. I'm like you. Exactly like you. I live for myself and for you. The duty of memory? Perhaps. Better: the impossibility of not seeing the obvious. Life is death, death is life. And between these two stages, there is a tunnel. And in this tunnel, we scream. We must scream. We should never never stop screaming.)

Since Abdellah Taïa wrote *L'Armée du salut* in 2006, hysteria has connected his creative writing with his mother. It is his mother who has taught him how to scream in spite of everything – to write without fear of 'criticism and incessant sneers'[2] – and it is after the loss of his mother that life and death have come to interpenetrate in his writing, such as in *Infidèles* and *Un Pays pour mourir*. Thus, if the act of screaming bridges life and death, as in the above-mentioned quote, then the hysterical scream comes to embody an effort of space making – that is, a speech act that stakes out an experimental nation for Arab-Muslim queers.

But the world has changed since Taïa published *Un Pays pou mourir*. In 2015 a wave of terrorist attacks swept over Paris and France – from the attack on Charlie Hebdo on 7 January 2015 until the co-ordinated attacks on 13 November 2015 that killed 130 people and after which President François Hollande declared a state of emergency which was to last for two years. Within this state of emergency and with a sharpened anti-immigration rhetoric the space for Arab-Muslim queers has grown even smaller. This claustrophobic space is what Taïa grapples with in his two latest novels, *Celui qui est digne d'être aimé* (2017) and *La Vie lente* (2019). In many respects, these two novels rearticulate themes that have dominated

Taïa's writings since his debut in 2000, particularly the 'self-absorbed' as a site of queer commitment and its symbiotic relation to the mother figure and hysteria. Throughout Taïa's writing the mother figures hold love and mercy, hysteria, violence and tyranny. It is in the women, who through hysteria resists patriarchy, that Taïa finds his inspiration, and it is in these women that he mirrors his queer characters.

From exotic sexual object to calculated seduction

In *Celui qui est digne d'être aimé* and *La Vie lente* Taïa has displaced the narrative of the 'emancipated Arab boy' altogether. Contrary to the coming-into-existence story of *L'Armée du salut*, *Celui qui est digne d'être aimé* is the story of a tormented life and of a protagonist who has turned calculated and cruel after a life of being the exotic sexual object of French men's desire while simultaneously being treated as just another immigrant who does not belong in France and whose sexual attraction will diminish the older he gets. Thus, whereas *L'Armée du salut* through naivety and a redefinition of freedom in the West parodies the stereotypic 'narrative of arrival', where 'being queer' presupposes coming out in public, arriving in the city centre of Paris, and leaving one's religion, culture, family and community behind, *Celui qui est digne d'être aimé* narrates the life of a forty-year-old Arab-Muslim queer in Paris who is as trapped as ever.

Celui qui est digne d'être aimé is an epistolary novel that over the course of four letters moves back in time (from 2015 to 1990) to find the source of the evil controlling the life of forty-year-old Ahmed. In the first letter Ahmed writes to his mother, who passed away five years earlier. Similarly to Taïa's earlier novels, this letter displaces the gendered space of traditional patriarchy. Contrary to the classical narrative of an oppressive patriarch and his submissive wife, such as in Driss Chraïbi's *Le Passé simple*, Taïa questions what it means to be in 'power' through hysterical mother figures. In *Celui qui est digne d'être aimé* the mother's hysteria is made more explicit while the narrator's relation to her is rendered complicated. In this novel the mother is cold, cynical and calculated rather than controlled by her feelings. The novel depicts a rather unsympathetic mother who dominates others to avoid being dominated herself. But as Ahmed reproduces his mother's strategies to survive in an unkind world, the first letter of *Celui qui est digne d'être aimé* is also a self-critique. Whereas Jallal in *Infidèles* has been separated from humanity through the loss of his mother, Ahmed is both lost without his mother and because he mirrors himself in her. In this respect, *Celui qui est digne d'être aimé* is a melancholic story of how Arab-Muslim women and queers are trapped by the same patriarchal and neocolonial structures that they disturb.

Ahmed is predetermined to do as his mother, and it is through the radically 'self-absorbed' position that he breaks the hearts of his lovers in order to be able to exist himself.

> Je revenais à ce cœur égoïste que tu m'as donné, Malika. Et, crois-le ou pas, cela me soulageait chaque fois. Partir. Quitter. Rompre. Casser le lien. Ne rien laisser à l'autre. Retourner à la case depart. Seul. Avec mon cœur terrible, terrifiant.[3]

(I returned to that selfish heart you gave me, Malika. And, believe it or not, that relieved me every time. Leave. Quit. Break up. Cut the tie. Leave nothing to the other. Return to square one. Alone. With my terrible, terrifying heart.)

Similarly to how Driss in *Le Passé simple* hits out violently against whoever crosses his way, Ahmed takes pleasure in leaving his lovers behind even though he is left alone himself. Ahmed is as angry at the world as Driss is, and just as Driss's agency is predetermined by the oppression of his father and the hypocrisy of the French colonial power, Ahmed's acts are predetermined by the dictatorship of his mother and the exoticizing gazes of his lovers. But while Driss revolts to become a man in his own right, Ahmed faces a future where he will be completely alone – too old to be the sexual object of French men's desire and thus without a weapon to control others.

The second letter is written in 2010 by one of Ahmed's 'victims', Vincent, a man he seduces in the Parisian metro and has a one-night stand with. Vincent is older than Ahmed and is immediately captivated by the vulnerability and determination of this beautiful young man. But Vincent falls as much in love with the idea of saving someone like Ahmed, without recognizing the underlying exoticization which Ahmed – in a seductive gesture – calls romantic. However, similarly to how the emotional vulnerability of Taïa's characters disarms the reader, Vincent realizes that the vulnerability that he understood as intimacy between the two was probably nothing but a perfect performance. But Vincent is still in love and writes a letter in a desperate hope to win Ahmed back. Thus, whereas Abdellah in *L'Armée du salut* in all his naivety is accused of exploiting sex tourism the moment he frees himself of its hold, Ahmed appears less naive than calculated in his seduction of Vincent. Ahmed might be trapped by the exoticizing gazes of French men, but he effectively frees himself from these by parodying the expectations of his lovers until the power balance has turned in his favour. That is, similarly to how the sexual storytelling of authors such as Taïa and Rachid O. plays into the expectations of their readers, Ahmed reproduces exotic stereotypes about Arab-Muslim queers in order to seduce French men only to leave them behind heartbroken. Thus, whereas *L'Armée du salut* corresponded to a consumption demand of testimonial literature about clandestine Arab sexuality, and Taïa therefore has been accused of self-orientalization and of perpetuating the 'native informant' trope, *Celui qui est digne d'être aimé* is explicitly postcolonial in its critique of how these exoticizing gazes destroy the lives of Arab-Muslim queers.

The third letter further explains why Ahmed plays with other people's feelings – breaks their hearts before they come to close and break his. This letter is a farewell letter to his boyfriend Emmanuel, written an early morning in 2005. Ahmed and Emmanuel have been together for thirteen years. It is thanks to Emmanuel that Ahmed lives in Paris, speaks French perfectly, knows French literature and lives a life in material wealth. When Ahmed at the age of seventeen meets Emmanuel, who is older, rich and important, he is happy and convinced that Emmanuel is his ticket to a better life far away from poor Salé. But instead of finding happiness he is uprooted. Emmanuel convinces him to study French literature instead of Arabic literature, takes him to Paris and encourages him to change his name because Ahmed is too difficult to pronounce for the French. Emmanuel creates a perfect little Frenchman out of Ahmed. But what is left is 'Midou' (a shortage of 'Hamidou', the definite form of Ahmed, which is easier to pronounce but also too foreign to Emmanuel), who has lost his intimacy with the Arabic language, his family and culture and instead has become a parody of Tintin's little dog 'Milou'.

However, contrary to his childhood friend, Lahbib, Ahmed does not choose death. He runs away from Emmanuel and for better and worse becomes a mirror of his mother. There is no salvation in *Celui qui est digne d'être aimé* and the most touching letter in the novel is the fourth letter written by Lahbib in 1990. Lahbib, *al-habib*, the loved one, the one who deserves to be loved, was Ahmed's closest friend and confident in Morocco. But Lahbib has turned seventeen, and he is no longer the feminine boy, that his French lover desires. He has become 'too old' and in all his desperation he commits suicide. The letter to Ahmed is his suicide letter. He cannot stay with his lover Gérard, but he cannot return to the 'prison' he and Ahmed came from either. The only thing left is to tell fifteen-year-old Ahmed about the humiliation and the unequal power balance, in order to prepare him for what will come and for him to revenge Lahbib.

Significantly, in *Celui qui est digne d'être aimé* Ahmed's older brother, the first-born son, 'the one who deserves to be loved' by the mother, is also the silent son. Masculine, quiet and in control of his feelings. It was this silent masculinity that Taïa spoke up against, when he started to write and later came out publicly; the silence that both protects against homophobic assaults and reproduces the cultural and religious norms that ostracize LGBT persons. With *Celui qui est digne d'être aimé* he takes this a step further and questions whether or not we are willing to hear that it is not only patriarchal and heteronormative traditions but also oppressive neocolonial structures that complicate life as an Arab, Muslim, immigrant and homosexual. As Lahbib says in *Celui qui est digne d'être aimé*, 'Le monde n'aime et n'appricie que ceux qui savent raconter les gros mensonges avec la plus grande assurance. Nous devons être comme ça, toi et moi. . . . Mon frère Ahmed . . . Des grands menteurs.' (The world loves and appreciates only those who know how to tell big lies with the greatest confidence. We must be like that, you and me. . . . My brother, Ahmed . . . Great liars.)[4] Because who wants to hear the truth, and who can survive by telling it?

Hysteria and terrorism

Whereas *Celui qui est digne d'être aimé* begins with a letter to Ahmed's mother, the mother is more or less absent in *La Vie lente*, and it is not until the end of the novel that the reader finds out that Mounir's hysteria and urge to act out stems from this absence. With *La Vie lente* Taïa has written an intensely neurotic book about a sensitive and hysterical, calculated and lost man in Paris.

La Vie lente is the story of a remarkable friendship and an intense conflict between Mounir Rochdi and Madame Marty. Mounir is a forty-year-old Moroccan homosexual who is completely lost in Paris. Madame Marty is a poor eighty-year-old woman, who lives alone in a tiny studio of 14 square metres and with a toilet in the hall. Mounir becomes particularly connected to this upstairs neighbour, who both reminds him of his mother and reveals how radically displaced he is. Their relationship is a loving relationship between a mother, who has lost her relation to her son, and a son, who has lost his mother. They are both lonely and invisible in a society that does not care for their stories. But it is also a violent relationship between a hysterical man, driven to madness by the noises of his upstairs neighbour, and a frightened old woman, who ends up calling the police because she is afraid that her downstairs neighbour is a terrorist.

In *La Vie lente* the neuroses and hysterical outbursts of Mounir function as both mask and therapeutic room, and, similarly to *Celui qui est digné d'être aimé*, it is through hysteria that Taïa challenges dominant narratives of femininity and masculinity, of normality and monstrosity, of East and West. The urge to scream, exaggerate and hurl insults at others is something Mounir has taken with him from his childhood in Morocco. It functions as a mask that protects him in a brutal world.

> Au lieu de laisser le Pouvoir nous tuer, on le faisait nous-mêmes. On se déchirait à longueur de journée, à longueur d'année. On ne parlait pas. On aboyait. Et il n'y avait que cela qui était compris, respecté, voire admire.
>
> Petit adolescent gay efféminé et persécuté par des hommes hétérosexuels affamés de sexe, ce n'est que lorsque j'avais décidé d'être violent à mon tour, violent par les mots, qu'on avait changé d'attitude vis-à-vis de moi. Plus j'étais ordurier dans mon langage, plus on me foutait la paix. Plus je parlais comme les égouts, moins on me violait.[5]

> (Instead of letting the State kill us, we did it ourselves. We tore each other all day long, all year long. We didn't talk. We barked. And that was the only thing which was understood, respected, even admired.
>
> Little effeminate gay teenager and persecuted by heterosexual men hungry for sex, it was only when I decided to be violent myself, violent with words, that they changed attitude toward me. The more vulgar my language was, the more they left me alone. The more I spoke like the sewers, the less they raped me.)

Similarly to how *Ḥadīth al-ʿatmah* and *Infidèles* counter silence with the ambivalence of screaming, Mounir's urge to scream is ambiguous. On the one hand, he has learnt how to scream to resist violence and rape. In this respect, screaming is the opposite of the self-imposed silence that Taïa experienced as a teenager. But on the other hand, screaming is also an act of desperation to Mounir. It is his last resort, the mask he has to wear to survive in a homophobic world, and as such it is the opposite of voiced resistance and testimony. His screams are his silence.

But in Paris it has become a mask to restrain his urge to scream, and Mounir struggles with having adjusted to this new world to such an extent that he has lost himself.

Bien élevé. Bien éduqué. Docile, quoi. Fade. Mou. Ennuyeux. Pas de coquilles. Plus de fierté arabe en toi. Tu es sans espoir. Tu ferais mieux de te jeter par la fenêtre puisque, depuis trois ans, tu as renoncé à cette flamme en toi, ce petit côté sauvage qui faisait que tu leur résistais un peu quand même.[6]

(Well-mannered. Well-educated. Docile, what. Bland. Soft. Boring. No balls. No more Arab pride in you. You are hopeless. You better throw yourself out the window because for three years you have renounced this flame in you, this little wild side that made you resist them a little anyway.)

Mounir's hysterical outbursts parody both the Moroccan world where he grew up and the role the well-integrated Muslim is supposed to play if he does not want to be accused of being a terrorist. But underneath this story hysteria is also what binds Mounir to his mother. It was the language she understood, and the therapy of being understood through hysteria is lost with her. What is left is a mask of hysteria that Mounir hides behind and that terrifies his neighbours. Thus, whereas the violent words that shock Madame Marty and make her call the police are empty to Mounir, the Parisian coolness – the cold zombie life of centre Paris – leaves no room for a hysterical homosexual Moroccan.

Similarly to the characters in *Un Pays pour mourir*, Mounir finds himself alone and invisible. In Paris nobody talks to him or approaches him, and days go by in complete silence – an all-encompassing silence that makes him mad, triggers his hysteria and makes him scream. But in an effort to escape this silence, Mounir turns towards the immigrant community of *la banlieue*, attends prayer in a mosque and considers renouncing his homosexuality – all in the hope to reconnect with his origins and annul his uprootedness. But instead of being recognized as a doubly displaced Arab-Muslim queer, he is accused of leading a double life, and his neuroses and hysterical outbursts make the police suspect that his homosexuality and intellectual manners are a mask made up to cover that he is plotting a terrorist attack.

Similarly to Taïa's earlier works, *La Vie lente* is a poetic rambling which plays with the relationship between fiction and reality. Not just in the loss of a mother does one find Taïa's own story but in all of Mounir's biography – he grew up in Salé, is homosexual, has migrated to Paris and has written his PhD at Sorbonne about Fragonard and the French libertine novel of the eighteenth century. He is the well-integrated, intellectual, homosexual Arab. He is 'free' and about to suffocate. But the most interesting part of Taïa's play with fiction and reality lies not in the autofictional parts of the novel but in the story about the police inspector Antoine. Is Mounir's love for and relationship with Antoine a fiction within a fiction? A way to give the French police after the 2015 attacks a human face? Or does the police inspector who interrogates Mounir live his life on a lie?

Mounir and Antoine meet in the RER A and are immediately sexually attracted to each other. This meeting parallels how Mounir as a teenager let an older man 'have' him in a crowded bus from Rabat to Salé, found intimacy in being groped and ejaculated on by a complete stranger. But with Antoine it is not a fleeting affair. For three months Mounir finds companionship in Antoine and refuge from the silence that permeates his life. But Mounir has turned Parisian – intellectual and arrogant – and unwillingly pushes Antoine away. Contrary to *L'Armée du salut* where Abdellah increasingly comes to stand out as a naive next to Jean who takes him to art galleries and museums, Mounir humiliates Antoine by exposing Antoine's lack of knowledge about Louvre.

In *La Vie lente* the only constant is the silence that surrounds Mounir's life – even his (imagined) affair with Antoine begins in silence and ends in silence. But it is another silence than the one Taïa experienced as a teenager and which he broke when he came out publicly in 2006. It is a silence that has materialized itself after the death of Mounir's mother and is reinforced by life in Paris, where people keep to themselves and nobody screams. Mounir is the embodiment of the impossible location of diasporic Arab-Muslim queers in France, trapped by a globalized rhetoric of a 'sexual clash of civilizations' that constructs the Arab-Muslim 'other' as both misogynist and homophobic. As such Mounir's position as silenced and invisible is the diametric opposite of the iconic status Taïa achieved when he came out publicly. Or perhaps the other side of the coin. Significantly, *La Vie lente* concludes with the police inspector Antoine saying, 'la silence, c'est de la lâcheté' (silence, that's cowardice),[7] because Mounir has turned silent during the interrogation. But who is the coward? Whether Mounir screams or remains silent, he is just another immigrant and potential terrorist whom Antoine denies ever having known. The whole world around Mounir is silent, and without a mother who understands his hysteria, he is nothing but a monstrous 'other'.

NOTES

Introduction

1 *Mon Maroc* and *Le Rouge du tarbouche* have been translated into English in a collected volume and published as *Another Morocco: Selected Stories* in 2017.

2 According to Éditions du Seuil (13 November 2018), Abdellah Taïa's works have been translated into English, German, Castillian, Basque, Catalan, Danish, Italian, Dutch, Romanian, Swedish, Polish, Portuguese and Arabic.

3 Abdelkébir Khatibi, *Maghreb pluriel* (Paris, 1983).

4 Julia Kristeva, *Desire in Language: A Semiotic Approach to Literature and Art* (Oxford, 1987 (1980)), p. 65.

5 Jean-Paul Sartre, *Qu'est-ce que la littérature* (Paris, 2008 (1948)).

6 Other works which focus on historical and contemporary conceptions of *iltizām* are Georges Khalil, Friederike Pannewick and Yvonne Albers (eds), *Commitment and Beyond: Reflections On/Of the Political in Arabic Literature Since the 1940s* (Wiesbaden, 2015) and Tarek El-Ariss, *Trials of Arab Modernity: Literary Affects and the New Political* (New York, 2013), to mention but a few.

7 Robert J. C. Young, 'World Literature and Postcolonialism', in Theo D'haen, David Damrosch and Djalal Kadir (eds), *The Routledge Companion to World Literature* (London and New York, 2012), p. 215.

8 David Damrosch, *What Is World Literature* (Princeton and Oxford, 2003), p. 4.

9 Rebecca Walkowitz, 'Interview with Rebecca Walkowitz, Author of Born Translated', *Columbia University Press 'Blog Archive'*, 28 July 2015.

10 Rebecca Walkowitz, *Born Translated: The Contemporary Novel in an Age of World Literature* (New York, 2015), p. 31.

11 Ibid., p. 21.

12 Homi K. Bhabha, *The Location of Culture* (London, 2004 (1994)).

13 Ibid., p. 53.

14 Benedict Anderson, *Imagined Communities: Reflections on the Origin and Spread of Nationalism* (New York, 1991 (1983)).

15 With this focus, I hope to contribute to a growing academic focus on the need to study Maghrebin literature in its multilingual expression in order to counter its marginalization within hegemonic single-language literary systems. Within the study of Moroccan literature, see, for instance, Abdallah Mdarhri Alaoui, *Apect du roman marocain, (1950-2003): Approche historique, thématique et esthétique* (Rabat, 2006), Khalid Zekri, *Fictions du réel: Modernité romanesque et écriture du réel au Maroc 1990-2006* (Paris, 2006), Karima Laachir, 'The Aesthetics and Politics of "Reading Together" Moroccan Novels in Arabic and French', *The Journal of North African Studies* 21/1 (2016), pp. 22–36, and Gonzalo Fernández Parrilla, 'The Novel in Morocco as Mirror of a Changing Society', *Contemporary French and Francophone Studies* 20/1 (2016), pp. 18–26.

16   Yoav Di-Capua, 'The Intellectual Revolt of the 1950s and the "Fall of the Ubadā"', in Georges Khalil, Friederike Pannewick, and Yvonne Albers, *Commitment and Beyond: Reflections On/Of the Political in Arabic Literature Since the 1940s* (Wiesbaden, 2015), pp. 89–104.

17   Jean Déjeux, 'L' Emergence du je dans la littérature maghrébine de langue française', *Itinéraires et contacts de cultures* 13/1er semestre (1991), pp. 23–9 and 'Au Maghreb, la langue française "langue natale du je"', Martine Mathieu (ed.), *Littératures autobiographiques de la francophonie* (Paris, 1994), pp. 181–93.

18   Georges Gusdorf, 'Conditions and Limits of Autobiography', in James Olney (ed.), *Autobiography: Essays Theoretical and Critical* (Princeton, 1980), pp. 28–48. Whereas Western scholarship has considered Gusdorf's article the foundation of modern autobiography studies and a key to defining autobiography as a Western genre with roots in Christian tradition, Dwight F. Reynolds (ed.) in *Interpreting the Self. Autobiography in the Arabic Literary Tradition* (Berkeley, Los Angeles and London, 2001) points to the Eurocentric underpinnings of Gusdorf's article and argue that it constitutes a reorientation in Western literary criticism rather than a foundation of a new study: 'Autobiography's shift from a general category of literature as conceived by Goethe, Herder, and Dilthey to the culturally specific genre advocated by Gusdorf, May, and Pascal represents a highly significant, and politically suspect, turning point in western intellectual history' (pp. 18–19). For an investigation of autobiography in Arabic literary history, see Reynolds (ed.), *Interpreting the Self.*

19   Said Graiouid, 'We Have Not Buried the Simple Past: The Public Sphere and Post-Colonial Literature in Morocco', *Journal of African Cultural Studies* 20/2 (2008), p. 150.

20   Réda Bensmaïa, *Experimental Nations: Or, the Invention of the Maghreb* (New Jersey, 2003), p. 104.

Chapter 1

1   Éric Fassin, 'Sexual Democracy and the New Racialization of Europe', *Journal of Civil Society* 8/3 (2012), pp. 285–8; Denis M. Provencher, *Queer Maghrebi French. Language, Temporalities, Transfiliations* (Liverpool, 2017); and Mehammed Amadeus Mack, *Sexagon: Muslims, France, and the Sexualization of National Culture* (New York, 2017).

2   Éric Fassin, 'National Identities and Transnational Intimacies: Sexual Democracy and the Politics of Immigration in Europe', *Public Culture* 22/3 (2010), pp. 507–29.

3   Jasbir K. Puar, *Terrorist Assemblages: Homonationalism in Queer Times* (Durham, 2007).

4   Mack, *Sexagon.*

5   Provencher, *Queer Maghrebi French.*

6   Yoav Di-Capua, *No Exit: Arab Existentialism, Jean-Paul Sartre, and Decolonization* (Chicago, 2018).

7   Jarrod Hayes, *Queer Nations: Marginal Sexualities in the Maghreb* (Chicago, 2000), p. 1.

8   Ibid., p. 15.

9   Ernest Renan, *Qu'est-ce qu'une nation? Et autres essais politiques* (Paris, 1992).

10   Homi K. Bhabha, *The Location of Culture* (London and New York, 2004 (1994)), p. 229.

11   Ibid., p. 202.

12   Ibid., p. 208.

13   Hayes, *Queer Nations*, p. 8.

14   A few examples of analyses of Moroccan postcolonial novels as 'national allegories' are Danielle Marx-Scouras, 'A Literature of Departure: The Cross-Cultural Writing of Driss Chraïbi', *Research in African Literatures* 23/2 (1992), pp. 131–44; Tetz Rooke, 'Moroccan Autobiography as National Allegory', *Oriente moderno XVI (LXVII)* 2–3 (1997), pp. 289–305; and Ellen McLarney, 'Politics of Le Passé Simple', *The Journal of North African Studies* 8/2 (2003), pp. 1–18. These three examples differ considerably from each other and demonstrate the various analytical possibilities when approaching Moroccan postcolonial novels as 'national allegories.' McLarney's analysis of Driss Chraïbi's *Le Passé simple* is worth emphasizing because she applies the 'national allegory' to highlight the internal heterogeneity of the text as well as its 'non-representability.'

15   Fredric Jameson, 'Third-World Literature in the Era of Multinational Capitalism', *Social Text* 15 (1986), p. 69 (italics in original).

16   Aijaz Ahmad, 'Jameson's Rhetoric of Otherness and the "National Allegory"', *Social Text* 17 (1987), p. 10.

17   Réda Bensmaïa, *Experimental Nations: Or, the Invention of the Maghreb* (New Jersey, 2003), p. 68.

18   Jameson, 'Third-World Literature in the Era of Multinational Capitalism', p. 73.

19   Ibid., p. 68.

20   Homi K. Bhabha, 'Representation and the Colonial Text: A Critical Exploration of Some Forms of Mimeticism', in Frank Gloversmith (ed.), *The Theory of Reading* (Sussex, 1984), p. 103.

21   Ibid., p. 95.

22   Franco Moretti, 'Conjectures on World Literature', *New Left Review* 1 (2000), p. 56.

23   Bensmaïa, *Experimental Nations*, p. 6.

24   Ibid., p. 7.

25   Ibid., p. 8.

26   Abdelkébir Khatibi, *Maghreb pluriel* (Paris, 1983), p. 63 (italics in original).

27   Ibid., p. 50.

28   See, for instance, Jean Déjeux, 'L' Emergence du je dans la littérature maghrébine de langue française', *Itinéraires et contacts de cultures* 13 (1er semestre), pp. 23–9, and 'Au Maghreb, la langue française "langue natale du je"', in Martine Mathieu (ed.), *Littératures autobiographiques de la francophonie* (Paris, 1994), pp. 181–93.

29   Debra Kelly, *Autobiography and Independence: Selfhood and Creativity in North African Postcolonial Writing in French* (Liverpool, 2005), p. 11.

30   Philippe Lejeune, *L'Autobiographie en France* (Paris, 1971).

31   Arnaud Schmitt, 'Making the Case for Self-Narration Against Autofiction', *A/B: Auto/Biography Studies* 25/1 (2010), pp. 122–37.

32   Philippe Lejeune, *Le pacte autobiographique* (Paris, 1975), p. 14.

33   Ibid.

34   Ibid., p. 27.

35   Ibid., p. 36.

36   Yumna al-Eid, 'The Autobiographical Novel and the Dual Function', in Robin Ostle, Ed de Moor, and Stefan Wild (eds), *Writing the Self. Autobiographical Writing in Modern Arabic Literature* (London, 1998), p. 160.

37   Serge Doubrovsky, *Fils* (Paris, 2001 (1977)), p. 10.

38   Abdellah Taïa and Jason Napoli Brooks, 'An Interview with Abdellah Taïa', *Asymptote*, July (2012).

39   Philippe Vilain, *L'Autofiction en théorie, suivi de deux entretiens avec Philippe Sollers et Philippe Lejeune* (Chatou, 2009), p. 14.

40   Ibid., p. 13.

41   Roland Barthes, 'The Death of the Author', *Image, Music, Text* (New York, 1977), pp. 142–8 (originally published in 1967).

42   Jacques Derrida, 'The Law of Genre', *Critical Inquiry* 7/1 (1980), pp. 55–81.

43   Paul de Man, 'Autobiography as De-Facement', *MLN* 94/5 (1979), pp. 919–30.

44   Ibid., p. 921.

45   Gérard Genette, *Fiction et diction* (Paris, 1991).

46   Vincent Colonna, *Autofiction & autres mythomanies littéraires* (Auch, 2004).

47   Schmitt, 'Making the Case for Self-Narration Against Autofiction'.

48   Ibid., p. 129.

49   Ibid.

50   Ibid., p. 135.

51   Abdellah Taïa and Dale Peck, 'In Conversation: Abdellah Taïa and Dale Peck', in *PEN World Voices Festival of International Literature* (New York, 2011).

52   al-Eid, 'The Autobiographical Novel and the Dual Function', p. 159.

53   Gonzalo Fernández Parrilla, 'Breaking the Canon: Zafzaf, Laroui and the Moroccan Novel', in Stephan Guth and Gail Ramsay (eds), *From New Values to New Aesthetics. Turning Points in Modern Arabic Literature. 2. Postmodernism and Thereafter* (Wiesbaden, 2011), p. 9.

54   al-Eid, 'The Autobiographical Novel and the Dual Function', p. 160.

55   Mohamed Ould Bouleiba, *Critique littéraire occidentale - critique littéraire arabe: 'Texte croisés'* (Paris, 2000), pp. 66–7.

56   Ibid., p. 124.

57   Ibid., 69. Paul Klee opens his *Creative Confession* (1920) with the statement: 'Art does not reproduce the visible; rather, it makes visible.'

58   Yumna al-Eid, *al-riwāyah al-'arabiyyah: al-mutakhayyal wa-bunyatuh al-fanniyyah* (Beirut, 2011), p. 8.

59   See for instance Abdelkébir Khatibi, *Le Roman maghrébin* (Paris, 1968); Roger Allen, *The Arabic Novel: An Historical and Critical Introduction* (Syracuse, 1995 (1982)); and Sabry Hafez, *The Genesis of Arabic Narrative Discourse: A Study in the Sociology of Modern Arabic Literature* (London, 1993).

60   al-Eid, *al-riwāyah al-'arabiyyah*, p. 7.

61   Ibid., p. 8.

62   Hafez, *The Genesis of Arabic Narrative Discourse*, p. 27.

63   Jonathan Culler, *The Pursuit of Signs: Semiotics, Literature, Deconstruction* (Ithaca, 2002), p. 114.

64   Ibid.

65   Julia Kristeva, *Desire in Language: A Semiotic Approach to Literature and Art.* Reprint (Oxford, 1987 (1980)), p. 65.

66   Hayes, *Queer Nations*, pp. 15–16.

67   Ibid., p. 16.

68   Fassin, 'National Identities and Transnational Intimacies'.

69   Hayes, *Queer Nations*, p. 6.

70   Arno Schmitt and Jehoeda Sofer (eds), *Sexuality and Eroticism Among Males in Moslem Societies* (New York and London, 1992), p. 4.

71   Ibid., p. 8.
72   Ibid., pp. 5–6; Hayes, *Queer Nations*, p. 4.
73   Schmitt and Sofer, *Sexuality and Eroticism Among Males in Moslem Societies*, pp. 2–3.
74   Ibid., p. 6.
75   See for instance Stephen O. Murray and Will Roscoe, *Islamic Homosexualities: Culture, History, and Literature* (New York, 1997), Hayes, *Queer Nations,* and Joseph A. Massad, *Desiring Arabs* (Chicago, 2007).
76   In Massad's terminology the 'Gay International' refers to the universalization of 'gay rights' promoted by Western gay movements. As such, it simultaneously points to the Orientalist discourse that produced the missionary task of defending the rights of 'gays and lesbians' all over the world, and to the Western male white-dominated organizations that promote this discourse. *Desiring Arabs*, pp. 160–90.
77   Ibid., pp. 49–50.
78   Ibid., pp. 162–3.
79   See also Mehammed Amadeus Mack, *Sexagon: Muslims, France, and the Sexualization of National Culture* (New York, 2017).
80   Jean Zaganiaris, *Queer Maroc: Sexualités, genres et (trans)identités dans la littérature marocaine* (Paris, 2013), p. 10.
81   Judith Butler, 'Imitation and Gender Insubordination', in Henry Abelove, Michèle Aina Barale and David M. Halperin (eds), *The Lesbian and Gay Studies Reader* (New York and London, 1993 (first published in 1991)), pp. 307–20.
82   Ibid., p. 308.
83   Michel Foucault, *Histoire de la sexualité, tome 1: La Volonté de savoir* (Paris, 1994).
84   Butler, 'Imitation and Gender Insubordination', p. 311 (italics in original).
85   Ibid., p. 312.
86   Judith Butler, *Gender Trouble: Feminism and the Subversion of Identity* (New York, 1990), p. 33.
87   Ibid., p. 5.
88   Ibid., p. 9.
89   Ibid.
90   Butler, 'Imitation and Gender Insubordination', p. 310 (italics in original).
91   Ibid., p. 311.
92   Ibid.
93   Ibid., p. 312.
94   Ibid.
95   Ibid., p. 313 (italics in original).
96   Massad, *Desiring Arabs*.
97   Edward W. Said, *Orientalism* (New York, 1978).
98   Sara Ahmed, *The Cultural Politics of Emotion* (New York, 2012 (2004)), p. 10.
99   Ibid., p. 103.
100 Ibid., p. 104.
101 Ibid., p. 105.
102 Ibid., p. 106 (italics in original).
103 Ibid.
104 Eve Kosofsky Sedgwick, 'Shame and Performativity: Henry James's New York Edition Prefaces', David McWhirter (ed.), *Henry James's New York Edition: The Construction of Authorship* (Stanford, 1995), p. 210.
105 Maja Mons Bissenbakker-Frederiksen, 'Krumme tæer. Skam i krydsfeltet mellem queer, feministiske og postkoloniale teorier', *Kvinder, køn og forskning* 1 (2013), p. 29.

106   Sara Ahmed, *Queer Phenomenology: Orientations, Objects, Others* (Durham, 2006), p. 175.

107   Bissenbakker-Frederiksen, 'Krumme tæer. Skam i krydsfeltet mellem queer, feministiske og postkoloniale teorier', p. 34.

108   See Chapter 5.

109   Ahmed, *The Cultural Politics of Emotion*, p. 102.

110   Ibid.

111   Ibid., p. 109.

Chapter 2

1   Fatima El-Tayeb, '"Gays Who Cannot Properly Be Gay." Queer Muslims in the Neoliberal European City', *European Journal of Women's Studies* 19/1 (2012), pp. 79–95.

2   An earlier version of this section and the section 'Homosexuality "à la marocaine"' was published in *Expressions maghrébines* 16/1 (2017), pp. 107–25, as 'Breaking the Silence: Between Literary Representation and LGBT Activism. Abdellah Taïa as Author and Activist'.

3   Florence Bergeaud-Blackler and Victor Eck, 'Les "faux" mariages homosexuels de Sidi Ali au Maroc: enjeux d'un scandale médiatique', *Revue des mondes musulmans et de la Méditerranée* 129 (2011), pp. 203–21.

4   Ibid.

5   Bouchra Hida, 'Mobilisations collectives à l'épreuve des changements au Maroc', *Revue Tiers Monde* HS, 5, p. 171.

6   Zakaria Choukrallah, 'Pourquoi les homos font peur', *Actuel* 44 (2010), p. 43.

7   Justin McGuinness, 'Réprésentation et résistance sur mithly.net: analyse du discours d'un site communautaire marocain', in Sihem Najar (ed.), *Les nouvelles sociabilités du Net en Méditerranée* (2012), p. 119.

8   Ibid.

9   Ibid., p. 125.

10   Hida, 'Mobilisations collectives à l'épreuve des changements au Maroc', p. 173.

11   Ibid., p. 174.

12   Ibid., p. 173.

13   Zineb El Rhazoui and Habibou Bangré, 'Zineb El Rhazoui: "Nous ne défendons pas que la liberté de 'dé-jeûner'"', *afrik.com* (2009).

14   Loubna Ghrib, 'Groundbreaking Video Series Breaks LGBTI Silence in Morocco', *OutRight International* (2014).

15   Xavier Héraud, '"Ils existent", une web-série sur l'homosexualité et l'homophobie au Maroc', *yagg.com* (2015).

16   Adjil Kribi, 'Campagne contre l'homophobie au Maroc: "Je dis que les homosexuels ont les mêmes droits que moi"', *HuffPost Maghreb* (2014).

17   Youssef Roudaby, 'Aswat publie une vidéo pour sensibiliser les LGBT sur leurs droits au Maroc', *HuffPost Maroc* (2016).

18   The protest was filmed and uploaded on YouTube on 6 June 2015: https://www.you tube.com/watch?v=fgPGbYgi5jA (accessed 20 December 2018).

19   Bainier, Corentin, 'Homosexuality and Femen: Morocco debates "public decency"', *The Observers* (2015).

20   Pauline, 'Les militants marocains de défense des LGBT pour ou contre l'action des Femen?', *TelQuel* (2015).

21   Ibid.

22   Ibid.

23   Ibid.

24   Anaïs Lefébure, 'LGBT – L'autorisation pour se constituer en association lui est refusée, mais le collectif Akaliyat continue la lutte', *HuffPost Maroc* (2017); Marien Gouyon and Sandrine Musso, 'Luttes contre le sida et luttes LGBT au Maroc. Notes exploratoires sur les enjeux d'une imbrication', *L'Année du Maghreb* 17 (2017), paragraph 43.

25   Personal interview with Ismaël Bakkar, project coordinator at MALI, in Rabat on 18 October 2016.

26   Bergeaud-Blackler and Eck, 'Les "faux" mariages homosexuels de Sidi Ali au Maroc: enjeux d'un scandale médiatique', p. 29 (the number refers to the numbered paragraphs (1–30) in the online version of the article).

27   Ibid., p. 5.

28   Ibid.

29   Ibid., p. 6.

30   Ibid., p. 25.

31   Abdellah Taïa, 'A Boy to Be Sacrificed', *The New York Times* (24 March 2012).

32   Ibid.

33   Ibid.

34   Abdellah Taïa and Aaron Hicklin, 'Why Abdellah Taia Had to Die in Order to Live', *out.com* (26 January 2010).

35   Taïa's autobiographical novel *Une melancholie arabe* opens with a different version of this event and is an interesting example of how fiction can function as a constitutive element of self-narration, thus making it undesirable to neatly distinguish between fiction and fact. For an analysis of the opening scene of *Une melancholie arabe*, see, for instance, Ralph Heyndels, 'Configurations et transferts de la sexualité, du genre et du désir dans l'ouverture d'Une mélancolie arabe d'Abdellah Taïa, ou "le dépassement des frontières"', *Expressions maghrébines* 16/1 (2017), pp. 85–105.

36   Abdellah Taïa and Brian Whitaker, 'Interview with Abdellah Taia', *al-bab.com* (January 2009).

37   Abdellah Taïa and Georgia Phillips-Amos, 'Abdellah Taïa by Georgia Phillips-Amos', *bombmagazine.org. BOMB - Artists in Conversation* (3 May 2016).

38   Ibid.

39   *L'Armée du salut* (2006), for instance, jumps from a vacation, where the protagonist is thirteen, to the point where he is a university student and travels to Geneva (see Chapter 3), and *Une Mélancolie arabe* (2008) jumps from the story of the protagonist being raped by a group of boys at the age of twelve to his adult life in Paris, Morocco and Egypt. In *La Vie lente* (2019), however, life as a teenage homosexual in Morocco is defining for the adult life of the protagonist Mounir in Paris – whether men paying him for sex, the mosque and prayer as a temporary safe space from the same men, or casual sex with a stranger in an crowded public bus as a stolen moment of intimacy and love.

40   Karim Boukhari, 'Portrait. Homosexuel envers en contre tous', *TelQuel* 277 (2007), p. 41.

41   Ibid., p. 43.

42   Muhammad al-Khodayri and Abdallah Taïa, '·abdallah al-ṭāyʿa: "yasṭafalū" al-ʾislāmīīn!' *al-ʾakhbār* (12 June 2012).

43   The quotation can be found in the 2014 article "'*L'Armée du salut*,' l'homosexualité au festival du film de Tanger', accessible at http://www.bladi.net/l-armee-du-salut-ho mosexualite.html (accessed 14 October 2018).

44   On 30 September 2012 *2M* broadcasted a documentary about Taïa.

45   Quoted in Boukhari, 'Portrait. Homosexuel envers en contre tous', p. 44.

46   Ibid., p. 45.

47   Quoted in Ilham Mellouki, 'La génération du "Je"', *TelQuel* 249 (2007).

48   Examples of earlier first-person narratives – fictional, autobiographical and transgeneric – are Driss Chraïbi: *Le Passé simple* (1954), Mohammed Khaïr-Eddine: *Agadir* (1967), Abdelkébir Khatibi: *La Mémoire tattouée* (1971), Mohamed Choukri: *Al-khubz al-ḥāfi* (1973), Leila Abouzeid: *'Ām al-fīl* (1983) and Mohamed Berrada: *Luʿbat al-nisyan* (1987), to mention but a few.

49   Khalid Zekri, *Fictions du réel: Modernité romanesque et écriture du réel au Maroc 1990-2006* (2006), p. 55.

50   Quoted in Mellouki, 'La génération du "Je"'.

51   Zekri, *Fictions du réel*, p. 79.

52   Gonzalo Fernández Parrilla, 'Breaking the Canon: Zafzaf, Laroui and the Moroccan Novel', in Stephan Guth and Gail Ramsay (eds), *From New Values to New Aesthetics: Turning Points in Modern Arabic Literature. 2. Postmodernism and Thereafter* (Wiesbaden, 2011), p. 9 (online version).

53   Zekri, *Fictions du réel*, p. 79.

54   Fernández Parrilla, 'Breaking the Canon', p. 9.

55   Ibid., pp. 7–8. See the first part of Chapter 4.

56   Valérie K. Orlando, *Francophone Voices of the 'New Morocco' in Film and Print: (Re) presenting a Society in Transition* (New York, 2009), p. 113.

57   Ibid., p. 112.

58   Zekri, *Fictions du réel*, p. 50.

59   Ibid., p. 51.

60   Ibid., p. 50.

61   Jean Zaganiaris, *Queer Maroc: Sexualités, genres et (trans)identités dans la littérature marocaine* (Paris, 2013), pp. 51–2.

62   Ibid., p. 52.

63   See Chapter 5.

64   Quoted in Orlando, *Francophone Voices of the 'New Morocco' in Film and Print*, p. 107.

65   Karim Nasseri, *Noces et funerailles* (Paris, 2001), p. 63.

66   See Chapter 3.

67   Mohamed Choukri, quoted in Ferial Ghazoul and Barbara Harlow (eds), *The View from within* (Cairo, 1994), p. 220.

68   Ibid.

69   Nirvana Tanoukhi, 'Rewriting Political Commitment for an International Canon: Paul Bowles's "For Bread Alone" as Translation of Mohamed Choukri's "Al-Khubz Al-Hafi"', *Research in African Literatures* 34/2 (2003), pp. 127–44.

70   http://www.seuil.com/collection/collection-597 (accessed 30 July 2017).

71   Abdellah Taïa, 'L'Homosexualité expliquée à ma mère', *TelQuel* 367 (2009), p. 22.

72   Derrida's main purpose in discussing the 'supplement' in *De la grammatologie* (1967) was to problematize Rousseau's definition of a supplement as something secondary

added to something 'original' or 'natural'. According to Derrida, the supplement not only reveals an originary lack (as nothing can be added to something that is complete in itself) but also has an undecidability attached to it, as it cannot be decided whether the supplement is an accretion or a substitution. With respect to Taïa, his writings cannot be divided into 'primary' (original) and 'secondary' (something added), but the different genres of his writings supplement each other as simultaneous accretion and substitution.

73   Taïa, 'L'Homosexualité expliquée à ma mère', p. 22.
74   Ibid.
75   Zakaria Choukrallah, 'Pourquoi les homos font peur', *Actuel* 44 (2010).
76   Jean-Pierre Péroncel-Hugoz, 'Pédérastie et pudeur: la prêt-à-penser a encore frappé . . ', *Actuel* 47 (2010), p. 50.
77   Ibid.
78   Ibid.
79   Ibid.
80   Ibid.
81   Abdellah Taïa, 'Le retour du maréchal Lyautey', *Actuel* 47 (2010), p. 51.
82   Ibid.
83   Ibid.
84   Ibid.
85   Abdellah Taïa and Dale Peck, 'In Conversation: Abdellah Taïa and Dale Peck', *PEN World Voices Festival of International Literature* (New York, 2011).
86   See Chapter 4.
87   Abdellah Taïa and Antoine Idier, '"Sortir de la peur": Construire une identité homosexuelle arabe dans un monde postcolonial. Entretien avec Abdellah Taïa', *Revue critique de fixxion française contemporaine* 12 (2016), p. 204.
88   Ibid.
89   See, for instance, Valérie K. Orlando, 'Review of Abdellah Taïa "L'Armée Du Salut"', *African Studies Review* 57/2 (2014), pp. 245–50, and Gibson Ncube, 'Writing Queer Desire in the Language of the "Other": Abdellah Taïa and Rachid O', *Rupkatha Journal. On Interdisciplinary Studies in Humanities* vi/1 (2014), pp. 87–96.
90   Denis M. Provencher, *Queer Maghrebi French. Language, Temporalities, Transfiliations* (Liverpool, 2017), p. 6.
91   For an elaboration on the question of language, see Chapter 4.
92   Taïa and Idier, '"Sortir de la peur"', p. 197.
93   Ibid.
94   Ibid., p. 198.

Chapter 3

1   See Chapter 2 and Tina Dransfeldt Christensen, 'Breaking the Silence: Between Literary Representation and LGBT Activism. Abdellah Taïa as Author and Activist', *Expressions maghrébines* 16/1 (2017), pp. 107–25.
2   Mehammed Amadeus Mack, *Sexagon: Muslims, France, and the Sexualization of National Culture* (New York, 2017), p. 131.
3   Réda Bensmaïa, *Experimental Nations: Or, the Invention of the Maghreb* (New Jersey, 2003), p. 6.

4   Mack, *Sexagon*, p. 139.
5   Ibid., p. 136.
6   I am aware that recent literary critics, such as Salim Jay in *Dictionnaire des écrivains marocains* (Paris, 2005), p. 128, have questioned the canonized 'entrance' in the 1950s of the novel as a modern literary genre. However, this does not change the fact that the novel is a modern genre in Morocco and that the 1950s were significant for the development of the novelistic genre in both Arabic and French in Morocco.
7   Abdelkébir Khatibi, 'Roman maghrébin et culture nationale', *Souffles* 3 (1966), pp. 10–11, and Bensmaïa, *Experimental Nations*, p. 1. In *La violence du texte: Etudes sur la littérature marocaine d'expression française* (Paris, 1981), p. 15, Marc Gontard, for instance, mentions Henry de Montherlant's *La Rose de sable* (written between 1930 and 1932; published in 1968) and Robert Grasillach's *La Conquérante* (1943) as examples of 'exotic portraits' of Maghrebins in French literature. For further examples, see also Edward Said, *Orientalism* (New York, 1978) and Abdelkébir Khatibi, *Figures de l'étranger dans la littérature française* (Paris, 1987).
8   Abdelkébir Khatibi, *Le Roman maghrébin* (Paris, 1968), p. 9.
9   Ibid., p. 11.
10 Ibid., p. 10.
11 Ibid., p. 11. A similar point has been made by Bensmaïa in *Experimental nations*, p. 6 (see Chapter 1).
12 Ibid.
13 Ibid., p. 39.
14 See Chapter 4.
15 Gonzalo Fernández Parrilla, 'The Challenge of Moroccan Cultural Journals of the 1960s', *Journal of Arabic Literature* 45/1 (2014), p. 110.
16 Said Graiouid, 'We Have Not Buried the Simple Past: The Public Sphere and Post-Colonial Literature in Morocco', *Journal of African Cultural Studies* 20/2 (2008), p. 146.
17 Gonzalo Fernández Parrilla, 'Breaking the Canon: Zafzaf, Laroui and the Moroccan Novel', in Stephan Guth and Gail Ramsay (eds), *From New Values to New Aesthetics: Turning Points in Modern Arabic Literature. 2. Postmodernism and Thereafter* (Wiesbaden, 2011), p. 7.
18 In *Le Roman maghrébin*, p. 27, Khatibi distinguishes between three novelistic categories corresponding with three historical periods: (1) from 1945 to 1953 the ethnographic novel is predominant; (2) from 1954 to 1958 novelistic writing is preoccupied with the problem of acculturation; and (3) from 1958 to 1962 a militant literature centred around the Algerian War of Independence dominates the literary scene. However, as the struggle for independence in Morocco and Tunisia differed considerably from that in Algeria, which spanned over a longer period and was radically more violent, the third category is primarily of relevance for Algerian literature.
19 Khatibi, *Le Roman maghrébin*, p. 44.
20 See, for instance, M'hamed Alaoui Abdalaoui, 'The Moroccan Novel in French', *Research in African Literatures* 23/4 (1992), pp. 9–33, and Graiouid, 'We Have Not Buried the Simple Past', pp. 145–58.
21 See, for instance, Jacqueline Kaye and Abdelhamid Zoubir, *The Ambiguous Compromise: Language, Literature, and National Identity in Algeria and Morocco* (New York, 1990).
22 Gontard, *La violence du texte*, p. 44.

23 Ibid., pp. 13–14.
24 Kaye and Zoubir, *The Ambiguous Compromise*.
25 Abdallah Mdarhri Alaoui, *Aspects du roman marocain, (1950–2003): Approche historique, thématique et esthétique* (Rabat, 2006), pp. 16–17.
26 Ibid., p. 17.
27 Ibid., p. 18.
28 Khatibi, *Le Roman maghrébin*, p. 27; Graiouid, 'We Have Not Buried the Simple Past', p. 149.
29 Albert Memmi, *Portrait du colonisé* (Paris, 1966 (1957)).
30 Frantz Fanon, *Les Damnés de la terre* (Paris, 1961).
31 Khatibi, *Le Roman maghrébin*, p. 29.
32 Abdellatif Laâbi, 'Réalités et dilemmes de la culture nationale (I)', *Souffles* 4 (1966), p. 6.
33 See Chapter 4.
34 Gontard, *La violence du texte*, p. 16.
35 Ellen McLarney, 'Politics of Le Passé Simple', *The Journal of North African Studies* 8/2 (2003), p. 1.
36 Quoted in McLarney, 'Politics of Le Passé Simple', p. 1.
37 Driss Chraïbi and Abdellatif Laâbi, 'Driss et nous: Questionnaire établi par Abdellatif Laâbi', *Souffles* 5 (1967), p. 6.
38 Jarrod Hayes, 'Rachid O. and the Return of the Homopast: The Autobiographical as Allegory in Childhood Narratives by Maghrebian Men', *Contemporary French and Francophone Studies* 1/2 (1997), p. 505.
39 See Chapter 4.
40 Abdellatif Laâbi, 'Défense du "Passé simple"', *Souffles* 5 (1967), p. 20.
41 Khatibi, *Le Roman maghrébin*, p. 27.
42 Ibid.
43 Kaye and Zoubir, *The Ambiguous Compromise*, p. 47.
44 McLarney, 'Politics of Le Passé Simple', p. 2.
45 Michael J. Willis, *Politics and Power in the Maghreb: Algeria, Tunisia and Morocco from Independence to the Arab Spring* (New York, 2012), p. 30.
46 Tellingly, this parody is not all that different from how Khatibi's meta-reflections on 'le nouveau roman' in the epilogue of *Amour bilingue* seek to deconstruct established literary genres as well as displace the question of acculturation (see Chapter 4).
47 Driss Chraïbi, *Le Passé simple* (Paris, 1954), pp. 88–9.
48 Danielle Marx-Scouras, 'A Literature of Departure: The Cross-Cultural Writing of Driss Chraïbi', *Research in African Literatures* 23/2 (1992), pp. 131–44, and McLarney, 'Politics of Le Passé Simple', pp. 1–18.
49 McLarney, 'Politics of Le Passé Simple', p. 2.
50 Chraïbi, *Le Passé simple*, p. 18 (italics in original).
51 Ibid., p. 19.
52 Ibid., p. 23.
53 Ibid., p. 204.
54 Ibid., pp. 207–8.
55 See for instance Ian Campbell, *Labyrinths, Intellectuals and the Revolution. The Arabic-Language Moroccan Novel, 1957–72* (Leiden and Boston, 2013), on the labyrinth in the modern Moroccan Arabic novel, and Bensmaïa, *Experimental Nations*, p. 30, on the Medina in modern Maghrebin francophone literature: 'It is a space they can come to know only by straddling it, and it will turn out to

have hidden affinities with the space of thought. Viewed from a certain angle, the geography of the city merges with the equally indistinguishable geography of thought and its very (im)possibility.'

56 Chraïbi, *Le Passé simple*, p. 208.
57 Marx-Scouras, 'A Literature of Departure', p. 133.
58 Chraïbi, *Le Passé simple*, p. 208 (italics in original).
59 Ibid., p. 212.
60 Ibid., p. 213.
61 Ibid.
62 Ibid., p. 218.
63 Ibid., p. 18.
64 Ibid., p. 266.
65 Ibid., p. 264.
66 Ibid., p. 30.
67 Ibid., p. 79.
68 Ibid., p. 134.
69 Ibid., p. 14.
70 Ibid., p. 20.
71 McLarney, 'Politics of Le Passé Simple', p. 7.
72 Chraïbi, *Le Passé simple*, p. 48.
73 Ibid., p. 172.
74 McLarney, 'Politics of Le Passé Simple', p. 7.
75 Ibid.
76 Hayes, 'Rachid O. and the Return of the Homopast', p. 505.
77 Chraïbi, *Le Passé simple*, p. 45.
78 Ibid., p. 48.
79 Ibid., p. 139.
80 Ibid., p. 153.
81 Ibid., p. 161.
82 Ibid., p. 171.
83 Ibid., pp. 253–4.
84 Ibid., p. 253.
85 Ibid., pp. 255–6.
86 Ibid., p. 262.
87 Ibid., pp. 264–5.
88 Jay, *Dictionnaire des écrivains marocains*, pp. 138–9.
89 Chraïbi, *Le Passé simple*, p. 273.
90 Hayes, 'Rachid O. and the Return of the Homopast', p. 505.
91 Chraïbi and Laâbi, 'Driss et nous', p. 5.
92 Driss Chraïbi and Lionel Dubois, 'Interview de Driss Chraïbi (Accordée à Lionel Dubois le 23 juin 1983)', *CELFAN Review* 5/2 (1986), p. 25, and Marx-Scouras, 'A Literature of Departure', p. 135.
93 Chraïbi and Laâbi, 'Driss et nous', p. 5.
94 Chraïbi, *Le Passé simple*, p. 43.
95 Ibid., p. 32.
96 Ibid., p. 70.
97 Ibid., p. 32.
98 Ibid., p. 44.
99 Ibid., p. 151.

100   Ibid., p. 44.
101   Ibid., p. 147.
102   Ibid., p. 58.
103   Ibid., p. 153.
104   Ibid.
105   Ibid., p. 78.
106   Ibid., pp. 242–3.
107   Ibid., p. 249.
108   Marx-Scouras, 'A Literature of Departure', p. 135.
109   Chraïbi, *Le Passé simple*, p. 254.
110   Ibid., p. 149.
111   Ibid.
112   Ibid., p. 261.
113   An earlier and shorter version of this analysis has been published as: Tina Dransfeldt Christensen, '"Writing the Self" as Narrative of Resistance: L'Armée du Salut by Abdellah Taïa', *The Journal of North African Studies* 21/5 (2016), pp. 857–76.
114   Abdellah Taïa, *L'Armée du salut* (Paris, 2006), p. 11.
115   Ibid., p. 14.
116   Ibid., p.15.
117   Ibid., p. 22.
118   Ibid.
119   Mohamed Choukri, *Al-khubz al-ḥāfi* (Beirut, 2009 (1973)), p. 12.
120   Taïa, *L'Armée du salut*, pp. 36–7.
121   Cecily Devereux, 'Hysteria, Feminism, and Gender Revisited: The Case of the Second Wave', *ESC: English Studies in Canada* 40/1 (2014), p. 20.
122   Ibid.
123   Ibid., p. 25.
124   Taïa, *L'Armée du salut*, p. 22.
125   Ibid., p. 27–30.
126   Ibid., p. 35.
127   Ibid., p. 50–1.
128   Abdellah Taïa Abdellah, and Dale Peck, 'In Conversation: Abdellah Taïa and Dale Peck', *PEN World Voices Festival of International Literature* (New York, 2011).
129   Taïa, *L'Armée du salut*, p. 61.
130   Ibid., p. 84.
131   Ibid., p. 100.
132   Ibid., p. 106.
133   Ibid., p. 108.
134   Ibid., p. 108–9.
135   Ibid., p. 109.
136   Ibid., p. 122.
137   Ibid., p. 123.
138   Ibid., p. 151.
139   Ibid., p. 153.
140   Ibid., p. 152.
141   For an elaboration of the question of reinventing freedom, see my analysis of *Un Pays pour mourir* in Chapter 4.
142   Ibid., p. 130.
143   Ibid.

Chapter 4

1 Réda Bensmaïa, *Experimental Nations: Or, the Invention of the Maghreb* (New Jersey, 2003), p. 13 (italics in original).
2 Abdelkébir Khatibi, *Le Roman maghrébin* (Paris, 1968).
3 Bensmaïa, *Experimental Nations*.
4 Albert Memmi, *Portrait du colonisé* (Paris, 1966 (1957)), p. 148.
5 Bensmaïa, *Experimental Nations*, p. 2.
6 Ibid.
7 Abdellatif Laâbi, 'Prologue', *Souffles* 1 (1966), pp. 3–6.
8 Abdellatif Laâbi, 'Réalités et dilemmes de la culture nationale (I)', *Souffles* 4 (1966), p. 12.
9 Abdellatif Laâbi, 'Avant-propos', *Souffles* 22 (1971), pp. 3–5.
10 Abdelkébir Khatibi, 'Roman maghrébin et culture nationale', *Souffles* 3 (1966), p. 11.
11 Bensmaïa, *Esperimental Nations*, p. 15.
12 Ibid.
13 Khatibi, *Le Roman maghrébin*, p. 23.
14 Said Graiouid, 'We Have Not Buried the Simple Past: The Public Sphere and Post-Colonial Literature in Morocco', *Journal of African Cultural Studies* 20/2 (2008), p. 147.
15 Gonzalo Fernández Parrilla, 'The Challenge of Moroccan Cultural Journals of the 1960s', *Journal of Arabic Literature* 45/1 (2014), p. 109.
16 For a more detailed overview of Moroccan cultural journals, in both Arabic and French, from the 1930s to the 1960s, see Fernández Parrilla, 'The Challenge of Moroccan Cultural Journals of the 1960s'.
17 Ibid., p. 110.
18 Ibid.
19 Ibid., p. 111.
20 Ibid., p. 109.
21 Ibid., p. 112.
22 Ibid., pp. 112–13.
23 Khatibi, *Le Roman maghrébin*, p. 34.
24 Fernández Parrilla, 'The Challenge of Moroccan Cultural Journals of the 1960s', p. 113.
25 Ibid., p. 114.
26 Ibid., p. 115.
27 Ibid., p. 107.
28 Ibid., p. 118.
29 Ibid.
30 Ibid., p. 119.
31 Ibid.
32 Ibid., p. 122.
33 Ibid.
34 Ibid.
35 Susan Gilson Miller, *A History of Modern Morocco* (Cambridge, 2013), p. 168.
36 Kenza Sefrioui, *La revue Souffles: Espoirs de révolution culturelle au Maroc* (Casablanca, 2013), p. 23, and Ibid., pp. 167–8.
37 Olivia Harrison and Teresa Villa-Ignacio, *Souffles-Anfas: A Critical Anthology from the Moroccan Journal of Culture and Politics* (Redwood City, 2016), p. 2.

38 Tahar Ben Jelloun, for instance, published his first poems, 'L'Aube des dalles' (The dawn of slabs) and 'La Planète des singes' (Planet of the apes), in *Souffles* (12, 1968, and 13–14, 1969), a few years before the publication of his first novel, *Harrouda* (1973).

39 Miller, *A History of Modern Morocco*, p. 170.

40 Harrison and Villa-Ignacio, *Souffles-Anfas*, p. 6.

41 Sefrioui, *La revue Souffles*, p. 123.

42 Ibid., p. 123.

43 Abdellatif Laâbi, 'Préface', Sefrioui, *La revue Souffles*, p. 8.

44 Harrison and Villa-Ignacio, *Souffles-Anfas*, p. 3.

45 Sefrioui, *La revue Souffles*, p. 35.

46 Ibid., p. 30.

47 Abdellatif Laâbi, 'La presse nationale entre le business et le dogme', *Souffles* 4 (1966), p. 39.

48 Laâbi, 'Prologue', p. 3.

49 Sefrioui, *La revue Souffles*, p. 20.

50 Laâbi, 'Prologue', p. 6.

51 Ibid., p. 6.

52 Laâbi, 'Prologue', p. 5 (italics in original).

53 Memmi, *Portrait du colonisé*, p. 145.

54 Laâbi, 'Réalités et dilemmes de la culture nationale (I)', p. 7 (italics in original).

55 Memmi, *Portrait du colonisé*, p. 144.

56 Laâbi, 'Réalités et dilemmes de la culture nationale (I)', p. 12.

57 Hédi Abdel-Jaouad, 'Mohammed Khaïr-Eddine: The Poet as Iconoclast', *Research in African Literatures* 23/2 (1992), p. 146.

58 Mohamed Berrada, 'al-laghū wal-aswāt', *Souffles* 10–1 (1968), pp. 27–9, and Muhammad Zafzaf, 'fī al-ẓahīra, wa kānit al-shams', *Souffles* 10–1 (1968), pp. 30–2.

59 Marc Gontard, *La violence du texte: Etudes sur la littérature marocaine d'expression française* (Paris, 1981), p. 21.

60 Abdellatif Laâbi, 'Littérature maghrébine actuelle et francophonie', *Souffles* 18 (1970), p. 36.

61 Jacques Alessandra, 'Abdellatif Laâbi: A Writing of Dissidence', *Research in African Literatures* 23/2 (1992), p. 159.

62 See Alessandra, 'Abdellatif Laâbi', on the chaos-rebirth imagery of Laâbi's poetry.

63 Abdellatif Laâbi, 'Marasmes', *Souffles* 1 (1966), p. 22.

64 Laâbi, 'Littérature maghrébine actuelle et francophonie', p. 37.

65 Laâbi, 'Avant-propos', p. 3.

66 Ibid., p. 4.

67 Khatibi, 'Roman maghrébin et culture nationale', p. 11.

68 Ibid., p. 11.

69 Abdelkébir Khatibi, *Penser le Maghreb* (Rabat, 1993), p. 88.

70 Ibid., p. 82.

71 Ibid.

72 Abdelkébir Khatibi, 'Un étranger professionnel', *Études françaises* 33/1 (1997).

73 In *Maghreb pluriel*, pp. 47–8, Khatibi defines 'decolonial deconstruction' as 'une pensée radicalement critique vis-à-vis de la machine idéologique de l'impérialisme et de l'ethnocentrisme, une décolonisation qui serait en même temps une déconstruction des discours qui participent, de manières variées et plus ou moins dissimulées, à la domination impériale, qui est entendue ici également dans son

pouvoir de parole' (a radically critical thought vis-à-vis the ideological machinery of imperialism and ethnocentrism, a decolonization which at the same time would be a deconstruction of the discourse which participates, in various and more or less hidden ways, in imperial domination, which is understood here also in its power of speech). In this respect, Khatibi's 'decolonial deconstruction' is not dissimilar to Latin American decoloniality and its political and epistemological critique.

74 Bensmaïa, *Experimental Nations*, pp. 103–4.
75 Gayatri Chakravorty Spivak, *A Critique of Postcolonial Reason: Toward a History of the Vanishing Present* (Cambridge, 1999), p. 6.
76 See Tina Dransfeldt Christensen, 'Towards an Ethics of Bilingualism: An Intertextual Dialogue between Khatibi and Derrida', *Interventions* 19/4 (2017), pp. 447–66.
77 Waïl S. Hassan, 'Translator's Introduction', in Abdelfattah Kilito, *Thou Shalt Not Speak My Language* (Syracuse, 2008), p. xiv.
78 Lucy Stone McNeece, 'Decolonizing the Sign: Language and Identity in Abdelkebir Khatibi's La Mémoire Tatouée', *Yale French Studies* 83 (1993), pp. 12–29.
79 This is a quote from the last sentences of the novel: 'Folie de la langue, mais si douce, si tendre en ce moment. Bonheur indicible! Ne dire que cela: Apprends-moi à parler dans tes langues.' (Madness of language, but how sweet, how tender in this moment. Unspeakable happiness! Don't say only that: teach me to speak in your languages) (Abdelkébir Khatibi, 'Amour bilingue', *Œuvre de Abdelkébir Khatibi I: Romans et récits*, second edition (Paris, 2008 (1983)), p. 283).
80 Bensmaïa, *Experimental Nations*, p. 104.
81 Khatibi, 'Amour bilingue', pp. 207–8.
82 Ibid., p. 207.
83 Bensmaïa, *Experimental Nations*, p. 107.
84 Khatibi, 'Amour bilingue', p. 265.
85 Ibid., p. 266.
86 Ibid., pp. 211–12.
87 Ibid., p. 211.
88 Ibid., p. 266.
89 Ibid., p. 281.
90 Ibid. p. 279.
91 Khatibi, *Maghreb pluriel*, pp. 177–207.
92 Bensmaïa, *Experimental Nation*, p. 125.
93 Hassan, 'Translator's Introduction', p. xviii.
94 Abdelfattah Kilito, *The Author and His Doubles: Essays on Classical Arabic Culture*, trans. Michael Cooperson (Syracuse, 2001), p. 108.
95 Hassan, 'Translator's Introduction', p. xviii.
96 Ibid., p. xix.
97 Bensmaïa, *Experimental Nations*, p. 122.
98 Khatibi, 'Amour bilingue', p. 236.
99 Bensmaïa, *Experimental Nations*, p. 123.
100 Khatibi, 'Amour bilingue', p. 221.
101 Bensmaïa, *Experimental Nations*, p. 123.
102 Gonzalo Fernández Parrilla, 'The Novel in Morocco as Mirror of a Changing Society', *Contemporary French and Francophone Studies* 20/1 (2016), p. 18.
103 With the amended Constitution of 2011 Amazigh was recognized as an official language together with Arabic. Moreover, linguistic and cultural 'minorities' occupy a prominent place in the amended Constitution, where Morocco is defined as the

following: 'Arab-Islamic, Amazigh and Saharan-Hassani, nourished and enriched by its African, Andalusian, Hebraic and Mediterranean affluents.' (Ibid., p. 22).

104 Moha Ennaji, *Multilingualism, Cultural Identity, and Education in Morocco* (New York, 2005), p. xi.

105 Megan C. MacDonald, 'Publish or Paris: Reflections on the Politics of Transnational Literary Culture between Morocco and France', *Francosphères* 2/1 (2013), p. 2.

106 Fernández Parrilla, 'The Novel in Morocco as Mirror of a Changing Society', p. 19.

107 Ato Quayson, 'Periods versus Concepts: Space Making and the Question of Postcolonial Literary History', *PMLA* 127/2 (2012), p. 346.

108 See, for instance, Jean Déjeux, *Littérature maghrébine de langue française: Introduction générale et auteurs* (Sherbrooke, 1980), M'hamed Alaoui Abdalaoui, 'The Moroccan Novel in French', *Research in African Literatures* 23/4 (1992), pp. 9–33, and Valérie K. Orlando, *Francophone Voices of the 'New Morocco' in Film and Print: (Re)presenting a Society in Transition* (New York, 2009).

109 Karima Laachir, 'The Aesthetics and Politics of "Reading Together" Moroccan Novels in Arabic and French', *The Journal of North African Studies* 21/1 (2016), p. 22.

110 Khalid Zekri, *Fictions du réel: Modernité romanesque et écriture du réel au Maroc 1990–2006* (Paris, 2006), pp. 70–8.

111 Ibid., p. 73.

112 Ibid., p. 77.

113 Ibid., p. 41.

114 Ibid., pp. 41–2.

115 MacDonald, 'Publish or Paris', pp. 6–7.

116 Ibid., p. 7.

117 See, for instance, Zekri, *Fictions du réel*, p. 43, MacDonald, 'Publish or Paris', p. 4, and Fernández Parrilla, 'The Novel in Morocco as Mirror of a Changing Society', p. 24.

118 Cited in MacDonald, 'Publish or Paris', p. 10.

119 Zekri, *Fictions du réel*, p. 42.

120 MacDonald, 'Publish or Paris'.

121 Abdelfattah Kilito, *Je parle toutes les langues, mais en arabe* (Arles, 2013), p. 22.

122 Ibid., p. 21.

123 Ibid., p. 18.

124 Kilito, *Je parle toutes les langues, mais en arabe*, p. 22, and Fernández Parrilla, 'The Novel in Morocco as Mirror of a Changing Society', p. 20.

125 Kilito, *Je parle toutes les langues, mais en arabe*, pp. 20–1.

126 Abdellah Taïa and Antoine Idier, '"Sortir de la peur": Construire une identité homosexuelle arabe dans un monde postcolonial. Entretien avec Abdellah Taïa', *Revue critique de fixxion française contemporaine* 12 (March 2016), p. 201.

127 Kilito, *Je parle toutes les langues, mais en arabe*, p. 14.

128 Muhammad al-Khodayri and Abdallah Taïa, 'ʿabdallah al-ṭāyʿa: "yasṭafalū" al-ʿislāmīn!', *al-ʾakhbār* (12 June 2012).

129 Taïa and Idier, 'Sortir de la peur', p. 198.

130 Ibid., p. 201.

131 Ibid., p. 202.

132 Ibid., p. 200.

133 Ibid., p. 201.

134 Ibid., p. 198.

135 Gibson Ncube, 'Writing Queer Desire in the Language of the "Other": Abdellah Taïa and Rachid O', *Rupkatha Journal. On Interdisciplinary Studies in Humanities* vi/1 (2014), pp. 87–96.

136	Valérie K. Orlando, 'Review of Abdellah Taïa "L'Armée Du Salut"', *African Studies Review* 57/2 (2014), 248–9.
137	Ilham Mellouki, 'La génération du "Je"', *TelQuel* 249 (2007).
138	al-Khodayri and Abdallah Taïa, ''abdallah al-ṭāy'a: "yastafalū" al-'islāmīn!'
139	Taïa and Idier, 'Sortir de la peur', p. 201.
140	Abdellah Taïa, *Un Pays pour mourir* (Paris, 2015), p. 13.
141	Ibid., p. 16.
142	Jean-Pierre Boulé, 'Writing Selves as Mourning and Vita Nova: Abdellah Taïa's Un Pays Pour Mourir', *Contemporary French Civilization* 41/1 (2016), pp. 25–47.
143	Abdellah Taïa (ed.), *Lettres à un jeune marocain* (Paris, 2009), pp. 199–212.
144	Taïa, *Un Pays pour mourir*, p. 11.
145	Ibid., p. 17.
146	Ibid., p. 14.
147	Ibid., p. 13.
148	Taïa (ed.), *Lettres à un jeune marocain*, p. 204.
149	Ibid., p. 205.
150	Taïa, *Un Pays pour mourir*, p. 17.
151	Ibid., p. 32.
152	Abdellah Taïa and Fadwa Islah, 'L'écrivain Abdellah Taïa nous parle des sans-papiers, de racisme et d'islamophobie', *Al Huffington Post, Maghreb – Maroc* (18 January 2015).
153	Ibid.
154	Taïa, *Un Pays pour mourir*, p. 33.
155	Ibid., p. 34.
156	Ibid., p. 35–6.
157	Ibid., p. 47.
158	Ibid., p. 47–8.
159	See Chapter 2.
160	Taïa, *Un Pays pour mourir*, p. 46.
161	Ibid., p. 50.
162	Ibid., p. 38.
163	Ibid., p. 77.
164	Ibid., p. 78.
165	See Chapter 2.
166	Taïa, *Un Pays pour mourir*, p. 79.
167	Ibid., p. 95.
168	Ibid., p. 53.
169	Ibid., p. 61.
170	Ibid., pp. 99–100.
171	Ibid., p. 109.
172	Ibid., pp. 112–13.
173	Ibid., p. 123.
174	Zekri, *Fictions du réel*, p. 37.
175	Khatibi, 'Un étranger professionnel', p. 126.

Chapter 5

1	Susan Slyomovics, *The Performance of Human Rights in Morocco* (Philadelphia, 2005), p. 9.

2 See Chapter 2.
3 Bettina Dennerlein, 'Remembering Violence, Negotiating Change: The Moroccan Equity and Reconciliation Commission and the Politics of Gender', *Journal of Middle East Women's Studies* 8/1 (2012), p. 12.
4 This is an abbreviated version of a study conducted in the summer of 2005, initiated by – but independent from – the ERC and made available to ERC members to inform the final recommendations of the commission. The aim of the abbreviated version is to share the results with a wider public. First published in Arabic and then in English on ccdh.ma (National Human Rights Council) (Dennerlein, 'Remembering Violence, Negotiating Change', p. 25).
5 Nadia Guessous, *Women and Political Violence during the Years of Lead in Morocco* (Rabat, 2009), p. 16.
6 Dennerlein, 'Remembering Violence, Negotiating Change', p. 24.
7 Guessous, *Women and Political Violence during the Years of Lead in Morocco*, p. 31.
8 Ibid., p. 46.
9 Ibid., p. 47.
10 Ibid., p. 48.
11 Ibid., pp. 52–3.
12 Ibid., p. 54.
13 Ibid., p. 55.
14 Ibid., pp. 63–8.
15 Ibid., p. 56.
16 Laura Menin, 'Rewriting the World: Gendered Violence, the Political Imagination and Memoirs from the 'Years of Lead' in Morocco', *International Journal of Conflict and Violence* 8/1 (2014), pp. 1–15.
17 Ibid., p. 6.
18 Ibid.
19 Women were given both a number and a man's name (see my analysis of Ḥadīth al-'atmah later in this chapter).
20 Guessous, *Women and Political Violence during the Years of Lead in Morocco*, p. 84.
21 Ibid., p. 87.
22 Ibid., p. 93.
23 Susan Slyomovics, 'Fatna El Bouih and the Work of Memory, Gender, and Reparation in Morocco', *Journal of Middle East Women's Studies* 8/1 (2011), p. 41.
24 See Chapter 4.
25 Pierre Vermeren, *Histoire du Maroc depuis l'indépendance* (Paris, 2016), p. 44; Susan Gilson Miller, *A History of Modern Morocco* (Cambridge, 2013), p. 169.
26 Ibid.
27 Miller, *A History of Modern Morocco*, p. 169.
28 Slyomovics, *The Performance of Human Rights in Morocco*, p. 58.
29 Miller, *A History of Modern Morocco*, pp. 177–8.
30 Slyomovics, *The Performance of Human Rights in Morocco*, p. 58.
31 Ibid., p. 21.
32 Fatna El Bouih, *Ḥadīth al-'atmah* (Casablanca, 2001), p. 14; Susan Slyomovics, 'The Argument from Silence: Morocco's Truth Commission and Women Political Prisoners', *Journal of Middle East Women's Studies* 1/3 (2005), p. 90; Slyomovics, 'Fatna El Bouih and the Work of Memory, Gender, and Reparation in Morocco', p. 41.
33 Slyomovics, *The Performance of Human Rights in Morocco*, p. 21.
34 El Bouih, *Ḥadīth al-'atmah*, p. 4; Slyomovics, *The Performance of Human Rights in Morocco*, p. 134.

35   Slyomovics, 'Fatna El Bouih and the Work of Memory, Gender, and Reparation in Morocco', p. 41.
36   Ibid., p. 42.
37   Slyomovics, *The Performance of Human Rights in Morocco*, p. 21.
38   Slyomovics, 'Fatna El Bouih and the Work of Memory, Gender, and Reparation in Morocco', p. 42.
39   Susan Slyomovics and Fatna El Bouih, '"This Time I Choose When to Leave." An Interview with Fatna El Bouih', *Middle East Report, Morocco in Transition* 31/218 (2001). This campaign and the UAF's continued activism to raise awareness of the need to improve women's rights culminated in the Moudawana Reform of 2004.
40   Slyomovics, *The Performance of Human Rights in Morocco*, p. 24.
41   Ibid., p. 75.
42   Ibid., p. 33. (Interview made by Slyomovics in 2001).
43   Slyomovics, 'Fatna El Bouih and the Work of Memory, Gender, and Reparation in Morocco', p. 46.
44   Ibid., p. 48.
45   Ibid.
46   Ibid., p. 46.
47   Ibid., p. 51.
48   Ibid., p. 52.
49   Ibid., p. 55.
50   Slyomovics, *The Performance of Human Rights in Morocco*, p. 5.
51   Ibid., p. 81.
52   Khalid Zekri, *Fictions du réel: Modernité romanesque et écriture du réel au Maroc 1990–2006* (Paris, 2006), p. 199.
53   Testimonies by and about women: Maria Charaf's *Être au feminine* (To be in feminine) (1997), Malika Oufkir and Michèle Fitoussi's *La Prisonnière* (*Stolen Lives. Twenty Years in a Desert Jail*) (1999), Fatéma Oufkir's *Les Jardins du roi* (The king's garden) (2000), Saïda Menebhi's *Poèmes, Lettres. Ecrits de prison* (Poems, letters. Prison writings) (2000), Khadija Menebhi's "Ishtishād imra'ah" (A woman's martyrdom) (1999) and *Morceaux choisis du livre de l'opression: Témoignage* (Selected pieces from the book of oppression: Testimony) (2001), Fatna El Bouih's *Ḥadīth al-ʿatmah* (2001), and Nour-Eddine Saoudi (ed.), *Femmes-Prison: Parcours croisés* (Women-prison: Crossed paths) (2005). In addition to these, *Ḥadīth al-ʿatmah* includes the testimonies of El Bouih's co-prisoners, Latifa Jbabdi and Widad Bouab, first published in 1994 in the Moroccan newspaper, *Ittihad Ichtiraki*. For a survey of Moroccan prison testimonies, see for instance Zekri, *Fictions du réel*, pp. 199–234) or Valérie K. Orlando, *Francophone Voices of the 'New Morocco' in Film and Print: (Re)presenting a Society in Transition* (New York, 2009), pp. 45–70.
54   Slyomovics and El Bouih, 'This Time I Choose When to Leave.'
55   Valérie K. Orlando, 'Feminine Spaces and Places in the Dark Recesses of Morocco's Past: The Prison Testimonials in Poetry and Prose of Saïda Menebhi and Fatna El Bouih', *The Journal of North African Studies* 15/3 (2010), p. 277.
56   Ibid.
57   El Bouih, *Ḥadīth al-ʿatmah*, p. 3.
58   Sara Ahmed and Jackie Stacey, 'Testimonial Cultures: An Introduction', *Cultural Values* 5/1 (2001), p. 6.
59   Ahmed, *The Cultural Politics of Emotion*, p. 32.
60   Ahmed and Stacey, 'Testimonial Cultures', p. 4.

61 Abdellatif Laâbi, *Le Chemin des ordailes* (Paris, 2003 (1982)), p. 143.

62 Slyomovics, *The Performance of Human Rights in Morocco*, pp. 149–52.

63 El Bouih, *Ḥadīth al-'atmah*, p. 33.

64 Ibid., p. 38.

65 Ibid., p. 45.

66 An earlier and significantly different version of this analysis was presented at the Eleventh EURAMAL conference at Universidad Autónoma de Madrid, Spain, in 2014 and has been published as: Tina Dransfeldt Christensen, 'Narrating the Unnarratable: The Role of Literary Memory in Moroccan Testimonial Writing. Ḥadīth Al-'atmah by Fāṭnah Al-Bīḥ', in Roger Allen, Gonzalo Fernández Parrilla, Francisco Rodriguez Sierra, and Tetz Rooke (eds), *New Geographies: Texts and Contexts in Modern Arabic Literature* (Madrid, 2018), pp. 237–49.

67 Ibid., p. 10.

68 Ibid., pp. 9–10.

69 Ibid., pp. 17–18.

70 Ibid., p. 58.

71 Slyomovics, 'The Argument from Silence', p. 91.

72 El Bouih, *Ḥadīth al-'atmah*, pp. 24–5.

73 This is also the title of the French translation of *Ḥadīth al-'atmah*: *Une femme nommée Rachid*.

74 El Bouih, *Ḥadīth al-'atmah*, pp. 14–15.

75 Slyomovics, *The Performance of Human Rights in Morocco*, p. 132.

76 El Bouih, *Ḥadīth al-'atmah*, p. 21.

77 Slyomovics, *The Performance of Human Rights in Morocco*, p. 133.

78 Ibid., p. 15.

79 Fatima Zahra Zryouil, 'Taqdīm', in Fatna El Bouih, *Ḥadīth al-'atmah* (Casablanca, 2001), p. 6.

80 Latifa Jbabdi, 'Al-makhfar wal-ta'dhīb wal-sijn wal-jallādūn', in Fatna El Bouih, *Ḥadīth al-'atmah* (Casablanca, 2001), p. 135.

81 Slyomovics, 'The Argument from Silence', p. 92.

82 Ibid., p. 90.

83 Ibid., pp. 91–2.

84 Ibid., p. 102.

85 Ibid., p. 23.

86 Jean Zaganiaris, *Queer Maroc: Sexualités, genres et (trans)identités dans la littérature marocaine* (Paris, 2013), p. 55.

87 Abdellah Taïa, *Infidèles* (Paris, 2012), p. 22.

88 Ibid., p. 15.

89 Ibid., pp. 11–12.

90 Ibid., p. 13.

91 See Chapter 2.

92 Taïa, *Infidèles*, p. 44.

93 Ibid., p. 28.

94 See Chapter 2.

95 Taïa, *Infidèles*, p. 39.

96 Abdellah Taïa and Erik Morse, 'Expat Lit: Abdellah Taïa', *Interview Magazine* (5 November 2009).

97 Taïa, *Infidèles*, p. 50.

98 Ibid., pp. 52–3.

99   Ibid., p. 57.
100 Ibid., p. 56.
101 Ibid., p. 61.
102 Ibid., p. 70.
103 Ibid., p. 86.
104 Ibid., p. 94.
105 Ibid., p. 65.
106 Ibid., p. 92.
107 Ibid., pp. 103–4.
108 Ibid., pp. 105–6.
109 Taïa and Morse, 'Expat Lit: Abdellah Taïa'; Abdellah Taïa, 'A Boy to Be Sacrificed', *The New York Times* (24 March 2012).
110 Taïa, *Infidèles*, p. 110.
111 Ibid., p. 117.
112 Jean-Pierre Boulé, 'Deuil et résolution dans Infidèles d'Abdellah Taïa', *@nalyses* 9/2 (2014), p. 286.
113 Taïa, *Infidèles*, p. 142.
114 See Chapters 2 and 4.
115 Taïa, *Infidèles*, p. 143.
116 Ibid., pp. 122–3.
117 Ibid., p. 167.
118 Ibid., p. 155.
119 Abdellah Taïa and Sam Metz, 'Our Monsters Are Like Us: An Interview with Abdellah Taïa', *Los Angeles Review of Books* (9 January 2017).
120 Ibid.
121 Taïa, *Infidèles*, p. 169.
122 Ibid., p. 170.
123 Ibid., p. 172.
124 Ibid.
125 Ibid., p. 186.

Conclusion

1   Abdellah Taïa, 'Ma chère mère, on ne voyait pas à sa juste mesure ton combat de femme', *RTBF La Première* (2019).
2   Abdellah Taïa and Fadwa Islah, 'L'écrivain Abdellah Taïa nous parle des sans-papiers, de racisme et d'islamophobie', *Al Huffington Post, Maghreb - Maroc* (2015).
3   Abdellah Taïa, *Celui qui est digne d'être aimé* (Paris, 2017), p. 31.
4   Ibid., p. 100.
5   Ibid., p. 22.
6   Ibid., p. 14.
7   Ibid., p. 267.

BIBLIOGRAPHY

Abdalaoui, M'hamed Alaoui, 'The Moroccan Novel in French', Jeffrey S. Ankrom (trans.), *Research in African Literatures* 23/4 (1992), pp. 9–33.

Abdel-Jaouad, Hédi, 'Mohammed Khaïr-Eddine: The Poet as Iconoclast', *Research in African Literatures* 23/2 (1992), pp. 145–50.

Abouzeid, Leila, *'Ām al-fīl*. Casablanca: Markaz al-thaqāfī al-'arabī, 2011 [first published in 1983].

Ahmad, Aijaz. 'Jameson's Rhetoric of Otherness and the "National Allegory"', *Social Text* 17 (1987), pp. 3–25. DOI: https://doi.org/10.2307/466475.

Ahmed, Sara, *Queer Phenomenology: Orientations, Objects, Others*. Durham: Duke University Press, 2006.

Ahmed, Sara, *The Cultural Politics of Emotion*. New York: Routledge, Taylor and Francis Group, 2012 [first published in 2004].

Ahmed, Sara and Jackie Stacey, 'Testimonial Cultures: An Introduction', *Cultural Values* 5/1 (2001), pp. 1–6. DOI: https://doi.org/10.1080/14797580109367217.

Allen, Roger, *The Arabic Novel: An Historical and Critical Introduction*, second edition. Syracuse: Syracuse University Press, 1995 [first published in 1982].

Alessandra, Jacques, 'Abdellatif Laâbi: A Writing of Dissidence', [Abdellatif Laâbi:traversée de l'oeuvre], Richard Bjornson (trans.), *Research in African Literatures* 23/2 (1992), pp. 151–66.

Anderson, Benedict, *Imagined Communities: Reflections on the Origin and Spread of Nationalism*, second edition. New York: Verso, 1991 [first published in 1983].

Bakhtin, Mikhail M., *The Dialogic Imagination: Four Essays*, trans. Caryl Emerson and Michael Holquist. Austin: University of Texas Press, 2008 [first published in 1981].

Bakkar, Ismaël, 'Personal interview with Ismaël Bakkar, project coordinator at MALI', in Rabat, Morocco (18 October 2016). Interview by Tina Dransfeldt Christensen.

Bainier, Corentin, 'Homosexuality and Femen: Morocco Debates "Public Decency"', *The Observers* (11 June 2015). https://observers.france24.com/en/20150611-homosexuality-femen-jennifer-lopez-morocco-public-decency (accessed 2 December 2018).

Barthes, Roland, 'The Death of the Author', in *Image, Music, Text*. New York: Hill & Wang, (1977) , pp. 142–8.

Ben Jelloun, Tahar, 'Aube des dalles', *Souffles* 12 (1968), pp. 38–43.

Ben Jelloun, Tahar, 'La Planète des singes', *Souffles* 13–14 (1969), pp. 23–4.

Ben Jelloun, Tahar, *Harrouda*. Paris: Denoël, 1973.

Ben Jelloun, Tahar, *La nuit sacrée*. Paris: Éditions du Seuil, 1987.

Ben Jelloun, Tahar, *Le Racisme expliqué à ma fille*. Paris: Éditions du Seuil, 1998.

Benjelloun, Abdelmajid, *Fī al-ṭufūlah*. Rabat: Maktabat al-Ma'ārif, 1975 [first published in 1957].

Bensalmia, Chadwane, 'Portrait. "J'ai été élevé dans la honte"', *TelQuel* 210 (2006), p. 55.

Bensmaïa, Réda, *Experimental Nations: Or, the Invention of the Maghreb*. Princeton: Princeton University Press, 2003.

Bergeaud-Blackler, Florence, and Victor Eck, 'Les "faux" mariages homosexuels de Sidi Ali au Maroc: enjeux d'un scandale médiatique', *Revue des mondes musulmans et de la Méditerranée* 129 (July 2011), pp. 203-21. DOI: https://doi.org/10.4000/remmm.7180.

Berrada, Mohamed, 'al-laghū wal-aswāt', *Souffles* 10-1 (1968), pp. 27-9.

Berrada, Mohamed, *Lu'bat al-nisyān*. Rabat: Dar al-'amān, 1987.

Bhabha, Homi K., 'Representation and the Colonial Text: A Critical Exploration of Some Forms of Mimeticism', in Frank Gloversmith (ed.), *The Theory of Reading*. Sussex: The Harvester Press, 1984, pp. 93-122.

Bhabha, Homi K., *The Location of Culture*. London and New York: Routledge, 2004 [first published in 1994].

Bissenbakker Frederiksen and Maja Mons, 'Krumme tæer. Skam i krydsfeltet mellem queer, feministiske og postkoloniale teorier', *Kvinder, køn og forskning* 1 (2013), pp. 25-36.

Boukhari, Karim, 'Portrait. Homosexuel envers en contre tous', *TelQuel* 277 (2007), pp. 40-6.

Boulé, Jean-Pierre, 'Deuil et résolution dans Infidèles d'Abdellah Taïa', *@nalyses* 9/2 (2014), pp. 276-307. https://uottawa.scholarsportal.info/ojs/index.php/revue-analyses/article/view/1010.

Boulé, Jean-Pierre, 'Writing Selves as Mourning and Vita Nova: Abdellah Taïa's Un Pays Pour Mourir', *Contemporary French Civilization* 41/1 (2016), pp. 25-47. DOI: https://doi.org/10.3828/cfc.2016.2.

Butler, Judith, *Gender Trouble: Feminism and the Subversion of Identity*. New York: Routledge, 1990.

Butler, Judith, 'Imitation and Gender Insubordination', in Henry Abelove, Michèle Aina Barale, and David M. Halperin (eds), *The Lesbian and Gay Studies Reader*. New York and London: Routledge, 1993, pp. 307-20.

Campbell, Ian, *Labyrinths, Intellectuals and the Revolution. The Arabic-Language Moroccan Novel, 1957-72*, Leiden and Boston: Brill, 2013.

Carbajal, Alberto Fernández, 'The Wanderings of a Gay Moroccan: An Interview with Abdellah Taïa', *Journal of Postcolonial Writing* 53/4 (2017), pp. 495-506. DOI: https://doi.org/10.1080/17449855.2017.1327966.

Chaoui, Abdelkader, *Kāna wa-akhawātuha*. Casablanca: Dār al-Nashr al-Maghribīyah, 1986.

Charaf, Maria, *Être, au féminin*. Casablanca: Éditions La Voie démocratique, 1997.

Choukrallah, Zakaria, 'Pourquoi les homos font peur', *Actuel* 44 (2010), pp. 42-4.

Choukri, Mohamed, *Al-khubz al-ḥāfi*. Beirut: Dar al-Saqi, 2009 [originally written 1973 and published in Arabic in 1981].

Chraïbi, Driss, *Le Passé simple*. Paris: Denoël, 1954.

Chraïbi, Driss, and Lionel Dubois, 'Interview de Driss Chraïbi (Accordée à Lionel Dubois le 23 juin 1983)', *CELFAN Review* 5/2 (1986), pp. 20-6.

Chraïbi, Driss, and Abdellatif Laâbi, 'Driss et nous: Questionnaire établi par Abdellatif Laâbi', *Souffles* 5 (1967), pp. 5-10.

Christensen, Tina Dransfeldt, '"Writing the Self" as Narrative of Resistance: L'Armée du Salut by Abdellah Taïa', *The Journal of North African Studies* 21/5 (2016), pp. 857-76. DOI: https://doi.org/10.1080/13629387.2016.1212707.

Christensen, Tina Dransfeldt, 'Breaking the Silence: Between Literary Representation and LGBT Activism. Abdellah Taïa as Author and Activist', *Expressions Maghrébines* 16/1 (2017), pp. 107-25. DOI: https://doi.org/10.1353/exp.2017.0006.

Christensen, Tina Dransfeldt, 'Towards an Ethics of Bilingualism: An Intertextual Dialogue between Khatibi and Derrida', *Interventions* 19/4 (2017), pp. 447–66. DOI: https://doi.org/10.1080/1369801X.2016.1277150.

Christensen, Tina Dransfeldt, 'Narrating the Unnarratable: The Role of Literary Memory in Moroccan Testimonial Writing. Ḥadīth Al–'atmah by Fāṭnah Al-Bīh', in Roger Allen, Gonzalo Fernández Parrilla, Francisco Rodriguez Sierra, and Tetz Rooke (eds), *New Geographies: Texts and Contexts in Modern Arabic Literature*. Madrid: Universidad Autónoma de Madrid, 2018, pp. 237–49.

Colonna, Vincent, *Autofiction & autres mythomanies littéraires*. Auch: Éditions Tristram, 2004.

Culler, Jonathan, *The Pursuit of Signs: Semiotics, Literature, Deconstruction*. Ithaca: Cornell University Press, 2002.

Dailleux, Denis, Abdellah Taïa and Mahmoud Farag, *Égypte. Les martyrs de la révolution*. Marseille: Le bec en l'air, 2014.

Damrosch, David, *What Is World Literature?* Princeton and Oxford: Princeton University Press, 2003.

Déjeux, Jean, *Littérature maghrébine de langue française: Introduction générale et auteurs*, 3. édition revue et corrigée. Sherbrooke Naaman, 1980.

Déjeux, Jean, 'L' Emergence du je dans la littérature maghrébine de langue française', *Itinéraires et contacts de cultures* 13 (1er semestre, 1991), pp. 23–9.

Déjeux, Jean, 'Au Maghreb, la langue française "langue natale du je"', in Martine Mathieu (ed.), *Littératures autobiographiques de la francophonie*. Paris: C.E.L.F.A./L'Harmattan, 1994, pp. 181–93.

Dennerlein, Bettina, 'Remembering Violence, Negotiating Change: The Moroccan Equity and Reconciliation Commission and the Politics of Gender', *Journal of Middle East Women's Studies* 8/1 (2012), pp. 10–36.

Derrida, Jacques, *De la grammatologie*. Paris: Les Éditions de minuit, 1967.

Derrida, Jacques, 'The Law of Genre', Avital Ronell (trans.), *Critical Inquiry* 7/1 (1980), pp. 55–81.

Derrida, Jacques, *Le monolinguisme de l'autre, ou, La prothèse d'origine*. Paris: Galilée, 1996.

Devereux, Cecily, 'Hysteria, Feminism, and Gender Revisited: The Case of the Second Wave', *ESC: English Studies in Canada* 40/1 (2014), pp. 19–45. DOI: https://doi.org/10.1353/esc.2014.0004.

Di-Capua, Yoav, 'The Intellectual Revolt of the 1950s and the "Fall of the Udabā"', in Georges Khalil, Friederike Pannewick, and Yvonne Albers (eds), *Commitment and Beyond: Reflections On/Of the Political in Arabic Literature Since the 1940s*. Wiesbaden: Dr. Ludwig Reichert Verlag, 2015, pp. 89–104.

Di-Capua, Yoav, *No Exit: Arab Existentialism, Jean-Paul Sartre, and Decolonization*. Chicago: The University of Chicago Press, 2018.

Doubrovsky, Serge, *Fils*. Paris: Gallimard Folio, 2001 [first published in 1977].

Eid, Yumna al-, 'The Autobiographical Novel and the Dual Function', in Robin Ostle, Ed de Moor, and Stefan Wild (eds), *Writing the Self. Autobiographical Writing in Modern Arabic Literature*. London: Saqi Books, 1998, pp. 157–77.

Eid, Yumna al-, *al-riwāyah al-'arabiyyah: al-mutakhayyal wa-bunyatuh al-fanniyyah*. Beirut: al-Fārābī, 2011.

El Bouih, Fatna, *Ḥadīth al-'atmah*. Casablanca: Nashr al-Fanak, 2001.

El Rhazoui, Zineb and Habibou Bangré, 'Zineb El Rhazoui: "Nous ne défendons pas que la liberté de 'dé-jeûner"', *afrik.com* (23 October 2009). http://www.afrik.com/article17805.html (accessed 17 October 2018).

El-Ariss, Tarek, *Trials of Arab Modernity. Literary Affects and the New Political*. New York: Fordham University Press, 2013.

El-Ariss, Tarek, 'Fictions of Scandal', in Georges Khalil, Friederike Pannewick, and Yvonne Albers (eds), *Commitment and Beyond: Reflections On/Of the Political in Arabic Literature Since the 1940s*. Wiesbaden: Dr. Ludwig Reichert Verlag, 2015, pp. 237–51.

El-Tayeb, Fatima, 'Gays Who Cannot Properly be Gay.' Queer Muslims in the Neoliberal European City', *European Journal of Women's Studies* 19/1 (2012), pp. 79–95. DOI: https://doi.org/10.1177/1350506811426388

Ennaji, Moha, *Multilingualism, Cultural Identity, and Education in Morocco*. New York: Springer US, 2005. DOI: 10.1007/b104063.

Fanon, Frantz, *Peau Noire, Masques Blancs*. Paris: Éditions du Seuil, 1952.

Fanon, Frantz, *Les Damnés de la terre*. Paris: F. Maspéro, 1961.

Fassin, Éric, 'National Identities and Transnational Intimacies: Sexual Democracy and the Politics of Immigration in Europe', *Public Culture* 22/3 (2010), pp. 507–29. DOI: https://doi.org/10.1215/08992363-2010-007

Fassin, Éric, 'Sexual Democracy and the New Racialization of Europe', *Journal of Civil Society* 8/3 (2012), pp. 285–8. DOI: https://doi.org/10.1080/17448689.2012.738887

Fernández Parrilla, Gonzalo, 'Breaking the Canon: Zafzaf, Laroui and the Moroccan Novel', in Stephan Guth and Gail Ramsay (eds), *From New Values to New Aesthetics. Turning Points in Modern Arabic Literature. 2. Postmodernism and Thereafter*. Wiesbaden: Harrassowitz Verlag, 2011, pp. 2–13 (online version). https://www.academia.edu/5412586/Moroccan_Literature._Breaking_the_canon_Zafzaf_Laroui_and_the_Moroccan_Novel (accessed 17 October 2018).

Fernández Parrilla, 'The Challenge of Moroccan Cultural Journals of the 1960s', *Journal of Arabic Literature* 45/1 (2014), pp. 104–28. DOI: https://doi.org/10.1163/1570064x-12341278.

Fernández Parrilla, 'The Novel in Morocco as Mirror of a Changing Society', *Contemporary French and Francophone Studies* 20/1 (2016), pp. 18–26. DOI: https://doi.org/10.1080/17409292.2016.1120547.

Foucault, Michel, *Histoire de la sexualité, tome 1: La Volonté de savoir*. Paris: Gallimard, 1994 [first published in 1976].

Genette, Gérard, *Fiction et diction*. Paris: Éditions du Seuil, 1991.

Ghallab, Abdelkrim, *Dafannā al-māḍī*. Beirut: al-Maktab al-tijārī, 1966.

Ghazoul, Ferial, and Barbara Harlow (eds), *The View from Within*. Cairo: AUC Press, 1994.

Ghrib, Loubna, 'Groundbreaking Video Series Breaks LGBTI Silence in Morocco', *OutRight International* (25 November 2014). https://www.outrightinternational.org/content/groundbreaking-video-series-breaks-lgbti-silence-morocco (accessed 17 October 2018).

Gontard, Marc, *La violence du texte: Etudes sur la littérature marocaine d'expression française*. Paris: L'Harmattan, 1981.

Gouyon, Marien, and Sandrine Musso, 'Luttes contre le sida et luttes LGBT au Maroc. Notes exploratoires sur les enjeux d'une imbrication', *L'Année du Maghreb* 17 (13 November 2017). DOI : 10.4000/anneemaghreb.3261 (Accessed 20 December 2018)

Graiouid, Said, 'We Have Not Buried the Simple Past: The Public Sphere and Post-Colonial Literature in Morocco', *Journal of African Cultural Studies* 20/2 (2008), pp. 145–58. DOI: https://doi.org/10.1080/13696810802522254.

Guessous, Nadia, *Women and Political Violence during the Years of Lead in Morocco*, published by CCDH (Advisory Council on Human Rights) and UNIFEM (United

Nations Development Fund for Women). Rabat, 2009. http://www.ccdh.org.ma/sites/default/files/documents/GUIDang.pdf (accessed 17 October 2018).

Gusdorf, Georges, 'Conditions and Limits of Autobiography', in James Olney (ed.), *Autobiography: Essays Theoretical and Critical*. Princeton: Princeton University Press, 1981, pp. 28–48.

Hafez, Sabry, *The Genesis of Arabic Narrative Discourse: A Study in the Sociology of Modern Arabic Literature*. London: Saqi Books, 1993.

Harrison, Olivia, and Teresa Villa-Ignacio, *Souffles-Anfas: A Critical Anthology from the Moroccan Journal of Culture and Politics*. Redwood City: Stanford University Press, 2016.

Hassan, Waïl S., 'Translator's Introduction', Abdelfattah Kilito, *Thou Shalt Not Speak My Language*. Syracuse: Syracuse University Press, 2008, pp. vii–xvii.

Hayes, Jarrod, 'Rachid O. and the Return of the Homopast: The Autobiographical as Allegory in Childhood Narratives by Maghrebian Men', *Contemporary French and Francophone Studies* 1/2 (1997), pp. 497–526. DOI: https://doi.org/10.1080/10260219708455907

Hayes, Jarrod, *Queer Nations: Marginal Sexualities in the Maghreb*. Chicago: University of Chicago Press, 2000.

Héraud, Xavier, '"Ils existent", une web-série sur l'homosexualité et l'homophobie au Maroc', *yagg.com* (18 January 2015). http://yagg.com/2015/01/18/ils-existent-une-web-serie-sur-lhomosexualite-et-lhomophobie-au-maroc/ (accessed 19 December 2018)

Heyndels, Ralph, 'Configurations et transferts de la sexualité, du genre et du désir dans l'ouverture d' Une mélancolie arabe d'Abdellah Taïa, ou "le dépassement des frontières"', *Expressions maghrébines* 16/1 (2017), pp. 85–105.

Hida, Bouchra Sidi, 'Mobilisations collectives à l'épreuve des changements au Maroc', *Revue Tiers Monde* HS/5 (2011), pp. 163–88.

Hiddleston, Jane, *Understanding Postcolonialism*. Stocksfield: Acumen Publishing Limited, 2009. DOI: http://dx.doi.org/10.1017/UPO9781844654284.

Jameson, Fredric, 'Third-World Literature in the Era of Multinational Capitalism', *Social Text* 15 (1986), pp. 65–88. DOI: https://doi.org/10.2307/466493.

Jay, Salim, *Dictionnaire des écrivains marocains*. Paris: Eddif, 2005.

Jbabdi, Latifa, 'Al-makhfar wal-taʿdhīb wal-sijn wal-jallādūn', in Fatna El Bouih, *Ḥadīth al-ʿatmah*. Casablanca: Nashr al-Fanak, 2001, pp. 120–35.

Kaye, Jacqueline, and Abdelhamid Zoubir, *The Ambiguous Compromise: Language, Literature, and National Identity in Algeria and Morocco*. New York: Routledge, 1990.

Kelly, Debra, *Autobiography and Independence: Selfhood and Creativity in North African Postcolonial Writing in French*. Liverpool: Liverpool University Press, 2005.

Khaïr-Eddine, Mohammed, *Agadir*. Casablanca: Tarik éditions, 2010 [first published in 1967].

Khalil, Georges, Friederike Pannewick, and Yvonne Albers, *Commitment and Beyond: Reflections On/Of the Political in Arabic Literature Since the 1940s*. Wiesbaden: Dr. Ludwig Reichert Verlag, 2015.

Khatibi, Abdelkébir, 'Roman maghrébin et culture nationale', *Souffles* 3 (1966), pp. 10–11.

Khatibi, Abdelkébir, *Le Roman maghrébin*. Paris: F. Maspéro, 1968.

Khatibi, Abdelkébir, *Maghreb pluriel*. Paris: Denoël, 1983.

Khatibi, Abdelkébir, *Figures de l'étranger: dans la littérature française*. Paris: Denoël, 1987.

Khatibi, Abdelkébir, *Penser le Maghreb*. Rabat: Société marocaine des éditeurs réunis, 1993.

Khatibi, Abdelkébir, 'Un étranger professionnel', *Etudes françaises* 33/1 (1997), pp. 123–6. DOI: https://doi.org/10.7202/036059ar.

Khatibi, Abdelkébir, 'Amour bilingue', *Œuvre de Abdelkébir Khatibi I: Romans et récits*, second edition. Paris: Éditions de la Différence, 2008 [first published in 1983], pp. 205–83.

Khatibi, Abdelkébir, 'La Mémoire tatouée: Autobiographie d'un décolonisé', *Œuvre de Abdelkébir Khatibi I: Romans et récits*, second edition. Paris: Éditions de la Différence, 2008 [first published in 1971], pp. 9–113.

Khatibi, Abdelkébir, 'Un Été à Stockholm', *Œuvre de Abdelkébir Khatibi I: Romans et récits*, second edition. Paris: Éditions de la Différence, 2008 [first published in 1990], pp. 285–379.

Khodayri, Muhammad al-, and Abdallah Taïa, ' ʿabdallah al-ṭāy ʿa: "yasṭafalū" al- ʾislāmīīn!', *al- ʾakhbār* (12 June 2012) http://al-akhbar.com/node/95255 (accessed 17 October 2018).

Kilito, Abdelfattah, *The Author and His Doubles: Essays on Classical Arabic Culture*, trans. Michael Cooperson. Syracuse: Syracuse University Press, 2001.

Kilito, Abdelfattah, *Thou Shalt Not Speak My Language*, trans. Waïl S. Hassan. Syracuse: Syracuse University Press, 2008.

Kilito, Abdelfattah, *Je parle toutes les langues, mais en arabe*. Arles: Sindbad, 2013.

Klee, Paul, *Creative Confession - Paul Klee*. London: Tate Enterprises Ltd, 2013 [first published in 1920].

Kribi, Adjil, 'Campagne contre l'homophobie au Maroc: "Je dis que les homosexuels ont les mêmes droits que moi"', *HuffPost Maghreb* (7 May 2014). https://www.huffpostmaghreb.com/2014/05/07/homophobie-maroc_n_5280388.html (accessed 19 December 2018)

Kristeva, Julia, *Desire in Language: A Semiotic Approach to Literature and Art*, reprint. Oxford: Blackwell, 1987 [first published in 1980].

Laâbi, Abdellatif, 'Prologue', *Souffles* 1 (1966), pp. 3–6.

Laâbi, Abdellatif, 'Marasmes', *Souffles* 1 (1966), pp. 22–8.

Laâbi, Abdellatif, 'Réalités et dilemmes de la culture nationale (I)', *Souffles* 4 (1966), pp. 4–12.

Laâbi, Abdellatif, 'La presse nationale entre le business et le dogme', *Souffles* 4 (1966), pp. 38–40.

Laâbi, Abdellatif, 'Défense du "Passé simple"', *Souffles* 5 (1967), pp. 18–21.

Laâbi, Abdellatif, 'Réalités et dilemmes de la culture nationale (II)', *Souffles* 6 (1967), pp. 29–35.

Laâbi, Abdellatif, *L'œil et la nuit: itinéraire*. Inéditions Barbare & Comité de libération d'A. Laâbi, 1969.

Laâbi, Abdellatif, 'Littérature maghrébine actuelle et francophonie', *Souffles* 18 (1970), pp. 35–8.

Laâbi, Abdellatif, 'Avant-propos', *Souffles* 22 (1971), pp. 3–5.

Laâbi, Abdellatif, *Le Chemin des ordailes*, revised edition. Paris: Éditions de La Différence, 2003 [first published in 1982].

Laâbi, Abdellatif, 'Préface', Kenza Sefrioui, *La revue Souffles: Espoirs de révolution culturelle au Maroc*. Casablanca: Éditions du Sirocco, 2013, pp. 7–10.

Laachir, Karima, 'The Aesthetics and Politics of "Reading Together" Moroccan Novels in Arabic and French', *The Journal of North African Studies* 21/1 (2016), pp. 22–36. DOI: https://doi.org/10.1080/13629387.2015.1084098.

Lefébure, Anaïs, 'LGBT - L'autorisation pour se constituer en association lui est réfusée, mais le collectif Akaliyat continue la lutte', *HuffPost Maroc* (3 February 2017). https://www.huffpostmaghreb.com/2017/02/03/refus-autorisation-association-lgbt-a kaliyat_n_14597996.html (accessed 20 December 2018).

Lejeune, Philippe, *L'Autobiographie en France*. Paris: Armand Colin, 1971.

Lejeune, Philippe, *Le pacte autobiographique. Paris*. Paris: Éditions du Seuil, 1975.

MacDonald, Megan C., 'Publish or Paris: Reflections on the Politics of Transnational Literary Culture between Morocco and France', *Francosphères* 2/1 (2013), pp. 1–13. DOI: http://dx.doi.org/10.3828/franc.2013.2.

MacDonald, Megan C., 'Editors' Introduction', *Contemporary French and Francophone Studies* 20/1 (2016), pp. 1–6. DOI: https://doi.org/10.1080/17409292.2016.1120545.

Mack, Mehammed Amadeus, *Sexagon: Muslims, France, and the Sexualization of National Culture*. New York: Fordham University Press, 2017.

Man, Paul de, 'Autobiography as De-Facement', *MLN* 94/5 (1979), pp. 919–30. DOI: https://doi.org/10.2307/2906560.

Marx-Scouras, Danielle, 'A Literature of Departure: The Cross-Cultural Writing of Driss Chraïbi', *Research in African Literatures* 23/2 (1992), pp. 131–44.

Massad, Joseph A., *Desiring Arabs*. Chicago: University of Chicago Press, 2007.

McGuinness, Justin, 'Réprésentation et résistance sur mithly.net: analyse du discours d'un site communautaire marocain', in Sihem Najar (ed.), *Les nouvelles sociabilités du Net en Méditerranée*. Paris: Éditions Karthala et IRMC, 2012, pp. 117–42.

McLarney, Ellen, 'Politics of Le Passé Simple', *The Journal of North African Studies* 8/2 (2003), pp. 1–18. DOI: https://doi.org/10.1080/13629380308718505.

McNeece, Lucy Stone, 'Decolonizing the Sign: Language and Identity in Abdelkebir Khatibi's La Mémoire Tatouée', *Yale French Studies* 83 (1993), pp. 12–29. DOI: https://doi.org/10.2307/2930085.

Mdarhri Alaoui, Abdallah, *Aspects du roman marocain, (1950–2003): Approche historique, thématique et esthétique*. Rabat: Éditions Zaouia Art et Culture, 2006.

Mellouki, Ilham, 'La génération du "Je"', *TelQuel* 249 (2007).

Memmi, Albert, *Portrait du colonisé*. Paris: Jean-Jacques Pauvert, 1966 [first published in 1957].

Menebhi, Khadija, 'Ishtishād Imra'ah', *Nafāwiḍ* 3 (1999), pp. 121–7.

Menebhi, Khadija, *Morceaux choisis du livre de l'oppression: témoignage*. Rabat: Édition Multicom, 2001.

Menebhi, Saïda, *Poèmes, lettres, écrits de prison*. Rabat: Éditions Feed-Back, 2000.

Menin, Laura, 'Rewriting the World: Gendered Violence, the Political Imagination and Memoirs from the 'Years of Lead' in Morocco', *International Journal of Conflict and Violence* 8/1 (2014), pp. 1–15. http://www.ijcv.org/earlyview/351.pdf (accessed 17 October 2018).

Mernissi, Fatema, *Scheherazade Goes West. Different Cultures, Different Harems*. New York: Washington Square Press, 2001.

Miller, Susan, Gilson, *A History of Modern Morocco*. Cambridge: Cambridge University Press, 2013.

Moretti, Franco, 'Conjectures on World Literature', *New Left Review* 1 (2000), pp. 54–68.

Mouride, Abdelaziz, *On affame bien les rats!* Casablanca: Tarik éditions, 2000.

Murray, Stephen O., and Will Roscoe, *Islamic Homosexualities: Culture, History, and Literature*. New York: New York University Press, 1997.

Nasseri, Karim, *Noces et funerailles*. Paris: Denoël, 2001.

Ncube, Gibson, 'Writing Queer Desire in the Language of the "Other": Abdellah Taïa and Rachid O', *Rupkatha Journal. On Interdisciplinary Studies in Humanities* vi/1 (2014), pp. 87–96.

O., Rachid, *L'Enfant Ébloui*. Paris: Gallimard, 1995.

Orlando, Valérie K., *Francophone Voices of the 'New Morocco' in Film and Print: (Re)presenting a Society in Transition*. New York: Palgrave Macmillan, 2009.

Orlando, Valérie K., 'Feminine Spaces and Places in the Dark Recesses of Morocco's Past: The Prison Testimonials in Poetry and Prose of Saïda Menebhi and Fatna El Bouih', *The Journal of North African Studies* 15/3 (2010), pp. 273–88. DOI: https://doi.org /10.1080/13629380902745884.

Orlando, Valérie K., 'Review of Abdellah Taïa "L'Armée Du Salut"', *African Studies Review* 57/2 (2014), pp. 245–50. DOI: https://doi.org/10.1017/asr.2014.80.

Oufkir, Fatéma, *Les Jardins du roi: Oufkir, Hassan II et nous*. Neuilly-sur-Seine: Lafon, 2000.

Oufkir, Malika, and Michèle Fitoussi, *La prisonnière*. Paris: Grasset, 1999.

Ould Bouleiba, Mohamed, *Critique littéraire occidentale - critique littéraire arabe. 'Texte croisés.'* Paris: L'Harmattan, 2000.

Pauline, 'Les militants marocains de défense des LGBT pour ou contre l'action des Femen?', *TelQuel* (11 June 2015). https://telquel.ma/2015/06/11/defenses-droits-lgbt -les-militants-marocains-on-contre-laction-femen_1451330 (accessed 20 December 2018).

Péroncel-Hugoz, Jean-Pierre, 'Pédérastie et pudeur: la prêt-à-penser a encore frappé…', *Actuel* 47 (2010), p. 50.

Provencher, Denis M., *Queer Maghrebi French. Language, Temporalities, Transfiliations*. Liverpool: Liverpool University Press, 2017.

Puar, Jasbir K., *Terrorist Assemblages: Homonationalism in Queer Times*. Durham: Duke University Press, 2007.

Quayson, Ato, 'Periods versus Concepts: Space Making and the Question of Postcolonial Literary History', *PMLA* 127/2 (2012), pp. 342–8. DOI: https://doi.org/10.1632/pmla.2 012.127.2.342.

Renan, Ernest, *Qu'est-ce qu'une nation? Et autres essais politiques*, text of a conference delivered at the Sorbonne on 11 March 1882. Paris: Presses Pocket, 1992.

Reynolds, Dwight F. (ed.), *Interpreting the Self: Autobiography in the Arabic Literary Tradition*. Berkeley, Los Angeles and London: University of California Press, 2001.

Rooke, Tetz, 'Moroccan Autobiography as National Allegory', *Oriente moderno XVI (LXVII)* 2–3 (1997), pp. 289–305.

Roudaby, Youssef, 'Aswat publie une vidéo pour sensibiliser les LGBT sur leurs droits au Maroc', *HuffPost Maroc* (14 December 2016). https://www.huffpostmaghreb.co m/2016/12/14/lgbt-droits-maroc-aswat_n_13625128.html (accessed 19 December 2018).

Said, Edward W., *Orientalism*. New York: Pantheon Books, 1978.

Saoudi, Nour-Eddine, *Femmes - prison: parcours croisés*. Rabat: Marsam Editions, 2005.

Sartre, Jean-Paul, 'Orphée noir', in Léopold Sédar Senghor, *Anthologie de la nouvelle poésie nègre et malgache de langue française: Précédée de Orphée noir par Jean-Paul Sartre*. Paris: Presses universitaires de France, 1948.

Sartre, Jean-Paul, *Qu'est-ce que la littérature*. Paris: Gallimard, 2008 [first published in 1948].

Schmitt, Arnaud, 'Making the Case for Self-Narration Against Autofiction', *A/B: Auto/Biography Studies* 25/1 (2010), pp. 122–37. DOI: https://doi.org/10.1080/089895 75.2010.10815365.

Schmitt, Arno, and Jehoeda Sofer (eds), *Sexuality and Eroticism Among Males in Moslem Societies*. New York and London: The Haworth Press, 1992.

Sedgwick, Eve Kosofsky, 'Shame and Performativity', in David McWhirter (ed.), *Henry James's New York Edition: The Construction of Authorship*. Stanford: Stanford University Press, 1995, pp. 206–39.

Sefrioui, Ahmed, *La boîte à merveilles*. Paris: Éditions du Seuil, 1954.

Sefrioui, Kenza, *La revue Souffles: Espoirs de révolution culturelle au Maroc*. Casablanca: Éditions du Sirocco, 2013.

Slimani, Leïla, *Chanson douce*. Paris: Gallimard, 2016.

Slyomovics, Susan, 'The Argument from Silence: Morocco's Truth Commission and Women Political Prisoners', *Journal of Middle East Women's Studies* 1/3 (2005), pp. 73–95.

Slyomovics, Susan, *The Performance of Human Rights in Morocco*. Philadelphia: University of Pennsylvania Press, 2005.

Slyomovics, Susan, 'Fatna El Bouih and the Work of Memory, Gender, and Reparation in Morocco', *Journal of Middle East Women's Studies* 8/1 (2011), pp. 37–62.

Slyomovics, Susan, and Fatna El Bouih, '"This Time I Choose When to Leave." An Interview with Fatna El Bouih', Middle East Report, *Morocco in Transition* 31/218 (2001). http://www.merip.org/mer/mer218/time-i-choose-when-leave (accessed 17 October 2018).

Spivak, Gayatri Chakravorty, *A Critique of Postcolonial Reason: Toward a History of the Vanishing Present*. Cambridge: Harvard University Press, 1999.

Taïa, Abdellah, *Mon Maroc*. Paris: Séguier, 2000.

Taïa, Abdellah, *L'Armée du salut*. Paris: Éditions du Seuil, 2006.

Taïa, Abdellah, (ed.), *Lettres à un jeune marocain*. Paris: Éditions du Seuil, 2009.

Taïa, Abdellah, 'L'Homosexualité expliquée à ma mère', *TelQuel* 367 (2009), pp. 20–7.

Taïa, Abdellah, *Le Jour du roi*. Paris: Éditions du Seuil, 2010.

Taïa, Abdellah, 'Le retour du maréchal Lyautey', *Actuel* 47 (2010), p. 51.

Taïa, Abdellah, *Infidèles*. Paris: Éditions du Seuil, 2012.

Taïa, Abdellah, *Le Rouge du tarbouche*. Paris: Éditions Points 2012 [first published in 2004].

Taïa, Abdellah, 'A Boy to Be Sacrificed', Edward Gauvin (trans.), *The New York Times* (24 March 2012). http://www.nytimes.com/2012/03/25/opinion/sunday/a-boy-to-be -sacrificed.html (accessed 17 October 2018).

Taïa, Abdellah, *Un Pays pour mourir*. Paris: Éditions du Seuil, 2015.

Taïa, Abdellah, 'Personal interview with Abdellah Taïa', in Aarhus, Denmark (8 March 2016). Interview by Tina Dransfeldt Christensen.

Taïa, Abdellah, *Celui qui est digne d'être aimé*. Paris: Éditions du Seuil, 2017.

Taïa, Abdellah, *La Vie lente*. Paris: Éditions du Seuil, 2019.

Taïa, Abdellah, 'Ma chère mère, on ne voyait pas à sa juste mesure ton combat de femme', *RTBF La Première* (14 December 2019). https://www.rtbf.be/lapremiere/article/detail _abdellah-taia-ma-chere-mere-on-ne-voyait-pas-a-sa-juste-mesure-ton-combat-de-fe mme?id=10388649 (accessed 9 February 2020).

Taïa, Abdellah, and Jason Napoli Brooks, 'An Interview with Abdellah Taïa', *Asymptote* (July 2012). http://www.asymptotejournal.com/interview/an-interview-with-abdellah-taia/ (accessed 17 October 2018).

Taïa, Abdellah, and Aaron Hicklin, 'Why Abdellah Taia Had to Die in Order to Live', *out.com* (26 January 2010). http://www.out.com/entertainment/2010/01/26/ why-abdellah-taia-had-die-order-live (accessed 17 October 2018).

Taïa, Abdellah, and Antoine Idier, '"Sortir de la peur": Construire une identité homosexuelle arabe dans un monde postcolonial. Entretien avec Abdellah Taïa', *Revue critique de fixxion française contemporaine* 12 (March 2016), pp. 197–207.

Taïa, Abdellah, and Fadwa Islah, 'L'écrivain Abdellah Taïa nous parle des sans-papiers, de racisme et d'islamophobie', *Al Huffington Post, Maghreb - Maroc* (18 January 2015). http://www.huffpostmaghreb.com/2015/01/18/abdellah-taia-islamophobi_n_6495342.html (accessed 17 October 2018).

Taïa, Abdellah, and Sam Metz, 'Our Monsters Are Like Us: An interview with Abdellah Taïa', *Los Angeles Review of Books* (9 January 2017). https://blog.lareviewofbooks.org/interviews/monsters-like-us-interview-abdellah-taia/ (accessed 3 November 2018).

Taïa, Abdellah, and Frédéric Mitterrand, *Maroc, 1900–1960: Un certain regard.* Paris: Actes Sud, 2007.

Taïa, Abdellah, and Erik Morse, 'Expat Lit: Abdellah Taïa', *Interview Magazine* (5 November 2009). http://www.interviewmagazine.com/culture/abdellah-taia (accessed 17 October 2018).

Taïa, Abdellah, and Dale Peck, 'In Conversation: Abdellah Taïa and Dale Peck', *PEN World Voices Festival of International Literature* (New York, 2011). http://www.bookforum.com/video/7676/mode=large&top=7661&page_id=35 (accessed 17 October 2018).

Taïa, Abdellah, and Georgia Phillips-Amos, 'Abdellah Taïa by Georgia Phillips-Amos', *bombmagazine.org* (3 May 2016). http://bombmagazine.org/article/5723426/abdellah-ta-a (accessed 17 October 2018).

Taïa, Abdellah, and Youssef Roudaby, 'Dans son nouveau roman "Celui qui est digne d'être aimé", Abdellah Taïa fait le bilan d'une vie tourmentée', *2m.ma* (17 January 2017). https://www.2m.ma/fr/culture/20170117-dans-son-nouveau-roman-celui-qui-est-digne-detre-aime-abdellah-taia-fait-le-bilan-dune-vie-tourmentee/ (accessed 1 March 2020).

Taïa, Abdellah and Brian Whitaker, 'Interview with Abdellah Taia', *al-bab.com* (January 2009). http://al-bab.com/interview-abdellah-taia (accessed 17 October 2018).

Tanoukhi, Nirvana, 'Rewriting Political Commitment for an International Canon: Paul Bowles's "For Bread Alone" as Translation of Mohamed Choukri's "Al-Khubz Al-Hafi"', *Research in African Literatures* 34/2 (2003), pp. 127–44.

Todorov, Tzvetan, *Introduction à la littérature fantastique.* Paris: Éditions du Seuil, 1975 [first published in 1970].

Trabelsi, Bahaa, *Une vie à trois.* Bruxelles: Éditions Labor, 2002 [first published in 2000].

Vermeren, Pierre, *Histoire du Maroc depuis l'indépendance*, quatrième édition. Paris: La découverte, 2016.

Vilain, Philippe, *L'Autofiction en théorie, suivi de deux entretiens avec Philippe Sollers et Philippe Lejeune.* Chatou: Les Éditions de la transparence, 2009.

Walkowitz, Rebecca L., *Born Translated: The Contemporary Novel in an Age of World Literature.* New York: Columbia University Press, 2015.

Walkowitz, Rebecca L., 'Interview with Rebecca Walkowitz, Author of Born Translated', Columbia University Press *'Blog Archive'* (28 July 2015). http://www.cupblog.org/?p=17080 (accessed 17 October 2018).

Willis, Michael J., *Politics and Power in the Maghreb: Algeria, Tunisia and Morocco from Independence to the Arab Spring.* New York: Columbia University Press, 2012.

Young, Robert J. C., 'World Literature and Postcolonialism', in Theo D'haen, David Damrosch, and Djelal Kadir. (eds), *The Routledge Companion to World Literature*, London and New York: Routledge, 2012, pp. 213–22.

Zafzaf, Muhammad, 'fi al-ẓahīra, wa kānit al-shams', *Souffles* 10–1 (1968), pp. 30–2.

Zaganiaris, Jean, *Queer Maroc: Sexualités, genres et (trans)identités dans la littérature marocaine*. Paris: Des Ailes sur un Tracteur, 2013.

Zekri, Khalid, *Fictions du réel: Modernité romanesque et écriture du réel au Maroc 1990–2006*. Paris: L'Harmattan, 2006.

Zekri, Khalid, 'Le sujet et son corps dans le roman marocain'. *Itinéraires. Littérature, textes, cultures* 3 (2011), pp. 45–59. DOI: https://doi.org/10.4000/itineraires.1502.

Zryouil, Fatima Zahra, 'Taqdīm', in Fatna El Bouih, *Ḥadīth al-ʿatmah*. Casablanca: Nashr al-Fanak, 2001, pp. 5–8.

INDEX

2M   31

Abou Seif, Salah   29
Abouzeid, Leila   34, 35, 164 n.48
acculturation   58, 66, 80–1, 86, 87, 101,
    106, 167 n.46
    novel of acculturation, the   xi, 50,
    53–7, 166 n.18
L'Action du Peuple   82, 83
active/passive model   12, 23, 73, 112
Actuel   23, 41, 162, 165
Africa   86, 110
Ahmad, Aijaz   3, 159
Ahmed, Sara   xiv, 2, 17–20, 22, 125, 137
    Ahmed, Sara and Jackie Stacey   126
Aïn Bordja   61
Akaliyat   23, 26
ʾ*Akhbār al-Yaum*   31
al-ʿAlam   51
al-Ayyam   ix, 32
Algeciras   75
Algeria   2, 50, 52, 81, 103, 107, 110, 113,
    166 n.18
Amazigh   xii, 81, 92, 99, 172 n.103
Amour bilingue   xiv, xv, 16, 35, 79–80,
    89–99, 107, 109, 115, 134, 167 n.46,
    172 n.79
androgyny/androgyne/androgynous   16,
    97, 98, 115–16, 134
Anfās   80–9
anti-colonial resistance/struggle   2, 51,
    60, 79, 82
anti-imperialist struggle   88–9
Aqlām   83, 84
'Arab sexuality'   ix, 12, 13, 39, 41, 47, 49,
    76, 151
L'Armée du salut   vi, x, xiv, xv, 11, 31, 36,
    37, 49, 50, 66–78, 98, 105, 106, 108,
    117, 149–51, 155, 163 n.39
art for art's sake   xii–xiii, 4–5, 104
art for society's sake   xiii, 4–5

ʾ*Aṣwāt*   23–6
Attajdid   31
authenticity/authentic   ix, xiv, xv, 4, 9, 13,
    16, 21–2, 27–8, 30, 38, 43–5, 49–51,
    53, 59, 66–7, 83, 91, 99, 118
autobiography/autobiographical   ix, xiii,
    2, 3, 6–11, 16, 32–3, 38, 42, 46–7,
    70, 78, 80, 92, 107, 115, 144, 148,
    158 n.18, 164 n.48
    autobiographical novel   9–10, 51, 52,
    66, 163 n.35
    autobiographical pact   xiv, 6, 9, 33
autofiction   1, 7–8, 154
auto-exoticism, *see* exoticism
avant-gardism/avant-gardist   ix, xi, xv, 9,
    33, 35, 79, 83–5, 95, 98, 116
Azemmour   137

Baida, Abdellah   25
Bargachi, Samir   23
Barthes, Roland   7
Basri, Driss   141
Beirut   100
Belabbès, Youssef   84
Ben Ahmed   121
Ben Barka, Mehdi   84
Benchekroun, Siham   32
Beni Mellal   24
Benjelloun, Abdelmajid   33, 50, 51
Ben Jelloun, Tahar   39, 52, 84, 87, 89,
    100, 171 n.38
Benmoussa, Chakib   27
Bensaid, Marwan   24
Bensalmia, Chadwane   ix, 8
Bensmaïa, Réda   xiv, 2, 3–5, 9, 49, 80–1,
    90, 92, 93, 96, 98, 167 n.55
Berber, *see* Amazigh
Bergeaud-Blackler, Florence and Victor
    Eck   22, 27, 30
Berrada, Mohamed   34, 87, 164 n.48
bestiality   16, 95–7

Bhabha, Homi K.   xii, xiv, 2–3, 5, 9–10
bi-langue   80, 92, 94–9, 109, 111,
    115, 116
bilingualism/bilingual   xiii, xv, 16, 80, 87,
    89, 91–3, 96–7, 99, 101–2, 115–16
biography   6, 52, 137, 154
birth   2, 64, 71, 93, 94, 95, 96, 97, 132,
    133, 142
    rebirth   87, 94, 171 n.62
Bissenbakker Frederiksen, Maja
    Mons   19
born translated   xi, xii, 11
Bouab, Widad   122, 176 n.53
Boudaa, Nguia   122
Boudjedra, Rachid   52
Boukhari, Karim   31
Boukhari, Khadija   122
Boulé, Jean-Pierre   108, 145
Brussels   135, 145
Butler, Judith   xiv, 2, 14–19, 30, 45, 47,
    58, 138

Cairo   145
Campbell, Ian   167 n.55
Casablanca   ix, 24, 26, 27, 62, 83,
    121–2, 146
Casablanca civil prison (Ghbila)
    122, 126
Chahine, Youssef   29
Chaoui, Abdelkader   124
Charaf, Maria   176
Charlie Hebdo   149
Choukri, Mohamed   34, 37–8, 6–70,
    164 n.48
Chraïbi, Driss   xiv–xv, 34, 37, 49–50,
    52–66, 83, 98, 100, 103, 136, 150,
    159 n.14, 164 n.48
circumcision   35–6, 110
clandestine   1, 23, 49, 68, 76, 151
colonialism/colonial   xiii, xv, 3–4, 38,
    44, 53, 55, 57, 59–61, 63, 79, 83, 85,
    86–7, 97, 101–3, 151
colonized   xv, 5, 14, 15, 50, 51, 53–4,
    58–9, 79, 80, 85, 86, 92, 97
colonizer   xv, 5, 50, 51, 52, 53, 55, 79, 92,
    97, 105
Colonna, Vincent   7
coming out   ix, xiv, 1, 8, 14, 21, 22,
    27–32, 46, 77, 111, 145, 150

commitment (*iltizām, littérature engagé*)
    xi, xiii, xv, 2, 18, 21, 22, 26, 33, 37,
    67, 85, 89, 91, 137, 157 n.6
    see also queer, queer commitment
confessional novel   77–8
cultural journals   79, 82–5, 170 n.16

Dailleux, Denis   x
Damrosch, David   xi
Dar El Mokri   122
dārija   xii, 81, 92, 99, 102, 105, 129
Da'wat al-Ḥaqq   82
Décaux, Alain   90
decolonization/decolonized/decolonizing/
    decolonial   2, 5, 62, 79, 81, 85–9,
    90, 95, 171–2 n.73
deconstruction/deconstruct/
    deconstructed   4–6, 10, 13, 15, 33,
    46–7, 51, 58, 76, 87, 89, 90, 95, 98,
    104, 106, 129, 145, 148, 167 n.46,
    171–2 n.73
dehumanization   134, 142
Déjeux, Jean   xiii
democracy/democratic   9, 22, 42
Démocratie   54
Dennerlein, Bettina   119
Derb Moulay Cherif   121–4, 129–30, 133
Derrida, Jacques   2, 7, 164–5 n.72
deviance   3, 24, 26, 66, 138, 148
deviant   12, 24, 41, 43, 70, 145
Dialmy, Abdessamad   25
diary   6, 30, 71, 78
diaspora   1
discourse/discursive
    discourse and culture   57, 171–2 n.73
    discourse and hysteria   70
    discourse and literature   xi, xiv, 6, 8,
        10–11, 22, 56, 87, 95, 98
    discourse and political violence   119
    discourse and sexuality   11, 12–17,
        22, 35, 161 n.76
    discourse and shame   18
dissemination   2
Dlimi, Ahmed   141, 144
double critique   xiv, 5–6, 15–16, 34,
    38, 45–6, 54, 57, 95, 96, 132,
    138, 146
Doubrovsky, Serge   7–8
drag   16, 17, 112

Eaux vives 83
eclecticism xiv, 22, 32–3
Egypt x, 29, 104, 113, 142, 163 n.39
Eid, Yumna al- xiv, 2, 8–10, 14
Elalamy, Youssouf Amine 100
El-Ariss, Tarek 157 n.6
El Bouih, Fatna xiv, xvi, 117–18, 121–34,
    137, 142, 144, 146, 176 nn.39, 53
El Rhazoui, Zineb 24
emancipation/emancipated ix, xv, 36, 38,
    45–6, 65–6, 77–8, 98, 150
emotion/emotional 12, 17–18, 26,
    69, 70, 78, 79, 104, 107, 112,
    116, 120, 151
Equity and Reconciliation Commission
    (ERC) 119, 124, 125, 129, 175 n.4
erasure 14, 29–30, 80, 93, 95, 107, 109
eroticism/erotic 16, 80, 92, 93, 95–8
essentialism/essentialistic/essentializing
    15, 96, 119
ethnicity/ethnic 2, 11, 45, 49, 86, 96, 116
ethnographic novel, the xi, 50–3, 66,
    166 n.18
étranger professionnel, see professional
    foreigner
Eurocentrism/Eurocentric xiv, 3, 9, 12,
    158 n.18
Europe xiv, 21, 27, 58, 60, 63, 75, 76, 80,
    118, 134, 146
exhibitionism x, 31, 43, 68, 78
exile 56, 84, 108, 109, 129, 144, 145
exoticism 86
    auto-exoticism 49, 52, 54, 56
    exoticization 28, 76, 151
    exoticized 'other' 17, 111, 150
    exoticizing gazes 12, 39, 41, 151
    exotic portraits 37, 50, 80, 166 n.7
experimental nation, *see* nation
Ezzaouini, Maria 122

faggot 24, 74, 121, 146
Fanon, Frantz xv, 53
Farag, Mahmoud x
al-Fassi, Allal 82
Fassin, Éric 1, 11
father figure
    Abdelkébir Khatibi 94
    Abdellah Taïa 36, 67–70, 108, 109,
        113, 115, 138, 139, 140

Driss Chraïbi xv, 37, 55–8, 60–2, 63,
    65, 66, 70, 136, 151
    Fatna El Bouih 127, 128, 131
    Karim Nasseri 36, 37
    Mohamed Choukri 37, 38, 69, 70
    Rachid O. 36, 37
Femen 25–6
femininity/feminine 23, 29, 37, 65, 110,
    112, 118, 123, 125, 127, 136, 147,
    152, 153
feminism/feminist 13–14, 15, 70, 118,
    119, 121, 126, 130
Fernández Parrilla, Gonzalo 9, 34, 82–3,
    157 n.15, 170 n.16
Fez 27
Fitoussi, Michèle 176 n.53
folkloric 43, 51, 67, 86
Foucault, Michel 5, 14, 15, 94
France xv, xvi, 1, 21, 25, 30, 39, 46, 47,
    50, 54, 62, 73, 81, 84, 90, 95, 100,
    109, 124, 149, 150, 155
francophone ix, xii–xv, 1, 23, 24, 31, 33,
    41, 46, 50–1, 79, 80, 87, 90, 99–100,
    102, 104, 167–8 n.55
francophonie xv, 88–91, 96, 99,
    100–2, 106
French protectorate, the 44, 54, 56, 59,
    62, 63, 82
fuṣḥā 102, 105, 129

gay 14–16, 23–7, 35, 47, 110–12, 153
    Gay International 13, 45–6, 161 n.76
gender 2, 11, 18, 34, 36, 97, 118, *see also*
    normativity/normative, normative
    gender roles; violence, gendered
    violence
    gendered memories 117–26
    gender identities 12, 24–5, 110
    gender insubordination 14–17
    gender performativity,
        see performativity
    gender reassignment 109–13
    gender studies 1
genealogy 5, 15, 94, 115
Genette, Gérard 7
Geneva 67, 73, 75–7, 163 n.39
Ghallab, Abdelkrim 33, 34, 51
Ghbila, *see* Casablanca civil prison
    (Ghbila)

Gontard, Marc   52, 87, 166 n.7
Guessous, Nadia   119
Gusdorf, Georges   xiii, 158 n.18

Haddad, Malek   79
Ḥadīth al-ʿatmah   xiv, xvi, 117, 118,
    123–5, 127–34, 136, 147–8, 153,
    176 n.53
Hafez, Sabry   10
Hajji, Adil   32
hammam   35–6, 110, 142
Hassan, Waïl S.   96
Hassan II   xii, 8, 55, 84, 117, 121–4, 129,
    141, 144, 146
Hayes, Jarrod   2, 3, 11–12, 55, 61, 62
hegemony/hegemonic   xvi, 3, 5–6, 7, 10,
    11, 13, 14, 20, 22, 33, 47, 79, 92, 96,
    99, 100–1, 104, 106, 112, 117, 130,
    138, 147, 157 n.15
hetero/homo binary   13–14
Hetero-Nation, *see* nation
heteronormativity/heteronormative,
    see normativity/normative
heterosexuality/heterosexual   x, 2, 11, 21,
    30, 38, 41, 46, 73, 111, 138, 153
    heterosexual matrix   14–17
Heyndels, Ralph   163 n.35
Hicklin, Aaron   29
ḥizb al-Istiqlāl, *see* independence,
    Independence Party, the
Hollande, François   149
homonationalist   1
homonormativity/homonormative,
    see normativity/normative
homophobia/homophobic   1, 14, 21–6,
    28, 37, 39, 41, 43, 152, 153, 155
homosexuality/homosexual   ix, x, xiv, 1,
    4, 8, 11–17, 21–31, 35, 37–47, 49,
    66, 70, 72–3, 77, 97–8, 105–7, 110,
    114, 117, 118, 136, 138, 145, 149,
    152, 154, 163 n.39
honour   3, 17, 27, 43
humanism   4, 59
human rights   xii, 13, 20, 45, 47, 105,
    107, 117–19, 122–3, 125, 128,
    141, 146
hybridity/hybrid   xii, xiii, 7, 13–14, 92
hysteria   xvi, 11, 67, 68, 70, 77–8, 116,
    148–55

Ilā al-ʾamām   84, 122
iltizām, *see* commitment (*iltizām,
    littérature engagé*)
imitation   5, 10, 15–17, 34, 95
imperialism/imperialist   88, 171–2 n.73
impurity/impure,   98, 121, 137, *see also*
    purity
independence   51, 79–81
    Algerian War of Independence   2,
        103, 166 n.18
    Independence Party, the (*ḥizb
        al-Istiqlāl*)   51, 82
    Moroccan struggle for independence
        xii, xv, 34, 51, 54–5, 57, 77, 83
    post-independence literature   33, 82–3
individualism/individuality/individual/
    individualized   xiii, xiv, 3, 6, 17,
        20, 22, 23, 24, 26, 28, 32–3, 38, 40,
        41, 44, 45, 53, 122
Infidèles   x, xiv, xvi, 3, 36, 117–18,
    134–50, 153
intertextuality/intertextual   10–11, 34,
    37, 129
invisibility/invisible   xiv, 1, 10, 13, 14–15,
    21, 28–30, 45, 79–80, 85, 97–8, 104,
    107, 113–14, 119, 153–5
Iran   107, 114
Islam   2, 12, 21, 23, 26, 27, 31, 41, 43, 45,
    59, 82, 99, 118, 123, 134, 145–6
Islamic extremism   134, 145–6
Islamophobia   21
itinerary   87, 95

al-Jadida   31
Jameson, Fredric   3–4, 9
al-Jarida al-Oukhra   ix, 32
Jay, Salim   62, 166 n.6
Jbabdi, Latifa   122, 123, 130–1, 176 n.53
jinn   69, 114, 115

Kaddour, Youssfi   129, 141, 143–4
Kaye, Jacqueline and Abdelhamid Zoubir
    52, 56
Kelly, Debra   6
Kenitra central prison   122–4
Khaïr-Eddine, Mohammed   33, 34, 83–5,
    87, 164 n.48
Khalil, Georges, Friederike Pannewick and
    Yvonne Albers   157 n.6

Khatibi, Abdelkébir   x, xiv, xv, 2,
    5–6, 9, 15–16, 35, 45, 50–5, 79,
    80–4, 87, 89–99, 102–4, 106–9, 111,
    115–16, 134, 164 n.48, 166 nn.7, 18,
    167 n.46, 171–2 n.73, 172 n.79
KifKif   23–4
Kilito, Abdelfattah   96–7, 101–5
Klee, Paul   10, 160 n.57
Kristeva, Julia   xi, 10–11
Ksar El Kébir   26, 30

Laâbi, Abdellatif   33, 34, 54, 55, 62,
    79–81, 83–90, 95, 101, 102, 106,
    124, 126
Laachir, Karima   157 n.15
Lachgar, Ibtissame   24–5
Lefébure, Anaïs   163
Lejeune, Philippe   xiv, 2, 6–7, 9
lesbian   13–16, 24, 161 n.76
LGBT
    LGBT activism   xiv, 9, 14, 21–8, 41
    LGBT persons   23, 25, 26, 97, 120, 152
    LGBT rights   ix, xii, 13, 14, 21, 22, 26,
        40, 41, 43, 44, 47, 105
liberation   33, 50, 66, 88, 89–90, 141
littérature engagé, see commitment
    (*iltizām, littérature engagé*)

MacDonald, Megan C.   100
Mack, Mehammed Amadeus   1, 49
McLarney, Ellen   56, 60–1, 159 n.14
McNeece, Lucy Stone   92
madness, mad   69, 80, 91, 93, 98,
    110, 116, 143–4, 153–4,
    172 n.79
Madrid   23
Maghreb   xiii, 46, 50–1, 81, 86, 88,
    90, 91
Maghreb (journal)   82, 83
Maghrebin   1, 42, 46
    Maghrebin literature   xii, xiii, xv, 3–5,
        6, 11, 49–52, 55, 79–81, 87, 90–2,
        95, 98–9, 157 n.15, 166 nn.7, 18,
        167–8 n.55
Majallah li-l-Qiṣṣah wa-l-Masraḥ   83
majnūn   69
Man, Paul de   7
March 23 Movement   122
margin   5, 6, 15, 16, 34, 138

marginalization/marginalized   x, 19, 21,
    38, 50, 67, 70, 101, 107, 113, 115,
    117, 119, 128, 141, 157 n.15
Marrakesh   24, 73
martyr   x, 125–6, 176 n.53
Marxism   9, 84, 85, 121, 122
Marx-Scouras, Danielle   159 n.14
masculinity/masculine   x, xiii, 12, 23, 37,
    60, 65, 77, 111, 112, 118, 120, 125,
    130, 134, 136, 147, 152, 153
Mashreq   100
Massad, Joseph A.   2, 12–13, 17, 45,
    161 n.76
al-Massae   31
al-Mawqif   83
Mdarhri Alaoui, Abdallah   53, 157 n.15
Mecca   145
Medina   145
Mediterranean   xii, 11, 42, 172–3 n.103
Meknes prison   122
melancholy/melancholic   110, 148, 150
Mellouki, Ilham   33
Memmi, Albert   xv, 53, 79, 80–1, 86
memoirs   6, 124
memory   xvi, 10, 51, 70, 117–21, 124–6,
    128–30, 133, 140, 149
Menebhi, Khadija   176 n.53
Menebhi, Saïda   126, 176 n.53
Menin, Laura   120
Mernissi, Fatema   107
Middle East   2, 51
mimeticism/mimetically/mimetic   xii, 4,
    6, 50, 66
misogynistic   1, 39, 43, 126, 131, 133,
    142, 155
mission civilisatrice/civilizing
    mission   xiii, 54, 59, 60
Mitchum, Robert   138
Mithly   23, 41
Mitterrand, Frédéric   x
modernity/modernist   34, 38, 56, 82, 85
Mohammed V   56
Mohammed V University   73, 103
Mohammédia   24
Mohammed VI   xii, 9, 22, 84, 123
monarchy   55, 61, 83
Monroe, Marilyn   138, 140–1, 145, 147–8
monster   7, 41, 69, 76, 110, 112, 135–6,
    142, 145–6, 148

monstrosity   69, 118, 127, 131–2, 136,
    146, 148, 153
Moretti, Franco   4
Moroccan Arabic, *see dārija*
mosque   25, 146–7, 154, 163 n.39
mother figure
    Abdelkébir Khatibi   16, 93–4, 97
    Abdellah Taïa   xvi, 11, 28, 36–7,
        39–40, 67–70, 77, 108–9, 134–6,
        138–41, 144–6, 148–55
    Driss Chraïbi   57, 61, 62–6, 71, 77
    Fatna El Bouih   132–3
    Mohamed Choukri   69–70
    Rachid O.   37
mother tongue
    Abdelfattah Kilito   102
    Abdelkébir Khatibi   16, 92–5
    Abdellatif Laâbi   86
Mouride, Abdelaziz   124
Mouvement alternative pour les libertes
    individuelles (MALI)   23–6
Movement of Unity and Reform (MUR)
    31
Muruwwa, Husayn   xiii
Muslim   xiv, 1, 2, 8, 11, 23, 24, 39, 42, 45,
    47, 59, 146, 152
    Arab-Muslim queers   xvi, 1, 11, 21,
        38, 77, 149, 150, 151, 154, 155
    Arab-Muslim women   150
    Arab-Muslim writers   1, 46, 99
    Muslim immigrant   107, 110,
        113–15, 154
    'Muslim sexuality'   12, 43, 47
mystical poetry   98

'naive' realism   xi, 9, 22, 34–5, 111
naivety/naive   30, 34, 38, 52, 67, 74–8,
    107, 116, 135, 140, 146, 150–1, 155
Nasrallah, Yousry   29
Nasseri, Karim   22, 35–7, 42
nation   xii, 2, 6, 17, 79, 88, 90
    experimental nation   xiv, 2–6, 35, 80,
        90, 107, 109, 128, 148, 149
    Hetero-Nation   11, 16, 21, 34, 97,
        134, 148
    narrations of the nation   xvi, 1, 2, 3,
        5, 11–12, 22, 33–5, 117–18, 136,
        147–8
    national allegory   2–4, 159 n.14

national elite   55, 61
national identity   xii, 2–4, 11, 82,
    85, 91
nationalism   2
'nationalist realism'   33–4, 51
national reconciliation   xvi, 118, 144
nation building   xv, 2, 19–20, 81, 117,
    123, 125
    queering the nation   11–20, 34,
        36, 148
    transnation   5, 90, 96, 99, 115
    transnational   xi, xii, 46, 90, 96, 118
National Union of High School Students,
    the, *see Union nationale des
    étudiants au Maroc* (UNEM)
'native informant'   38, 49–50, 57, 59,
    68, 151
Nedjma   22, 32, 36
neocolonialism/neocolonial   xv, 43–4,
    62, 83, 89, 99, 101, 150, 152
Niny, Rachid   31
Nissaboury, Mostapha   83–5, 87
normativity/normative   x, 12, 14, 17, 19,
    96, 98, 112, 120, 137
    heteronormativity/heteronormative
        1, 11, 14–15, 29, 32, 35–8, 72–3,
        110–11, 120, 148, 152
    homonormativity/homonormative
        14–15, 17, 21, 73, 110–11
    non-normative   11, 17, 32–4, 36–8
    normative gender roles   36–7, 98,
        108, 115, 134, *see also* gender
    anti-normative   19, 137
North Africa, *see* Maghreb
North African, *see* Maghrebin
novel of acculturation, the,
    see acculturation
Ncube, Gibson   105

O., Rachid   9, 22, 32–3, 35–8, 42, 49,
    69, 151
oblivious foreigner   109–13
obliviousness   17, 30, 110–11
oppression   14, 15, 38, 45, 53, 55, 57, 59,
    61, 62, 70, 87, 118, 131, 132, 147, 151
Orlando, Valérie K.   105, 176 n.53
Oufkir, Fatéma   176 n.53
Oufkir, Malika   176 n.53
Oufkir, Mohamed   121, 122, 141

paratext/paratextual 6, 8–9
Paris ix, x, xiv, xvi, 1, 30, 31, 42, 45–7,
    67, 77, 82, 84, 100, 102–5, 107–8,
    113–14, 122, 124, 149–55, 163 n.39
parodic performance, *see* performativity/
    performative
parody xv, 16–17, 56, 58–9, 71, 98,
    111, 151–2, 154, 167 n.46,
    see also performativity, parodic
    performance
Parti de la justice et du développement
    (PJD) 23, 26, 31, 41, 43–5
Parti Démocratique d'Independence
    (PDI) 54
Le Passé simple xiv, xv, 34, 37, 49–51,
    53–68, 70–2, 76–8, 95, 98, 100, 103,
    136, 150–1, 159 n.14, 164 n.48
patriarchy 2, 11, 15, 37, 56, 70, 130, 150
    patriarch 69, 70, 150
    patriarchal 37, 49, 70, 117, 126,
    130–1, 150, 152
Un Pays pour mourir x, xiv, xv, 17, 19,
    79, 80, 98, 106–16, 117, 134, 145,
    149, 154
Peck, Dale 44
pederasty 12, 41
pénsee-autre x, xiv, 5, 16, 46, 92, 94–6
pensée en langues 5, 16, 92, 96
performativity/performative x, xiv, 15,
    17, 19, 46, 78, 126
    gender performativity 16
    parodic performance 16, 36, 47, 49,
    58, 66, 76, 95, *see also* parody
periphery/peripheral 1, 5, 6, 90, 95,
    100, 138
plurilingualism/plurilingual xiii, xv,
    98–9
Poésie toute 83, 87
poetry 54, 83–4, 87, 95, 98, 99, 115, 126,
    171 n.62
Polisario 138, 141
political activists 84, 119, 120–2, 126,
    129–30
political prisoner, *see* prison
political violence, *see* violence
poor 13, 30, 31, 38, 45, 67, 102–4,
    151, 152
'poor' French 79–80, 85, 98, 104, 106, 116
pop culture xiv, 22, 32

postcolonial
    postcolonial critics xi, 19, 45, 79,
    87, 103
    postcolonial identity 2, 45–6, 51
    postcolonial literature ix, xv, 3, 6, 54,
    82, 151, 159 n.14
    postcolonial Morocco 79, 101
    postcolonial studies xiv, 1, 99
    postcolonial theory 2
postmodernism/postmodern 4, 8, 32
pride 19, 41, 154, *see also* shame
prison 25, 76, 84, 118, 120, 121–9,
    131–3, 136, 140–2, 144, 146, 152
    criminal prisoners 118, 124, 131, 144
    imprisonment 23–5, 27, 36, 38, 43,
    84, 125–6, 129, 131, 141, 145
    political prisoner xv, 117–18, 120,
    123–6, 128, 130–1, 133–4, 142,
    144, 148
    prisoner 63, 120–1, 127, 132–3, 147
    prison guards 120, 130–2, 134
    prison testimony ix, xv, 117, 129,
    176 n.53
professional foreigner 90, 96, 98, 99, 109,
    111, 115–16
prostitute 31, 36, 74, 76–7, 107, 113–15,
    117, 134, 138, 141–2
prostitution 37, 38, 75, 98, 113–14
protectorate, *see* French protectorate, the
Provencher, Denis M. 1, 46
public sphere xvi, 8, 9, 12, 19, 26, 30,
    117–19, 147
purity xvi, 3, 98, 117, 125, 133, 137–8,
    see also impurity/impure

al-qasīdah 82
Quayson, Ato 99
queer, *see also* Muslim, Arab-Muslim
    queers; nation, queering the nation
    queer commitment x–xi, xiv, xv, xvi,
    1, 2, 9, 21, 22, 147, 150, *see also*
    commitment (*iltizām, littérature
    engagé*)
    queer desire 1, 97
    queer identities x, 1, 16, 22, 30, 43,
    77, 78, 80, 98, 117, 150
    queering extremism 144–7
    queer literature xiv, 21
    queerness 11, 72

queer resistance   11, 17, 19, 70, 72,
    75, 147–8
queer sexualities   xiv, 38, 42, 46, 80,
    107, 115, 134, 150
queer studies   1
queer theory   xiv, 2, 15
Qur'an   12, 99

Rabat   26, 41, 67, 73, 77, 122, 134, 154
    Rabat University   30
    Hassan Tower   25
Ramadan   24, 114
rape   28, 120–1, 122, 125, 130, 133–4,
    136, 142, 144, 147, 153, 163 n.39
reader   6–9, 32, 49–50, 53, 56, 68, 73, 74,
    77–8, 79, 81, 84, 89, 96, 98, 99, 104,
    107, 116, 125, 127, 131, 139, 144,
    151, 152
reception   xiv, 8, 50, 51, 56, 59, 62, 66
referentiality/referential   xiii, 6–10
regulatory regime   xiv, 14, 16, 36, 38,
    51, 148
religion   1, 2, 8, 11, 21, 25, 27, 38, 77,
    87, 150
Renan, Ernest   2, 158
repetition   16, 36, 125
representation   xi, xiv, 4, 6, 9, 11, 12,
    15–16, 21–2, 35–7, 40, 47, 49,
    50–2, 54, 64, 66, 69, 80, 81, 97–8,
    118, 134
revolution   x, 61, 114
revolutionary   36, 84, 87
Reynolds, Dwight F.   158 n.18
Risālat al-Maghrib   51, 82
Rooke, Tetz   159 n.14
Rumi, Jalal al-Din   134

Said, Edward W.   17, 44
salafi   34, 82–3
Salé   26, 67, 73, 77, 134, 151, 154
Saoudi, Nour-Eddine   120–1, 130,
    176 n.53
Sartre, Jean-Paul   xi, 63
Schmitt, Arnaud   2, 6, 8–9
Schmitt, Arno   11–12
Schmitt, Arno and Jehoeda Sofer   11
scream/screaming   68, 70, 109, 115–16,
    131–4, 137, 142, 143, 147–8, 149,
    153–5

'secret pact'   9, *see also* autobiography/
    autobiographical, autobiographical
    pact
Sedgwick, Eve Kosofsky   19, 43
Sefrioui, Ahmed   50, 52, 54–6, 83
Sefrioui, Kenza   84, 86
self-absorbed   x, xi, xiii, xiv, xv, xvi,
    1–2, 21–2, 30, 33, 40, 43, 50, 57,
    60, 65, 66–8, 71, 75, 78, 147, 150
self-narration   6–17, 163 n.35
self-orientalization   49–50, 54, 56, 68,
    78, 151
Serfaty, Abraham   84
sex tourism   73, 76, 151
sexual abuse, *see* violence, sexualized
    violence
sexual clash of civilizations   1, 11,
    77, 155
sexual deviance   3, 24, 26, 66, 138, 148
sexual deviant   12, 24, 41, 43, 70, 145
sexualized violence, *see* violence
shame   ix, xvi, 2, 11, 17–20, 22, 28, 30,
    38, 43, 69, 70, 72, 78, 112, 117,
    118, 121, 125, 131, 134, 136–7,
    142, 146
short story   ix, x, 33, 51, 82, 83
shādhdh al-jinsī, see sexual deviant
shudhudh al-jinsī, see sexual deviance
Sidi Ali   27
silence   x, xvi, 5, 10, 11, 15, 22–32,
    39–41, 43, 47, 56–7, 64, 69, 70,
    77, 87, 110, 117–18, 121, 124–8,
    130–4, 138, 142–4, 147–8, 152–5
'silent keepers of memory'   xvi, 117–18,
    125
silent witness   118, 125–6, 133
Slimani, Leïla   100
Slyomovics, Susan   117, 131
Sorbonne   2, 116, 154
Souffles   33, 54–5, 62–3, 79–90, 99, 105,
    121, 166 n.7
Spivak, Gayatri Chakravorty   91
stigmatization/stigmatized/
    stigmatize   xvi, 36, 74, 111,
    117–19, 121, 131, 134, 136,
    137, 139
storyteller   49, 56–7, 95, 107
storytelling   33, 49, 57, 78, 98, 107–8,
    126, 128, 151

subversion/subvert/subversive   xiii, xv, 3, 5, 16–17, 21, 33–6, 38, 49, 56, 67, 70, 80, 81, 92, 93, 97–8, 101, 105, 110–12, 116, 118, 127, 134, 136–8, 147, 148
Sufi   98, 115, 134
Switzerland   75, 77

taboo   xvi, 23, 25, 28, 32, 37, 39–40, 102, 105, 107, 121
Tafraout, Abderrahim   128
Tangier   26, 31, 71, 74–5
Taourirt   25
Tazmamart   122
TelQuel   ix, 8, 22, 23, 26, 30–2, 33, 39
terrorism   118, 146–7, 152–5
testimonial writing   xiii, 23, 49, 53, 117–18, 121, 124–6, 144, 148, 151, 176 n.53
testimony   xvi, 50, 70, 117–18, 122–4, 137, 141, 147–8, 153
Tétouan   23, 71, 72
textual violence   33, 79–80, 85, 87, 89, 95, 99, 101, 105–6
third world   3–4, 15, 84–6
torturers   118, 122, 127, 129–31, 142–4
torture/tortured   xvi, 10, 84, 120–31, 133–4, 141–5
Trabelsi, Bahaa   22, 32–3, 36, 38
transculturation   87, 89, 106
transgender   16, 107, 117
transgenerational model   12, 23, 37, 73
transidentity   79, 90
transnation, *see* nation
transnational, *see* nation

Union nationale des étudiants au Maroc (UNEM)   84, 121, 122
Union nationale des forces populaires (UNFP)   84
universal rights   xiv, 14, 21

Vermeren, Pierre   175
Vilain, Philippe   160
violence   xiv, 14–15, 21, 24, 28–9, 35, 37, 59, 68, 70, 80, 107, 110, 115, 145, 147, 150, *see also* textual violence
   gendered violence   69, 118, 123, 128, 131, 134, 139
   political violence   xvi, 10, 117–20, 123, 125–6, 134, 141, 147
   sexualized violence   120–1, 130, 136, 142, 144, 153
visibility/visible   10, 14–15, 26, 28, 69, 91, 100, 117, 160 n.57
vulnerability/vulnerable   18, 78, 79, 104, 107, 116, 151

Walkowitz, Rebecca L.   xi–xii
West, the/Western   xiii, xiv, 3–6, 9, 10–15, 17, 21, 31, 34, 38, 44–5, 47, 49–50, 56–7, 66, 73–4, 76–7, 98, 107, 123, 150, 153, 158 n.18, 161 n.76
witness   xvi, 18, 118, 125–6, 128, 133, 139
women's rights   44, 118–19, 123, 176 n.39
world literature   xi, xii, 3–5

xenophobia   118, 134, 146

Yacine, Kateb   103
Years of Lead   xii, xv, 19, 84, 117–26, 128, 134, 141, 144, 148
Young, Robert J. C.   xi

Zaganiaris, Jean   13, 36, 134
zamel   24, *see also* faggot
Zekri, Khalid   vi, 32, 35–6, 99–100, 110, 115, 157 n.15, 176 n.53
Zryouil, Fatima Zahra   130

Ingram Content Group UK Ltd.
Milton Keynes UK
UKHW020046130323
418471UK00005B/92